Expanding the View of Hohokam Platform Mounds

An Ethnographic Perspective

ANTHROPOLOGICAL PAPERS OF
THE UNIVERSITY OF ARIZONA
NUMBER 63

Expanding the View of Hohokam Platform Mounds

An Ethnographic Perspective

Mark D. Elson

THE UNIVERSITY OF ARIZONA PRESS
TUCSON
1998

About the Author

MARK D. ELSON has been engaged in archaeological research for more than twenty years, primarily in the American Southwest but also in the northeastern United States, Ecuador, and Argentina. He completed his undergraduate degree at the University of Rhode Island (1978) and received his master's (1980) and doctoral (1996) degrees in anthropology from the University of Arizona. Since 1984, Dr. Elson has been employed as a Senior Research Archaeologist at Desert Archaeology, Inc., in Tucson. He has directed archaeological projects on the Navajo Reservation, in the Flagstaff area, and in the Tucson, Phoenix, and Tonto Basins. Between 1988 and 1995 he directed the Rye Creek Project and the Roosevelt Community Development Study, and information from the latter formed the basis for his doctoral dissertation and portions of this book. In 1997 he became the director of a multiyear project south of the Wupatki area in northern Arizona. His research interests in the Southwest include prehistoric social organization and kinship systems, economic systems, and the formation of social boundaries.

About the Artist

ZIBA GHASSEMI, who produced the cover illustration and the platform mound reconstructions in Chapter 4, was born in Tehran, Iran, and came to the United States in 1979. She received her master's degree in architecture from the University of Arizona in 1995 and is an architect in Los Angeles.

Cover: The single-line drawing by Ziba Ghassemi shows a sequence of platform mounds. From bottom to top, structures depicted are from the mound-building groups of Ifaluk, Samoa, Natchez, Yap, the prehistoric Tonto Basin, and the Marquesas.

A grant from the U.S. Bureau of Reclamation provided support for printing this volume.

Publication of this book is made possible in part by the proceeds of a permanent endowment created with the assistance of a Challenge Grant from the National Endowment for the Humanities, a federal agency.

THE UNIVERSITY OF ARIZONA PRESS

Copyright © 1998

The Arizona Board of Regents
All Rights Reserved

This book was set in 10.7/12 CG Times.
∞ This book is printed on acid-free, archival-quality paper.
Manufactured in the United States of America

00 99 98   3 2 1

Library of Congress Cataloging-in-Publication Data

Elson, Mark (Mark D.)
    Expanding the view of Hohokam platform mounds : an ethnographic perspective / Mark D. Elson
        p. cm. -- (Anthropological papers of the University of Arizona; no. 63)
        Includes bibliographical references and index.
        ISBN 0-8165-1841-6 (pbk. acid-free paper)
        1. Hohokam culture. 2. Hohokam architecture. 3. Mound-builders--History. 4. Mound-builders--Southwest, New--History. 5. Mound-builders--Arizona--Tonto Basin--History. 6. Southwest, New--Antiquities. 7. Tonto Basin (Ariz.)--Antiquities.
    I. Title. II. Series
        E99.H68 E49 1998
        979.1'55--ddc21
                                98-19751
                                CIP

Contents

FIGURES

TABLES

Preface

In 1883, Adolph Bandelier observed that the Phoenix Basin platform mound of Pueblo Grande contained an artificially raised solid earth core with a cluster of rooms on its top. Four years later, Frank Hamilton Cushing, also working at the site of Pueblo Grande, undertook the first controlled archaeological excavation of a platform mound in the American Southwest. In contrast to Bandelier, Cushing proposed that the ruin was not an artificial platform but instead the structural remains of a great temple that served an elite class of priestly chiefs.

The work of these two early researchers initiated a controversy over platform mound function that has continued in various forms for more than a hundred years. Although subsequent excavations have demonstrated that platform mounds are artificially filled, the function of the mounds and the social organization of the groups who built them remain the subjects of heated debate in Southwest archaeology. The problem is so unresolved that the exact same data sets have been used by different researchers to argue for conflicting, and often opposite, interpretations of the same mounds. Two basic models have been proposed, each with a number of permutations: (1) platform mounds were residential features benefiting a class of elite leaders from socially ranked or stratified societies, or (2) platform mounds were largely vacant ceremonial features used by groups of limited social differentiation. Even though 24 platform mound sites have now been tested or excavated in Arizona, representing just over 20 percent of the sample of known mounds, and despite those decades of investigation, it is clear that archaeological excavation alone is not sufficient to resolve these issues.

I first became involved with platform mound research while serving as the project director for the Roosevelt Community Development Study, a cultural resource management project undertaken by Desert Archaeology, Inc. The United States Bureau of Reclamation sponsored the work as part of their larger Roosevelt Lake Project situated in the Tonto Basin of central Arizona, an area long known to contain a high density of prehistoric sites and more than 20 platform mounds. The impetus for the investigations was the raising of the dam at Roosevelt Lake to provide better flood control for the city of Phoenix. Increasing the height of the dam meant that close to 750 archaeological sites could be covered by the rising waters of the lake. Over the course of a decade, the Bureau spent approximately 13.5 million dollars to test, excavate, and analyze about 150 of these sites, including 7 with platform mounds. Additionally, for the past 15 years the Arizona Department of Transportation has been responsible for the excavation of another hundred or so Tonto Basin sites. The funding of these projects, as mandated by cultural resource legislation, and the commitment to archaeological research by both the Bureau and the Department of Transportation has now made the Tonto Basin one of the best and most intensively investigated areas not only in the American Southwest but in the entire United States.

The Roosevelt Lake investigations were divided into three separate projects, each with slightly different but overlapping research themes. In the early 1990s, contracts for this work were awarded to archaeologists from Desert Archaeology, Statistical Research, Inc., and the Office of Cultural Resource Management at Arizona State University. Desert Archaeology's portion of the project included 29 sites, 2 of them with platform mounds, within a continuous 6–km (3.7–mile) study area on the north bank of the Salt River. An adjoining area along the south bank of the Salt River containing 15 sites but with 3 platform mounds was investigated by Arizona State University. In combination, these two projects provided a unique and relatively complete examination of prehistoric settlement that resulted in the definition of the Eastern Tonto Basin settlement system.

During the analysis phase of the project, the Bureau's Roosevelt Research Team held meetings that included members of all three archaeological contractors. It soon became apparent that there was little agreement among us on the function of the platform mounds or the social organization of the associated groups. Various opinions existed both between and within the contracting firms: at Desert Archaeology, for example, some believed that the mounds were largely ceremonial features used by groups of limited social differentiation, whereas others believed that the mounds were lived on by ranked leaders of those groups, implying a much greater degree of social complexity. This led to lively discussion and argument, but little headway was made in convincing proponents of opposing views; eventually, each model was written up and published as a separate chapter in Desert Archaeology's final synthetic volume for the project.

Unlike the Southeastern United States, where ethnohistoric information from early explorers readily aids in the interpretation of the platform mounds and associated groups, no mound-building groups were present in the Southwest when the first European explorers arrived. According to the archaeological data, mounds ceased to be built several hundred years prior to the Spanish entrada. As we all grappled with the questions of platform mound function, social complexity, and the nature of group organization, I reasoned that perhaps there were regularities among historic mound-building groups in other parts of the world that could be used to help decipher those in the Southwest.

For my doctoral dissertation research, I selected a cross-cultural sample of mound-building groups with a level of social complexity similar to that of the prehistoric Southwestern groups, analyzed their attributes, and abstracted those that were commonly held by most or all of the groups (Elson 1996a). In this analysis, group attributes that were negatively correlated with mound-building were considered to be as important as those that were positively correlated. I then applied this information to the local Eastern Tonto Basin system and derived a new model for this settlement; it differed in a number of significant ways from my earlier models published as part of the Roosevelt project reports (Elson 1994; Elson, Gregory, and Stark 1995) and elsewhere (Elson and others 1996).

The primary criterion used in selecting the historic groups was that they had to be "middle-range," that is, somewhere between a "band" and a "state" in neoevolutionary terms, and had to have sufficient ethnographic or ethnohistoric information to form comparisons. The middle-range criterion was necessary to avoid analyzing groups that were either far above or far below the social complexity believed to be present in the prehistoric Southwest. A reconsideration for this volume of what constituted sufficient information for this purpose resulted in the elimination of two groups that I examined in my dissertation, but the results of the analysis did not change.

This book begins with a general overview and history of platform mound research in the American Southwest and discusses the various models used in platform mound interpretation. In Chapter 2, I present ethnographic and ethnohistoric information on seven platform-mound using groups who inhabited portions of Micronesia, Polynesia, South America, and the southeastern United States, including observations on environment, population size, social and political organization, economic systems, religious practices, and types and functions of platform mounds. Chapter 3 synthesizes the ethnographic and ethnohistoric research and abstracts the regularities in human behavior that pertain directly to platform mound function and social organization.

In Chapter 4, I review the results of the archaeological investigations in the Tonto Basin and focus on a single local settlement system in the eastern Tonto Basin that contained 5 platform mounds and 39 other sites. Each mound site is examined and previous models of mound function are discussed. Chapter 5 examines the Eastern Tonto Basin settlement system using data derived from the ethnographic and archaeological research. A new model for the prehistoric Classic period settlement of this system is offered and platform mound use and function are specifically addressed. The final chapter concludes with some thoughts on the prehistoric settlement of the Phoenix Basin and other Southwest platform mound systems. To provide a reference guide for other archaeologists who may want to make use of these resources, and in an effort to make more visible that "gray literature" of contract work, the Appendix contains a list, including chapters and authors, of the project reports prepared by Desert Archaeology, Statistical Research, and Arizona State University for the Roosevelt Project.

Acknowledgments

A great number of people through the years have contributed, both directly and indirectly, to this book. The research presented here is based on work undertaken by Desert Archaeology on the Roosevelt Community Development Study, and first I thank William Doelle, president of Desert Archaeology, for his logistical, technical, and intellectual support during the 14 years of our association. I have learned much about Southwestern archaeology from him.

The Tonto Basin has been a primary focus of my work since 1981, and I also express appreciation to other members of Desert Archaeology's Roosevelt research team: Jeffery Clark, David Gregory, James Heidke, Miriam Stark, Deborah Swartz, and Henry Wallace. Spirited discussion with all of these people, but particularly with Miriam Stark and David Gregory, strongly influenced the nature of this research. I am also indebted to my colleagues at Arizona State University, especially Owen Lindauer, David Jacobs, and Glen Rice, for their thorough work in the Livingston and Schoolhouse portions of the Eastern Tonto Basin.

Various other Desert Archaeology personnel were instrumental in the Roosevelt research and completion of this book, including Jenny Adams, Elizabeth Black, Donna Breckenridge, Dena McDuffie (who also computer-drafted Fig. 1.3), Lisa Eppley, Othelia Kiser, and Lisa Coleman. Several people skillfully drafted the figures used in this volume: Chip Colwell (Figs. 1.2, 2.1, 2.5, 2.6, 2.7, 4.1), Ronald Beckwith (Figs. 4.2, 4.5, 4.6, 4.7, 4.10, 5.3), and Elizabeth Gray (Figs. 2.2, 2.3, 2.4, 2.8). The computer-generated graphics were produced by Catherine Gilman of Desert Archaeology (Figs. 1.1, 3.1, 5.1) and by James Holmlund of Geo-Map, Inc. (Figs. 4.3, 4.8, 4.11, 4.12, 4.14). Figures 4.15-4.18 are from Arizona State University reports on the Roosevelt Project. Brenda Shears of Arizona State University helped me compile the reports presented in the Appendix. Ziba Ghassemi provided the single-line cover illustration and the fine reconstructions in Figures 4.4, 4.9, and 4.13.

The 40-member Roosevelt Study field crew and staff, although too numerous to name individually, spent a year working together in the Tonto Basin and are to be commended for compiling an excellent data base, one that will be used for many years to come. The project was undertaken for the Bureau of Reclamation on Tonto National Forest land. Bureau and Forest archaeologists Thomas Lincoln and J. Scott Wood provided essential support and help during the course of these investigations. Tom Lincoln and the Bureau have made special efforts to fund various publications, including portions of this book and others, and the archaeological profession appreciates their commitment to research. Discussions and disagreements with Scott Wood through the years have stimulated a better understanding of Tonto Basin prehistory.

Discussions with and comments from Barbara Mills, Charles Adams, Jeffrey Dean, Alice Schlegel, and Thomas Sheridan contributed enormously to this research, as did support and ideas from David Abbott, James Bayman, Sarah Herr, Trinkle Jones, Joanne Newcomb, Axel Nielsen, Terry Samples, Laura Stuckey, Helga Teiwes, William Walker, and David Wilcox. I must particularly acknowledge Bill Walker for suggesting that I use ethnographic data to investigate prehistoric platform mounds. Comments from two reviewers, Ben Nelson and Stephen Lekson, have been especially helpful. I thank Carol Gifford for the excellence of her editing skills and her anthropological mind, which have made this revised material a far better book than it was a dissertation. María Nieves Zedeño provided the Spanish translation of the Abstract.

Finally, I extend special appreciation to my parents, Norman and Winnie, for their support and patience through the years and to my wife and fellow archaeologist Deborah Swartz for her love and support. I trust Debbie's judgment implicitly; she was a major sounding board for much of what is presented here, as well as a safe haven in the storm.

CHAPTER ONE

Platform Mounds in the American Southwest

Throughout history and around the world, people have banded together to modify the earthen landscape upon which they lived. Among the most notable and often the most puzzling modifications are the mounds that have been purposefully raised above the surrounding ground surface. Globally, these cultural features vary widely in size, shape, construction method, and function. Some of the most well known are the huge serpentine and animal-shaped effigy mounds that have long captured the human imagination.

This book discusses a different subset of mound features called "platform mounds," which functioned in a structural manner to create a raised platform. Platform mounds were built in regions as diverse as the tropical islands of the Pacific Ocean, the temperate forests of the southeastern United States, the arid deserts of the Near East, the jungles and highlands of Mexico, and the rainforests of Southeast Asia, to name but a few of the better known examples. They range in time from many thousands of years B.C. to the present day and were built by groups with various forms of social organization. Clearly, mound construction is a pervasive and long-standing attribute of human populations.

Platform mounds are defined as any structure that was deliberately raised or filled to construct an elevated platform (Elson and Craig 1994: 19). They can be classified as a type of monumental architecture because their "scale and elaboration exceed the requirements of any practical functions . . . [they were] intended to perform" (Trigger 1990: 119). The significance of platform mounds lies in the fact that mound construction was almost certainly a group effort, one oriented toward a nonsubsistence-related task, that necessitated cooperation and structured leadership. Such leadership implies that groups that built platform mounds likely embodied some form of hierarchical social organization. But the function of the mounds and the nature of the social complexity that platform mound-building societies attained have been the subjects of archaeological debate since the earliest days of the discipline.

Prehistoric platform mounds are common in North, Central, and South America and are present in almost all portions of the United States with the exception of the northwest and Pacific coast regions. In the 1500s, Spanish explorers in the southeastern United States, such as Hernando de Soto and Juan Pardo, visited villages where platform mounds were still in use, providing a link with mound-building peoples of the prehistoric past (Hudson and Tesser 1994; Swanton 1946). Use of these accounts has greatly aided the archaeological interpretation of that area (Anderson 1994; Blitz 1993; Neitzel 1965; Scarry 1996).

In the southwestern United States we are not so fortunate, and ethnohistoric accounts of platform mound use and direct ethnographic continuity with prehistoric mound builders are lacking. Even though this architectural form did not persist into historic times, some 119 platform mounds from 96 prehistoric sites have been recorded (Doelle 1995a, Table F.1), almost all from central and southern Arizona in the region traditionally defined as the Hohokam culture area. Although there is variation among them, these mounds share enough similarities that they may be assigned to the same general class of cultural feature (Doelle and others 1995; Fish 1989; Gregory 1987, 1991; Gumerman 1991).

Platform mounds in the American Southwest are distributed across an area of approximately 45,000 square kilometers (17,370 square miles) largely confined to the Sonoran Desert, from the eastern Papaguería, Tucson Basin, and San Pedro River valley in the south, to the Phoenix and Tonto basins in the north (Fig. 1.1, Table 1.1). They have a raised surface area averaging 495 square meters, an average volume of fill of 1,362 cubic meters, and an average height above the surrounding ground surface of 1.9 meters (Table 1.2). Most, although not all, of the platform mounds are enclosed within a masonry or adobe compound wall, usually containing room spaces and open plaza areas, and they are often associated with other compounds without mounds that appear to be primarily residential areas (Fig. 1.2).

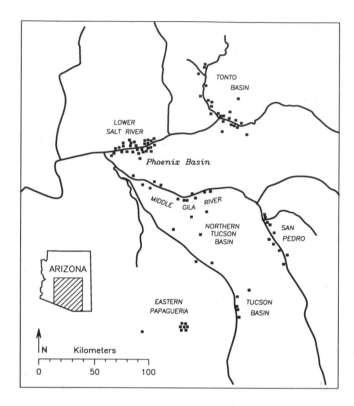

Figure 1.1. The regional distribution of Classic period platform mound sites in central and southern Arizona (after Doelle and others 1995, Fig. 13.1).

Table 1.1. Distribution of Central and Southern Arizona Classic Period Platform Mounds by Spatial Cluster

Cluster	Size (km²)[a]	Number of sites	Number of mounds
Lower Salt River (Phoenix Basin)	1150	30	43
Middle Gila River (Phoenix Basin)	1920	12	13
Tonto Basin	2560	23	26
Tucson Basin	770	5	7
Lower San Pedro River	900	10	14
Eastern Papaguería	140	8	8
N. Tucson Basin, Picacho Peak		6	6
Other[b]		2	2
Total		96	119

NOTE: Distribution does not include multistory structures (like those at Casa Grande and Pueblo Grande). Figures are from Doelle 1995a and Doelle and others 1995.

[a] Approximate size of area containing platform mounds within each cluster, excluding outliers.
[b] Other mounds located along Cherry Creek and Queen Creek are not shown in Figure 1.1.

Table 1.2. Surface Area, Volume, and Height of Platform Mounds in the Southwest

Measurements	Average	Range	Standard deviation	N
Surface area (sq. m)	495	47–4,945	797	60
Volume (cu. m)	1,362	77–14,000	2,884	44
Height (m)	1.9	0.4–3.7	0.7	44

NOTE: These figures are abstracted from tables in Doelle and others 1995.

Although a few platform mounds are dated as early as A.D. 950 to 1150, with some possibly dating as early as 750, most of them were built within a restricted period spanning two hundred years between 1150 and 1350, referred to in southern Arizona chronologies as the Classic period.

Determining the total number of mounds depends on how one interprets information on mounds that are no longer visible because of their destruction through vandalism or modern development. For example, there is a question whether Las Colinas in the Phoenix Basin once contained 4 platform mounds (the figure used in this analysis) and 8 large trash mounds (Gregory 1987) or 12 platform mounds (Doelle 1995a). Similar problems occur at other sites, and there are undoubtedly additional platform mounds not yet recorded, particularly in areas outside the Phoenix Basin. It is probably safe to say that there were more than 100 but fewer than 150 prehistoric platform mounds in central and southern Arizona.

Platform mounds in the American Southwest have been most commonly investigated through the use of standard archaeological techniques involving analyses of architecture, room and feature function, and patterns of artifact distribution (Bayman 1994; Ciolek-Torrello and others 1988; Craig and Clark 1994; Doyel 1974, 1981; Elson 1994; S. Fish and others 1992; Gregory 1987, 1988a; Jacobs 1994a, 1997; Lindauer 1995, 1996a, 1997a; Wilcox 1987). This study deviates from past analyses and investigates the function of platform mounds in historic groups through a world-wide, cross-cultural examination of ethnographic and ethnohistoric accounts. These historic groups share a number of common characteristics that have important archaeological implications (Chapters 2 and 3).

The use of cross-cultural attributes derived from groups living outside the American Southwest is appropriate for two reasons. First, unlike other areas in the Southwest, such as the northern pueblo regions, there are no known direct ethnographic analogs to the prehis-

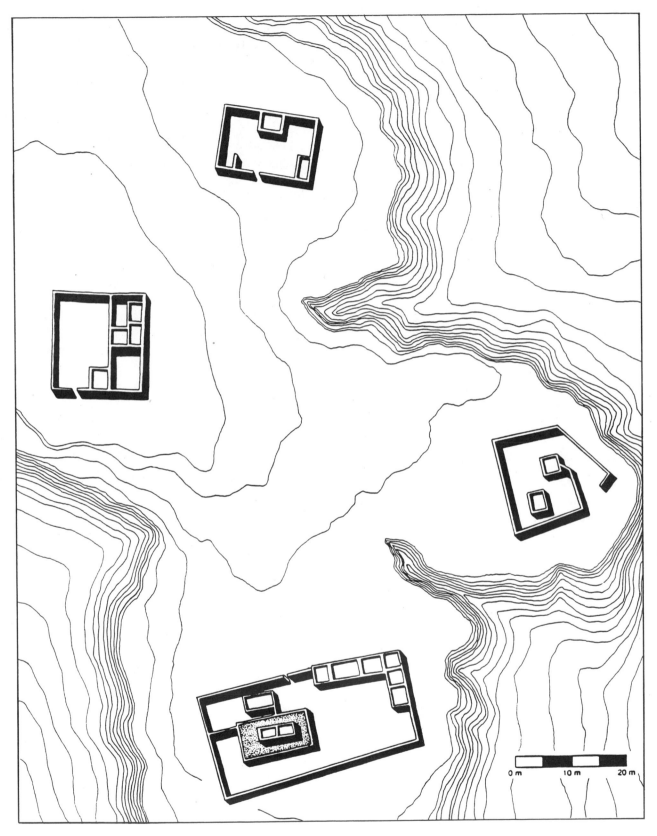

Figure 1.2. A schematic example of architectural structures in a platform mound site with four compounds and two rooms on top of the platform mound (*bottom center*).

toric groups who built the platform mounds. When Father Kino first entered southern Arizona in the late seventeenth century, for all practical purposes beginning the historic period, this area was occupied by O'odham (Pima and Papago) and Apache groups, neither of whom built platform mounds (Bayman 1994: 10–11). The O'odham are believed by some to be direct descendants of the Hohokam and have been widely used as the basis for ethnographic analogy in central and southern Arizona (Haury 1945). However, as noted by Suzanne Fish and others (1992: 39), "In contrast to Puebloan cultures of the northern Southwest, the nature of Hohokam institutions is not illuminated by ethnographic continuity in highly relevant spheres or by even early historic observations. Piman analogs are absent for mounds, compounds, and settlement hierarchy among the Hohokam." Doyel (1979: 550) further stressed this point when he said: "The Pima and Papago did. . . not build hundreds of miles of canals, 225 ballcourts, or over 60 platform mounds. . . . "

A second reason for using cross-cultural observations to model platform mound function lies in the nature of archaeological data. There are now 24 platform mound sites that have been tested or excavated in Arizona, most within the past 30 years (Doelle and others 1995, Table 13.1), but archaeologically derived knowledge alone has failed to provide resolution as to the nature and function of these features. The information is often too ambiguous for concrete interpretation, and, in fact, has led different investigators to derive different, and sometimes conflicting, interpretations using the same data sets. This ambiguity is at least partly due to the lack of ethnographic analogs on which models can be based or evaluated. In an attempt to dispel a common sentiment in Southwestern archaeology, one that dictates that *only* Southwestern groups are appropriate for ethnographic analogy, Feinman (1994: 242) wrote: "southwestern archaeologists should not be afraid to look outside their region for potentially productive models that may provide new interpretive perspectives."

HISTORY OF PLATFORM MOUND RESEARCH

Doelle and his colleagues (1995) recently provided a comprehensive review of prehistoric platform mound distribution in Arizona. They identified six primary spatial clusters (Fig. 1.1): the lower Salt River of the Phoenix Basin, the middle Gila River of the Phoenix Basin, the Tonto Basin, the Tucson Basin, the lower San Pedro River valley, and the eastern Papaguería

(Table 1.1). A somewhat diffuse and nonclustered distribution of mounds is also present between the Tucson and Phoenix basins in the northern Tucson Basin–Picacho Peak area; otherwise the clusters are discrete, suggesting the possibility that they represent internally cohesive systems (Doelle and others 1995: 436).

The Phoenix Basin, particularly along the Salt River, contains the highest density of platform mounds; the mounds here are larger and earlier than those in other regions and have a significantly longer developmental history (Doelle and others 1995; Doyel 1974; Gregory 1987). The Salt River mounds include Pueblo Grande and Mesa Grande, the two largest platform mounds in the Hohokam region, both estimated to contain approximately 14,000 cubic meters of artificial fill (Doelle and others 1995, Table 13.2, Fig. 13.26). As a comparison, Adamsville, the largest mound along the Gila River, contains around 4,000 cubic meters of fill. The largest mound in the Tonto Basin, Cline Terrace, is estimated to contain slightly more than 2,100 cubic meters of fill, and the Tom Mix and Los Robles mounds, the two largest in the northern Tucson Basin–Picacho Peak area, contain around 2,300 cubic meters. The largest mounds in the Tucson Basin, San Pedro River valley, and Papaguería for which measurements are available contain less than 900 cubic meters of fill.

Platform mounds have been the subject of archaeological investigation in the Hohokam region for more than a hundred years. Prior to the past 15 years, research focused primarily on mound clusters in the Phoenix Basin because it contained the largest and most visually impressive mounds. These features had been known to the professional archaeological community from at least the end of the nineteenth century (Downum and Bostwick 1993; Wilcox 1987). With the exception of the Tonto Basin, where platform mounds were also documented at an early date (Hohmann and Kelley 1988), the presence of mounds in other areas was not realized until much later: platform mounds in the Tucson Basin were first recognized in the 1940s, in the San Pedro River valley in the 1970s, and in the Papaguería in the 1980s. Therefore, the Phoenix Basin was a natural place to begin exploration. Also, the period prior to the mid-1970s was an era dominated by academic and privately sponsored archaeology, along with some government financing by the Civilian Conservation Corps during the 1940s, and funding was easier to procure for the larger and more impressive features. Until the beginning of the 1980s, two-thirds of the excavated or tested platform mounds were from this area (Doelle 1995a, Fig. F.1).

More recently, with the increasing emphasis on work funded by cultural resource management projects, the focus has shifted, and within the past 15 years archaeological investigations have centered on platform mounds in the northern Tucson Basin–Picacho Peak area and in the Tonto Basin (Ciolek-Torrello and Wilcox 1988; Elson, Stark, and Gregory 1995; S. Fish and others 1992; Jacobs 1994a, 1997; Lindauer 1995, 1996a). The Tonto Basin is now particularly well represented through excavations sponsored by the U.S. Bureau of Reclamation in the Roosevelt Lake area (Pedrick 1992); the results of that work form the basis of the research presented here. The reports prepared for the Bureau and published on this important area are listed in the Appendix. This intensive project has evened out the areal coverage, if not biased it toward the Tonto Basin, and today, of the 24 tested or excavated Classic period platform mound sites, 12 are in the Tonto Basin, 7 are in the Phoenix Basin, 2 are in the Tucson Basin, 2 are in the northern Tucson Basin–Picacho Peak area, and a single mound has been investigated in the Papaguería (Doelle and others 1995, Table 13.1). No mounds have been excavated in the San Pedro River area, but they have been documented from survey coverage and limited surface collections (Doelle and Wallace 1997).

To place the Tonto Basin investigations in a regional perspective, I briefly review the history of platform mound research in the Hohokam region of the American Southwest, giving special attention to those projects that substantially advanced the archaeology and general understanding of platform mounds. Doelle (1995a) and Doelle and others (1995) may be consulted for analyses of basic trends in platform mound research and for general historical information. For detailed historic accounts of Phoenix Basin platform mound research at the sites of La Ciudad and Pueblo Grande, see Wilcox (1987, 1993) and Downum and Bostwick (1993). Hohmann and Kelley (1988) discuss early platform mound research in the Tonto Basin.

The Early Years: Bandelier, Cushing, and Fewkes

Starting with the work of Adolph Bandelier and Frank Hamilton Cushing in the 1880s, the significance of platform mounds as centers of prehistoric settlement has long been recognized. Although most of the early research was undertaken along the Salt and Gila rivers of the Phoenix Basin, Bandelier (1892) also recorded a number of mounds in the Tonto Basin.

Bandelier was the first scientist to recognize that the mounds were artificially filled and contained structures on the mound tops (Wilcox 1993: 49). In 1883 Bandelier (1892: 444–445 in Wilcox 1993: 49–50) observed that the Pueblo Grande platform mound in the Phoenix Basin had been artificially mounded:

> it is easy to see, where the interior is exposed, that it is a solid mass of earth, and not a building with rooms. . . . I do not hesitate, therefore, to regard it as a solid mass raised on an artificial platform. The top of the mound bore a cluster of mounds and enclosures, a checkerboard village on a small scale.

A few years later, in 1887, Cushing conducted limited excavations at Pueblo Grande (called by him Los Pueblitos) prior to his more extensive work at Los Muertos, making it the first site in the Southwest to be excavated by a professional archaeologist (Wilcox 1993: 43). In direct contrast to Bandelier, however, whose work he was familiar with, Cushing believed that the mound was not an artificially raised platform but the remains of "a great central structure—a citadel or temple" (Cushing 1892: 52–54 in Wilcox 1993: 56). "It has also been held that these great central structures . . . had been reared on artificial platforms or terraces, whereas our excavations . . . had made evident the fact that the seeming terraces upon which they had been constructed were formed by the destruction of enormous walls" (Cushing in Haury 1945: 8). Drawing on his experience at Zuni and using ethnographic analogy, Cushing thought that the Hohokam "were a highly organized, stratified society run by a priestly class" (Howard 1992: 69; Wilcox and Shenk 1977: 24–25). Although Cushing died prior to completing the report on his Los Muertos and Pueblo Grande excavations, his notes and field records were later analyzed by Emil Haury for his 1934 doctoral dissertation (Haury 1945). In discussing Cushing's interpretation of the platform mounds, Haury (1945: 33) wrote, "The gross size of these adobe houses and their central position led Cushing to the assumption that they were the abodes of the priests and that the commoners occupied the less conspicuous neighboring buildings."

Their interpretive differences led to a public debate between Bandelier and Cushing and to the initiation of controversy over mound function that in many ways continues to the present day. Wilcox (1993: 58) diplomatically points out, however, that both men were essentially correct: although Bandelier's observations on the construction of the Pueblo Grande mound have since been substantiated through excavation, Cushing was also correct in suggesting that the mounds were used in a manner that most archaeologists believe to be at least partly ceremonial.

Archaeological work funded by the United States government at Casa Grande to repair and stabilize the ruin began in the last decade of the nineteenth century (Wilcox and Shenk 1977). This work was undertaken in 1891 by Cosmos Mindeleff (1896, 1897) and in 1906-1908 by J. Walter Fewkes (1907, 1912). Casa Grande contains two platform mounds in Compound B and what is probably another mound in Compound A (Doelle and others 1995: 395). The clearing of debris from within the Casa Grande by Mindeleff confirmed an earlier observation by Bandelier that the ground floor rooms had been artificially filled (Wilcox and Shenk 1977: 23, 38), suggesting that the Casa Grande itself was a platform mound. In his analysis of Casa Grande and the prehistoric culture that spawned it, Fewkes was apparently influenced by Cushing (Haury 1945: 32), although he introduced a more secular interpretation in his discussion of mound function: "An American feudal system developed in the Gila–Salado [Phoenix] Basin, marked by the erection of buildings belonging to some chief (civan) around which were clustered small huts, in which the common people lived" (Fewkes 1912: 152).

The Early Twentieth Century: Haury, Hayden, and the Salado

Platform mound research continued throughout the first half of the twentieth century with an average of two mound sites tested or excavated per decade (Doelle 1995a, Fig. F.1; Doelle and others 1995, Table 13.1). In the Phoenix Basin, Pueblo Grande continued to be sporadically investigated, with excavations at various times by Erich Schmidt, Odd Halseth, Julian Hayden, Albert Schroeder, and several others (Downum and Bostwick 1993). In the late 1920s, the mound at La Ciudad was investigated by Frank Midvale (Wilcox 1987), who, along with his mentor Omar Turney, also documented the distribution of both platform mound sites and prehistoric canals in the Phoenix Basin. The work by Midvale and Turney is highly important because in many cases it represents some of the only documentation of platform mounds long since destroyed by modern development.

In 1926, Erich Schmidt began the first excavations of platform mounds in the Lower Tonto Basin, placing test units into the sites of Armer Ranch, Bass Point, and Rock Island (Hohmann and Kelley 1988; Lindauer

1995), and in 1929 and 1930 Haury undertook limited excavation at the Rye Creek Ruin platform mound in the Upper Tonto Basin (Craig 1992; Gregory 1996; Haury 1930). In the Tucson Basin, Julian Hayden's (1957) detailed excavations at University Indian Ruin in 1940 extended the recorded distribution of platform mounds southward. Although Gabel (1931) had previously excavated rooms on top of each of the platform mounds at Martinez Hill South in the Tucson Basin, and Scantling (1940) excavated at the Papaguería mound site of Jack Rabbit Ruin, neither of these were perceived by their excavators to be platform mounds (Doelle 1995a: 355). It was not until Hayden (1957: 2), coming directly from his work at Pueblo Grande, began excavations at University Indian Ruin that platform mounds were recognized south of the Phoenix Basin.

The research of Schmidt (1928) in the Tonto and Phoenix basins, and later that of Winifred and Harold Gladwin (1935), resulted in the definition of the Salado culture. The Salado, as conceived by the Gladwins, were a migratory people from the Little Colorado area who manufactured white ware and polychrome ceramics, built masonry and adobe pueblos, and buried their dead in an extended position. Recognition of the Salado came through the discovery of white ware and polychrome pottery stratigraphically above the red-on-buff wares of the Hohokam (Hohmann and Kelley 1988; Schmidt 1928). The dissimilarity of cultural traits supported the idea of a different cultural group: the Hohokam lived in pit houses and cremated their dead, whereas masonry architecture and interment were associated with the white ware ceramics. In the traditional scenario posited by the Gladwins, the Salado migrated into the Tonto Basin around A.D. 1100, replacing the Hohokam who had previously abandoned the basin at the start of the Sacaton phase (about A.D. 950; Fig. 1.3). Using the Tonto Basin as a home base, the Salado then proceeded to migrate throughout southern Arizona, strongly influencing (and even truncating) Hohokam development in the Phoenix and Tucson basins by A.D. 1300.

Although debate continues sixty years later, most researchers now think that Salado represents more of a pan-southern Southwest regional horizon or religious cult rather than a defined cultural group or migratory people (Crown 1994: 214-217; Dean 1998; Elson, Gregory, and Stark 1995: 477-478). The Salado concept is important in the history of platform mound research because it introduced an ethnic variable into the explanatory equation. That is, although archaeologists considered the Hohokam to be the original builders of the platform

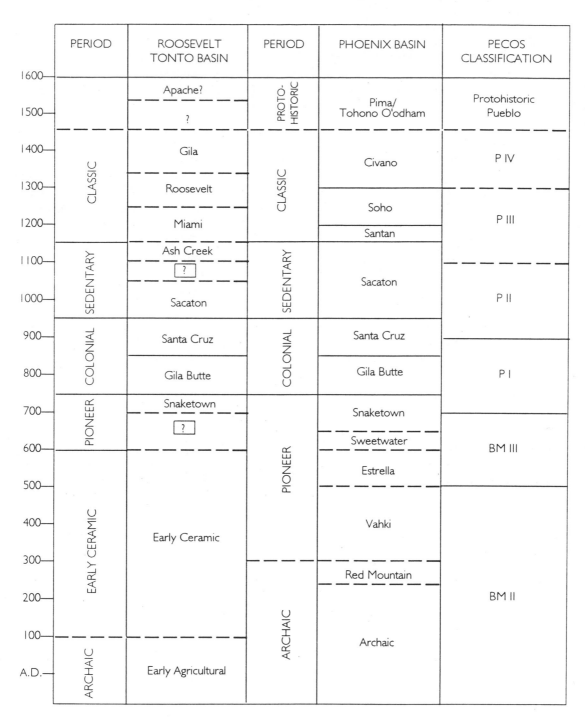

	PERIOD	ROOSEVELT TONTO BASIN	PERIOD	PHOENIX BASIN	PECOS CLASSIFICATION
1600		Apache?	PROTO-HISTORIC	Pima/ Tohono O'odham	Protohistoric Pueblo
1500		?			
1400	CLASSIC	Gila	CLASSIC	Civano	P IV
1300		Roosevelt		Soho	P III
1200		Miami		Santan	
1100	SEDENTARY	Ash Creek / ?	SEDENTARY	Sacaton	P II
1000		Sacaton			
900	COLONIAL	Santa Cruz	COLONIAL	Santa Cruz	P I
800		Gila Butte		Gila Butte	
700	PIONEER	Snaketown / ?	PIONEER	Snaketown	BM III
600				Sweetwater	
500	EARLY CERAMIC	Early Ceramic		Estrella	
400				Vahki	BM II
300			ARCHAIC	Red Mountain	
200					
100	ARCHAIC			Archaic	
A.D.		Early Agricultural			

Figure 1.3. Chronology and phase systematics for the Tonto Basin and selected areas of the American Southwest (after Elson 1995, Fig. 2.1).

mounds, they suggested that the Salado were the builders of the massive platform mound architecture that marked the transition from the Soho phase (A.D. 1200–1300) to the Civano phase (A.D. 1300–1450).

The use of the Salado as an explanatory mechanism is best exemplified by the work of Haury (1945) in his analysis of Cushing's Los Muertos excavations in the

Phoenix Basin and of Hayden (1957) in his investigation of University Indian Ruin in the Tucson Basin. Both characterized the Hohokam as the initial mound-builders, largely because on top of the mounds were "Hohokam-type houses" that were later torn down and replaced by the "multiple storied houses of massive adobe walls" of the Salado (Haury 1945: 35; Hayden 1957:

194). Concerning this massive Civano phase architecture, which Cushing had previously designated as the temples of the ruling priests, Haury (1945: 35) said, "These were the direct result of the Salado migration, undoubtedly built by the Salado, and the type of architecture appears simultaneously with other traits of their culture." To Haury, then, the platform mounds of the Civano phase resulted from the intrusion of a different ethnic group, rather than from the occupation of an elite or priestly class as advocated by Cushing and Fewkes. Haury further wrote, "While the possibility of such a condition [occupation by a priestly class] is not to be denied, it can be satisfactorily shown that the chief architectural difference is ethnic rather than one due to any direct internal social difference within a single group" (Haury 1945: 32–33). Why the Hohokam initially constructed platform mounds was still open to question, although Haury (1945: 35) suggested defense, waterlogged soils, or emulation of Mesoamerican groups as possibilities.

Hayden (1957) also thought that the Salado were responsible for constructing the massive late architecture found overlying Hohokam remains on the mound tops. Based on the lack of evidence for salt erosion at Pueblo Grande and on the fact that waterlogged soils would not have been a major problem at mound sites along the Gila River, he was more definitive in assessing overall mound function, writing that "no other purpose than that of defense may be seen in their erection" (Hayden 1957: 194). Like Haury, Hayden speculated that the platform mound concept probably came to the Hohokam from the south, although again he was more definitive and identified the nearby Trincheras area of northern Sonora as a likely source. Trincheras sites, although not platform mounds, are masonry fortifications built on elevated hilltops and ridges that have been traditionally interpreted as having a defensive function (Downum 1986, 1993). In Hayden's (1957: 194) words, "the artificial mounds of the Hohokam would appear to represent the adaptation of this idea to the flat, broad valley floors which the Hohokam farmed." Hayden reasoned that a defensive posture by the Hohokam was necessary because of Yuman invaders, although intrusions by both Salado and Apache groups were also mentioned as possible factors.

The 1970s: Doyel and the Escalante Ruin

The era of modern platform mound research in the Hohokam region essentially began with a publication by David Doyel (1974) in which he described the excavation of the Escalante Ruin by the Arizona State Museum in 1972. Escalante is a moderately sized mound along the Gila River, covering 875 square meters and containing an estimated volume of fill of 1,750 cubic meters; it stood approximately 2.0 meters high (Doelle and others 1995, Table 13.3). The entire Escalante mound system is one of the smallest in the Phoenix Basin, containing a single small village with a platform mound (the Escalante Ruin itself) and several associated compounds along an 11–km (6.8–mile) irrigation canal. In contrast, the Casa Grande mound system, one of the largest in the Phoenix Basin, has five platform mound villages and numerous smaller compounds along a 32–km (19.3–mile) canal (Crown 1987; Elson, Gregory, and Stark 1995, Fig. 14.2). Escalante is important, however, because it represents the first investigation of a platform mound site using modern archaeological methods.

Although the mound itself was not completely excavated, Doyel (1974: 116–117) documented that it was constructed with a series of retaining walls and internal cells that were filled with sterile deposits and cultural trash. Like the earlier work of Hayden and Haury, Doyel discovered that the top of the mound contained a Hohokam-style pit house overlain by solid-walled adobe structures (Doyel 1974: 125). He also recovered archaeomagnetic samples that provided some of the first absolute dates associated with platform mounds, although at that time the samples were dated on the DuBois curve, which is no longer thought to be accurate. An attempt to redate these samples using Colorado State University's 1986 archaeomagnetic curve produced ambiguous results (Eighmy and Doyel 1987, Table 2). The ceramic assemblage indicated a Civano phase (A.D. 1300–1450) date for the mound.

One of the most significant contributions of the Escalante investigations was Doyel's (1974: 175–177) perception that Classic period platform mounds in the Phoenix Basin were the result of a long sequence of in situ development. Noting the presence of small pre-Classic mounds at the sites of Snaketown and Gatlin, Doyel (1974: 176) posited "a general evolution" in platform mound construction through "900 years of the Hohokam cultural sequence." Neither Haury (1976) at Snaketown nor Wasley (1960) at Gatlin believed that these earlier platform mounds were residential, based primarily on the lack of structures on the mound tops; instead, a ceremonial function was inferred. Although the information was meager at the time of the Escalante excavations, evidence from platform mounds of the following Soho phase (A.D. 1150–1300) indicated to Doyel a similar nonresidential use. The Escalante excavations, however, showed that with the post–A.D. 1300 Civano phase came a change in mound function: "During the Civano phase, the function or organizational structure of these mounds may have been altered. . . . Typical domestic structures and typical daily activities were performed by the people who lived on top of the Escalante mound" (Doyel 1974: 177).

Doyel (1974, 1980: 31) further suggested that construction of the Escalante mound was undertaken communally by a number of related villages, probably joined together by a common canal system, which he defined as an "irrigation community." The overall Escalante community was integrated to some degree, then, with the hub of the settlement being the large Escalante mound itself. However, there was not much evidence that those who occupied the mound were of an elite class or had a special status: "Habitation rooms and a substantial number of common implements were found on top of the mound, while nothing was present that could be termed ceremonial. Thus, there is no indication that the mound served to house individuals or families of high status" (Doyel 1974: 170). Acknowledging that archaeological indicators of ceremonial- or status-related activities are often not recovered or difficult to interpret, Doyel went on to postulate that the mound-top occupants may have had limited authority through control of ritual knowledge and scheduling of group activities; he added, however, that supporting evidence for this idea was lacking at Escalante.

Most importantly, in direct contrast to the theories of Haury and Hayden, Doyel (1974: 189–190) disputed the Salado migration hypothesis as an explanation for changes in platform mound architecture. Even though typical Salado pottery, such as the Gila and Tonto polychromes, comprised the majority of the Escalante decorated ceramic assemblage, Doyel postulated the pottery was a local expression of a regional, pan-Southwest art form. Presaging sentiments expressed more completely in later work (Doyel 1976, 1978), particularly in his research on the Salado of the Tonto Basin and Globe-Miami areas, Doyel saw cultural continuity throughout the Escalante developmental sequence (Doyel 1974: 189):

> it is not sufficient to rely solely upon migration or expansion mechanisms as explanatory models for the diversity in cultural behavior during the Hohokam Classic period. . . . The pattern consists of Hohokam ceramics (Gila Plain, Gila Red, and

Casa Grande Red-on-buff), transitional Hohokam architecture with standard Hohokam features, standard Hohokam stone, bone and shell assemblages, a continuation of the Hohokam riverine subsistence and settlement system, and strong similarities in social organization. This continuity cannot be satisfactorily explained by the presence of an intrusive cultural pattern.

The 1980s: Gregory and Las Colinas

After a hiatus of nearly 10 years, the next significant period of platform mound research in the Hohokam region was initiated by David Gregory (1987, 1988a; Gregory and Nials 1985; Gregory and others 1985), based primarily on the 1982–1984 excavations by the Arizona State Museum at the site of Las Colinas. Las Colinas is one of the largest platform mound villages in the Phoenix Basin, containing at least four platform mounds within an estimated area of 3.5 to 5.0 square kilometers (Gregory and others 1985). It is likely that the village contained additional platform mounds, but they cannot be verified because they were long ago destroyed by modern construction. A large pre-Classic period village with a ballcourt underlies the Classic period component. Las Colinas is located at the west end of Canal System 2, approximately 12 km (7.5 miles) west of Pueblo Grande, which is at the head of the canal system (Howard and Huckleberry 1991).

Because of development within the city of Phoenix, only Mound 8 was still largely intact at the time of the Las Colinas excavations. Unfortunately, the top of the mound had been disturbed by historic house construction and it was not possible to excavate a full complement of mound-top features (Gregory 1988b: 36). Mound 8 was of moderate size, although slightly smaller than Escalante, and was estimated to cover 720 square meters and contain 1,584 cubic meters of fill (Doelle and others 1995, Table 13.2). It stood approximately 2.2 meters above the ground surface. The mound was partially excavated by the Arizona State Museum in 1968, and archaeologists determined that it had undergone several relatively complex episodes of rebuilding and expansion (Hammack and Sullivan 1981). Gregory conducted additional excavations and, with the evidence collected earlier, defined seven stages of mound growth. Each of the seven stages represented a period when the mound was functioning and stood "as a discrete and recognizable entity for some extended period of time" (Gregory and Abbott 1988: 23).

The work at Las Colinas represents one of the most complete excavations of a Phoenix Basin platform mound. Although it is now known that mound construction methods varied, depending on the type of mound and to a certain extent on its geographic location, Gregory's reconstruction of the building sequence illuminated one of the more common methods: "the initial construction of the mound and each subsequent modification began with the building of a retaining wall that defined the basic plan of the mound and created the internal space which was then filled to form the physical bulk of each structure" (Gregory and Abbott 1988: 23). Gregory (1988b: 26) also documented that the area where the mound was built, or the "mound precinct," was a designated specialized space for several hundred years prior to mound construction, perhaps from the earliest days of the Las Colinas occupation.

Most significantly, Gregory suggested that the Las Colinas mound bridged the gap between the earlier, small pre-Classic mound forms and the later, more massive Classic period forms, supporting Doyel's (1974) inference that Hohokam platform mounds had a long, in situ developmental sequence. According to Gregory (1987: 188), the first six stages of mound construction were essentially identical to what Wasley (1960) described at the pre-Classic Gatlin mound. These earlier mounds were round or had rounded corners and were formed by adding a post-reinforced retaining wall and then filling the space between the previous mound and the new wall. The seventh stage of the Las Colinas mound, however, was formed by the addition of a "massive, coursed adobe retaining wall in the shape of a well-defined rectangle" (Gregory 1987: 188). This massive adobe wall was similar to the Civano phase walls that Cushing uncovered at Los Muertos, that Doyel reported from Escalante, and that Hayden found at University Indian Ruin. The construction sequence was strengthened by a suite of archaeomagnetic dates that indicated the initial mound construction occurred late in the pre-Classic Sedentary period, perhaps between A.D. 1100 and 1150, whereas the final Stage VII mound was probably constructed sometime in the early-to-mid thirteenth century (Gregory 1987, Fig. 4).

As part of the Las Colinas research, Gregory (1987, 1988a; Gregory and Nials 1985) undertook a comprehensive study of Phoenix Basin platform mounds, focusing on architecture and on site and feature distribution. This work remains one of the most important contributions to platform mound research in the American Southwest. Gregory documented consistent patterning in mound layout, in site structure, and in the regular placement of mound villages every 5 km to 8 km (3 to 5 miles) along prehistoric Phoenix Basin irrigation canals. The construction of platform mounds and the control of irrigation systems could now be viewed as closely interrelated, with the leadership necessary to build and maintain canal systems probably stemming from the associated platform mound village (Gregory and Nials 1985: 383–386). Gregory (1987: 208) further noted comparatively that platform mounds outside of the Phoenix Basin, in areas with more limited irrigation potential, tended to be smaller with greater variation in mound form and overall site structure, implying that these mounds may have functioned in a different manner from those in the Phoenix Basin.

Patterning was also present in the rectangular shape and north-south orientation of the mound compound and in the location of the mound within the compound, which most commonly was in the western portion abutting or close to the western wall (Gregory 1987: 195). At sites with both platform mounds and ballcourts, which included most mound sites in the Phoenix Basin, there was also a consistent relationship between the location and orientation of the ballcourt and the placement of the mound. These patterns indicated that a conventionality prevailed throughout the Phoenix Basin that dictated the structure and function of the platform mounds (Gregory 1987: 208).

The Las Colinas excavations also provided support for Doyel's (1974) earlier suggestion that a change in function occurred between the early and late mound forms. "Earlier forms did not function as residential space, whereas the massive walled form of mound had this as a primary function. In all known cases, these mounds appear to have been the locus of residence for some social group or groups" (Gregory 1987: 208). Most importantly, because mound and canal construction required defined leadership and social group control, most likely from those occupying the mound, Gregory (1987: 209) concluded that the inhabitants of platform mound sites were clearly socially differentiated, with the authority of leaders probably legitimized through the religious system. Therefore, the shift from nonresidential to residential use of the mounds was critically important, signifying a change from a purely ritual function to one that may have involved both ritual and administrative control.

What is of interest is that this connection—of specific social groups with platform mounds—became a one-to-one identification sometime during the early decades of the thirteenth century. Thus the mounds were no longer strictly the focus of some specialized, probably ritual activities, but served as the actual locus of residence for certain groups as well. It is plausible, then, that this shift in the use of platform mounds represents a change in the role of certain groups within the society. . . . Whatever this set of roles may have been, they would have been symbolized and legitimized by residence upon the mounds (Gregory 1987: 209).

The 1980s and 1990s: Northern Tucson Basin and Picacho Peak Areas

Two projects in the 1980s and 1990s have led to a greater understanding of platform mound sites located in "peripheral" areas with limited irrigation potential. One is the excavation of the Brady Wash platform mound in 1984 by Richard Ciolek-Torrello, then with the Museum of Northern Arizona (Ciolek-Torrello and others 1988; Ciolek-Torrello and Wilcox 1988), and the other is the investigation of the Marana platform mound between 1988 and 1990 by Paul and Suzanne Fish of the Arizona State Museum (P. Fish and others 1992; S. Fish and others 1992). Several sites without mounds in the Marana community were also investigated by archaeologists from Arizona State University (Rice 1987a).

The Brady Wash Platform Mound

The Brady Wash platform mound, located in the Picacho Peak area north of the Tucson Basin proper, is an extremely small mound, in fact one of the smallest known. It consists of two underlying cells that were filled to elevate a surface of 47 square meters approximately 2 meters high (Ciolek-Torrello 1988: 307). The total volume of fill is estimated at 94 cubic meters (Doelle and others 1995, Table 13.7). The construction of internal cells, in contrast with the building of retaining walls as described by Gregory for Las Colinas, was another common method of forming platform mounds in the Hohokam region. Cells were essentially small, square-to-rectangular room spaces that were filled with cultural trash or sterile deposits to make an elevated surface. Most cells were built solely to elevate the mound surface, but functioning rooms were sometimes also turned into cells when abandoned. Cells were often used in conjunction with retaining walls, particularly at larger mounds; in small mounds, cells were generally the only construction method used.

According to Ciolek-Torrello (1988: 307), the Brady Wash mound may have been initially constructed in the late Soho phase, when it stood as an isolated feature; the following Civano phase saw the addition of the "compound wall . . . [and] massive rooms attached to the mound . . . ." Unlike mound sites in the Phoenix Basin, the Brady Wash mound was not associated with other compounds. Instead, it was surrounded by a dispersed, low density settlement containing isolated pit houses and adobe structures extending over an area of approximately one square kilometer.

There was extensive disturbance within the mound area (a cow had been buried in the mound itself) and most of the mound was not excavated (Gasser and Ciolek-Torrello 1988: 510–514, Fig. 61). Based on the somewhat limited findings, Ciolek-Torrello (1988: 307–308) suggested that the Brady Wash mound and mound compound were not residential, a perception contrary to the residential function proposed for other excavated Civano phase platform mounds in both the Phoenix (Las Colinas and Escalante) and Tucson (University Indian Ruin) basins. The assignment of a nonresidential function was based on the small size of the mound, the absence of a structure on its top, and the general lack of clay-lined hearths "typical of habitations throughout the community" in associated compound rooms. Instead, noting that the compound contained storage rooms and a number of large fire pits, Ciolek-Torrello (1988: 308) proposed that the mound and compound were used for "communal food processing" and functioned as a "community ceremonial, storage, and distribution center."

Because the excavation was incomplete and one of the rooms within the mound compound appeared to be a habitation room, Ciolek-Torrello acknowledged the possibility that limited residential occupation may have occurred within the mound area. But he maintained that even if several groups lived within the mound compound, they were "too few to represent an elite social group" (Ciolek-Torrello 1988: 310), although his basis for equating group size with elite status is unclear. The absence of an elite group was further indicated by the artifact assemblage, which was not significantly different from that of the outlying habitation areas. "The few households which may have occupied the mound did not exhibit much evidence of greater wealth or status than those living in surrounding areas. In fact, status goods were rare and the few burials and cremations found within the compound and associated trash areas contained no grave offerings" (Ciolek-Torrello 1988: 308).

Using the exact same data set, but drawing on some of the ambiguities in the Brady Wash excavation sample, Wilcox (1988) postulated a residential function for the Brady Wash platform mound, based on three lines of evidence. First, he speculated that the usable elevated area would have been much larger than just the 47-square-meter surface of the two platform mound cells if the roofs of adjoining rooms were also used, thereby discounting Ciolek-Torrello's size argument. Second, a hearth on the roof of one of the structures adjoining the mound indicated elevated habitation; other evidence for mound-top habitation may have been obscured by the incomplete and disturbed nature of the excavation sample. And finally, Wilcox (1988: 296) deduced, unlike Ciolek-Torrello, that the artifact assemblage did show "differential distribution of valuables, particularly shell and turquoise." Based on his interpretations, Wilcox (1988: 289) concluded that, "These data support a hypothesis that the occupants of Brady Wash became more socially ranked during the Classic period with the occupants at Locus S [the platform mound locus] managing the whole community. These changes mimic those happening in riverine settlements, although the size of the Brady Wash groups was clearly smaller." In this manner, Wilcox echoed earlier sentiments derived from his archival study of the large La Ciudad platform mound in the Phoenix Basin excavated by Frank Midvale in the 1920s. As he remarked about La Ciudad, "The structure of space usage . . . supports the inference that an elite social group resided on the mound" (Wilcox 1987: 168).

The Marana Platform Mound

The most comprehensive analysis of a platform mound complex in a primarily nonirrigable area is that of the Marana community in the northern Tucson Basin (Bayman 1992, 1994; P. Fish and others 1992; S. Fish and others 1985, 1989, 1992; Rice 1987a). The Marana platform mound is situated within the lower bajada of the Tortolita Mountains approximately 5 km (3 miles) east of the Santa Cruz River. The mound is centrally located within a village that extends parallel to the Santa Cruz for a distance of 1.5 km (about 1 mile). Along with the mound, the site contains seven residential clusters with an estimated 22 to 25 compounds (Bayman 1994: 19; P. Fish and others 1992: 63). Because most of these compounds have not been excavated, the exact number of rooms is unknown. The mound village is estimated to have contained between 400 and 750 inhabitants (P. Fish and others 1992: 63), although others suggest that these population figures are high because not all compounds were contemporaneous (Wallace 1995c: 812). An associated settlement system containing numerous smaller sites and agricultural field areas

extended from the Marana mound site approximately 25 km (15 miles) south up the Santa Cruz River.

The Marana mound itself was relatively small, encompassing 394 square meters with an estimated fill volume of 788 cubic meters; it was elevated to a height of approximately 2 meters (Doelle and others 1995, Table 13.7). From somewhat limited excavation evidence, the mound was postulated as a residential facility for "community leaders" based on the "presence of rooms and hearths on top of the platform mound, and domestic refuse in a nearby midden" (Bayman 1994: 19). Dated ceramics indicated the mound was constructed during the early Classic period Tanque Verde phase, around A.D. 1150 or 1200, and abandoned no later than 1325 prior to the advent of Gila Polychrome (Doelle and others 1995: 418). Based on archaeomagnetic determinations, the mound sustained a relatively brief occupation in the first half of the thirteenth century (P. Fish and others 1992: 63).

Extensive survey of more than 350 square kilometers surrounding the Marana mound recorded more than 700 archaeological sites (S. Fish and others 1992: 20). Of these, around 400 dated to the Tanque Verde phase and may have been contemporaneous with the platform mound (P. Fish and others 1992: 62). The distribution of these sites defined a very large Classic period platform mound community, of which the mound site itself was just one component. This community was separated from other contemporary communities of "equivalent sociopolitical units" by "buffer zones" of limited settlement (S. Fish and others 1992). In contrast to the linear irrigation communities of the Phoenix Basin, Suzanne Fish and her colleagues suggested that the Marana community was not primarily focused along the Santa Cruz River, but included both a riverine component and settlement extending away from the river into the bajada and foothills of the Tortolita Mountains. Settlement in this area, which covered approximately 145 square kilometers, was diffuse and therefore difficult to compare with the well-defined, canal-focused Phoenix Basin mound systems that averaged approximately 40 square kilometers (S. Fish and P. Fish 1992: 102).

Each of the six microenvironmental zones within the Marana community provided suitable conditions for different kinds of agriculture or resource procurement (S. Fish and others 1992: 31–34). Three of the zones contained residential settlement. Significantly, the midbajada zone, which contained "42,000 rock piles and 120,000 meters of linear rock alignments," was the scene of large-scale agave cultivation that probably represented subsistence specialization (Bayman 1994:

21). The platform mound itself and most of the habitations were within the lower bajada zone, which was suitable primarily for floodwater agriculture. Directly below, the riverine zone presented opportunities for both floodwater and irrigation agriculture. This zone contained several irrigation canals extending from headgates located near the site of Los Morteros, which was approximately 12 km (7.5 miles) south of the Marana mound (S. Fish and others 1992, Fig. 3.2). Los Morteros was one of the largest pre-Classic ballcourt villages in the northern Tucson Basin; although lacking a platform mound, the Classic period Tanque Verde phase occupation was relatively substantial and included several adobe compounds and a large hillside trincheras settlement (Wallace 1995b). The Marana mound itself was at the end of the canal system, placing it in a tenuous position to exert direct control over the water source unless some degree of community integration was present. However, large-scale canal irrigation like that in the Phoenix Basin was not possible on the Santa Cruz River, with its broad floodplain, shifting river channel, and less dependable surface flow (S. Fish and others 1992; Wallace 1995c: 813).

Suzanne Fish and others (1992: 39) documented a "three-tiered settlement hierarchy based on site size, architecture, and ceramics." This vertical differentiation was further supported by the work of Bayman (1992, 1994), who analyzed the distribution of "high value" exotic artifacts such as obsidian, shell, projectile points, and imported decorated ceramics. Bayman (1994: 37–38) discerned that residents of the platform mound village were both producers and consumers of these goods, whereas in the smaller habitations away from the mound, high value artifacts were either not commonly available or restricted in access. Bayman (1994: 37) suggested that these patterns represented the "development of a 'prestige economy' . . . or a system of 'social storage' . . . where the control of exotic goods is used to establish and maintain elite status and political power." He further postulated that "by regulating the distribution of rare and exotic goods, mound village residents could occupy an otherwise unfavorable zone for food production by trading small amounts of [high value] crafts for subsistence foodstuffs, raw materials, or finished utilitarian craft goods" (Bayman 1994: 37).

According to Suzanne and Paul Fish (1992: 102–104), one of the primary functions of the platform mound was to integrate the Marana community. The mound may have also served as a center from which the Marana elites competed with elites from nearby platform mound villages for resources and particularly

for population (S. Fish and P. Fish 1992: 104; see also Henderson 1993). Integration was necessary because of the lack of a unifying canal system and the presence of diverse environmental zones with varying subsistence potential. It was accomplished through both public ceremony, probably of a religious nature, and institutionalized leadership. The platform mound itself, in part because it was constructed through communal effort, served as a physical symbol of community integration.

The 1990s: Tonto Basin

The most intensive platform mound investigations in recent years have been in the Lower Tonto Basin of central Arizona (Fig. 1.1). This research, conducted under the mandate of cultural resource management legislation, was sponsored by the Bureau of Reclamation to mitigate the effects of raising the dam at Roosevelt Lake approximately 23 meters (77 feet), thereby increasing the zone of possible floodwater inundation (Pedrick 1992). Between 1991 and 1992, archaeologists from Desert Archaeology and Arizona State University excavated seven platform mound sites in this area: Meddler Point (Craig and Clark 1994), Pyramid Point (Elson 1994), Livingston (Jacobs 1994a), Pinto Point (Jacobs 1994a), Schoolhouse Point (Lindauer 1996a, 1997a), Bass Point (Lindauer 1995), and Cline Terrace (Jacobs 1997). In addition, mapping and limited test excavations were undertaken at the Oak Creek platform mound (Lindauer 1989) and, as part of the Rye Creek Project, the mound site of Rye Creek Ruin in the Upper Tonto Basin was mapped and test units were placed in three trash mounds (Elson and Craig 1992).

Information from these investigations constitutes one of the most comprehensive archaeological data bases in the greater Southwest. In all, about 150 prehistoric sites were tested or partially excavated. One well-defined local settlement system in the eastern Tonto Basin contained 44 sites, including 5 platform mounds (Meddler Point, Pyramid Point, Livingston, Pinto Point, and Schoolhouse Point) within a 6–km (3.7–mile) linear stretch of the Salt River. This area was investigated as part of two programs: the Roosevelt Community Development Study by Desert Archaeology (Elson, Stark, and Gregory 1995; Elson and Swartz 1994; Elson and others 1994) and the Livingston and Schoolhouse Point projects by Arizona State University (Jacobs 1994a; Lindauer 1996a, 1997a). The archaeology of the Tonto Basin is described in detail in Chapter 4. What is important to note here is that the diversity apparent in interpretations applied to mounds throughout the Southwest similarly applies to the more recently excavated mounds in the Tonto Basin.

FUNCTIONS OF HOHOKAM PLATFORM MOUNDS

There is general agreement among archaeologists working in the Hohokam region that platform mounds were specialized features constructed by suprahousehold group effort. The mounds probably served in some way, either through ceremonial or administrative means or perhaps a combination of the two, to integrate segments of the population and regulate irrigation and other subsistence activities. In this sense, platform mounds can be characterized as "high-level integrative features," following the work of Adler (1989) and Adler and Wilshusen (1990). Still, there is widespread variability in both mound morphology and archaeological interpretations of mound function. Doelle and his colleagues (1995) noted that although some of this variability, such as the use of particular construction methods or building materials, may be due to differences in local resources, much of the diversity in mound form and function, and therefore in archaeological interpretations of mounds, cannot currently be ascribed only to mound location.

Previous research in the Phoenix Basin, for example, has resulted in the following archaeological interpretations. Soho phase platform mounds were used primarily for nonresidential, probably ritual, activities (Doyel 1974; Gregory 1987). Civano phase platform mounds were used by religious specialists and were primarily nonresidential (Bostwick and Downum 1994; Howard 1992). Civano phase platform mounds were occupied by non-elites (Doyel 1974). Civano phase platform mounds were occupied by elites, possibly for combined religious and administrative functions (Gregory 1987; Wilcox 1987). Civano phase platform mounds were occupied by an elite class of priestly chiefs (Cushing 1892). Civano phase platform mounds were occupied by a new and intrusive ethnic group, the Salado (Haury 1945).

Interpretations for the northern Tucson Basin–Picacho Peak area included a Tanque Verde (Soho) phase platform mound occupied by managerial elites (Bayman 1994; S. Fish and others 1992; Rice 1987b). The only excavated Civano phase platform mound was thought to have been primarily nonresidential with little evidence for elite status (Ciolek-Torrello 1988), but a different analysis using the same information reported a residential occupation by an elite group (Wilcox 1988).

Differences in opinion are also registered for the Tonto Basin, where various models suggest the presence of residential and nonresidential mounds; elites and non-elites; and egalitarian, ranked, and stratified societies (Ciolek-Torrello and others 1994; Elson, Stark, and Gregory 1995; Hohmann and Kelley 1988; Jacobs and Rice 1994, 1997; Lindauer 1995, 1996a; Rice 1990a, 1990b; Whittlesey and Ciolek-Torrello 1992; Wood 1992; Wood and Hohmann 1985). And, like interpretations of the Civano phase Brady Wash mound in the northern Tucson Basin–Picacho Peak area, the same data set has been used to argue for either residential (Wallace 1995a) or nonresidential (Craig and Clark 1994; Elson, Gregory, and Stark 1995) occupation of the Meddler Point platform mound.

One of the primary areas of debate in previous research is the nature and degree of social complexity achieved by mound-building groups. Arguments abound concerning whether elites lived on the platform mounds, implying a high degree of social differentiation and therefore relatively high complexity, or whether the mounds were largely ceremonial and nonresidential. Furthermore, platform mounds are just one cultural expression in the larger debate over social complexity that has been raging for years throughout the greater Southwest (Cordell and others 1987; McGuire and Saitta 1996; Plog 1995; Reid and others 1989; Reid and Whittlesey 1990; Upham 1982). Although arguments over whether mound societies represent egalitarian groups (Whittlesey and Ciolek-Torrello 1992), simple or complex chiefdoms (Rice 1987b; Wilcox and Shenk 1977), or even states (Wood and Hohmann 1985; Wood and McAllister 1980) are no longer common in the literature in part because of problems with the "evolutionary stage" concept (Blanton and others 1996; Yoffee and Sherratt 1993), disputes over complexity remain.

For example, Ciolek-Torrello (1988: 310) wrote that the inhabitants of mound sites in areas with limited irrigation potential, such as Brady Wash, may have been at "a much lower level of social complexity" than those who occupied the Phoenix Basin platform mounds. This statement was mirrored by Doelle and others (1995: 439) when they suggested that there was greater social differentiation in the Phoenix Basin than in other mound systems. In the Tonto Basin, Craig (1995: 246-249) used Johnson's (1982, 1983) scalar stress model and notion of sequential hierarchies to explain the function of the Meddler Point platform mound and its role in the organization of irrigation systems, implying a relatively noncomplex social organization. Based primarily on the absence of material remains in the Tonto Basin that indicated social differentiation, low social complexity was also proposed by Ciolek-Torrello and others (1994); by Elson, Gregory, and Stark (1995: 447); and by Whittlesey and Ciolek-Torrello (1992).

On the other hand, relatively high complexity was posited for the Marana platform mound, also in an area of limited irrigation potential, through use of various permutations of the "peer-polity" interaction model (Renfrew and Cherry 1986) and the "prestige-goods" economy model (Friedman and Rowlands 1977) to explain patterning in artifact and site distribution (Bayman 1994; S. Fish and P. Fish 1992: 104; Rice 1987b). Competition between platform mound communities, as attested by Suzanne and Paul Fish (1992) and by Kathleen Henderson (1993), entailed increasing social complexity, as did the accumulation of surplus and the presence of significant economic differentiation. Researchers have postulated that abundant surplus, the differential distribution of status goods and power, and occasionally attached craft specialization were present at platform mound sites in the Phoenix and Tonto basins, indicating relatively high social complexity (Gregory 1987; Hohmann and Kelley 1988; Lindauer 1996a; Rice 1992; Wilcox 1991; Wood 1995; and Wood and Hohmann 1985).

THE QUESTION OF SOCIAL COMPLEXITY

Measuring social complexity through the archaeological record is in itself a complex process, and unidimensional models focusing on "levels" or "stages" of complexity add little to understanding the prehistoric situation. Complexity is polythetic, and a more appropriate question than asking "How complex were they?" is to ask "How were they complex?" (Nelson 1995: 599). This query involves "decoupling" or "unpacking" the elements of complexity into its constituent parts (Hastorf 1990; McGuire 1983; Nelson 1995; Upham 1990). Complexity has been viewed or modeled in a number of different ways by archaeologists: one is through a functionalist model that stresses group adaptation (Blanton and others 1981; Flannery 1972; Johnson 1982, 1983; Redman 1992); another is through a model focusing on individual action, or on a human actor as agent model (Brumfiel 1992; Clark and Blake 1994; Joyce and Winter 1996); and a third is through the use of the Marxist dialectic (McGuire and Saitta 1996). All of these approaches add to the understanding of social complexity and, despite debate, are not necessarily incompatible. Although the functionalists view complexity as a means for groups to adapt to varying

types of social and environmental stress (Flannery 1972; Johnson 1989), the role of the individual actor in this process cannot be discounted (Brumfiel 1992: 559; Hayden 1995; Price and Feinman 1995: 10), as is also stressed by some Marxist theorists (McGuire and Saitta 1996: 200).

At its most basic level, complexity is measured as the degree of internal differentiation, specialization, intensification, and centralization within a given social group (Flannery 1972). "Complexity refers to the extent to which there is functional differentiation among societal units" (Blanton and others 1981: 21). As complexity increases, there is an increase in group heterogeneity and inequality (McGuire 1983) and the differential distribution of goods, resources, and power (Adams 1966; Redman 1992). Scale and hierarchy also increase with increasing complexity (Nelson 1995). All of these processes result in the centralization of decision making into fewer and fewer hands under the control of a single leader or a small group of leaders as groups move from sequential hierarchies among essentially egalitarian and undifferentiated units to simultaneous hierarchies among unequal units (Johnson 1982, 1983). With increasing power and centralization, however, comes a corresponding increase in the potential of individual action as an agent of social change (Blanton and others 1996; Clark and Blake 1994; Hayden 1995; Joyce and Winter 1996; McGuire and Saitta 1996). This means that it is critical that the needs of both the individual and the larger social group be considered when examining complexity. In general, however, even with this new emphasis on individual action, most archaeologists use a systems-oriented definition of complexity that has changed little since it was defined by Flannery in the 1970s.

Truly "egalitarian" groups did not exist in the ceramic period Southwest, and most groups encompassed both egalitarian and hierarchical social dimensions (Flanagan 1989; Plog 1995: 190; Price and Feinman 1995: 4). Concerning historic period pueblo society, long used as a model for prehistoric Southwestern groups, Feinman (1992: 179) noted, "we ought not to conflate egalitarian ideologies with egalitarian social or economic behaviors." Therefore, in analyzing social complexity, the important distinction is not between egalitarian and non-egalitarian groups, but between groups with and groups without institutionalized or formalized hierarchical social organization (Price and Feinman 1995). Price and Feinman (1995: 4) define institutionalized hierarchies as those that are "inherited and socially reproduced," generally, in nonstate societies, through the kinship system.

Because all systems are complex, the use of relative measures such as "high" or "low" complexity is not really satisfactory. But, because these measures are so entrenched in the archaeological literature, they are difficult to avoid and, if defined, can serve as a useful shorthand. Therefore, for the purposes of this study, I use "low complexity" to refer to groups without institutionalized hierarchies. In these groups, leadership positions were based on achievement and not ascription or birthright, and, although status and power differences were present, there was not a formalized system of social ranking; resources were available to all on a generally equal basis. "High complexity" refers to groups with institutionalized hierarchies, inherited leadership (and sometimes class) positions, and social ranking. In these groups, resources were unequally distributed, with those of higher rank having a larger share of available goods and power. It is important to stress, however, that the term complexity is used here in a relative sense. That is, even when high complexity is suggested for groups in the prehistoric American Southwest, it is still significantly lower than that found in many groups on a world-wide scale (see Johnson 1989).

The relative degrees of social differentiation, hierarchical organization, and unequal distribution of resources and power can be used in a comparative manner to order social groups on a "complexity scale." I use these measures, out of the many that have been proposed to decouple and measure complexity, because these are the variables most commonly noted in ethnographic or ethnohistoric accounts that are also sometimes accessible in the archaeological record. Although the construct of the scale may be tenuous in a prehistoric context, it can be used effectively as an heuristic tool to compare both ethnographic groups and prehistoric mound-building societies.

MODELING PLATFORM MOUND FUNCTION

The function of platform mounds in the Hohokam region of the American Southwest is the subject of significant debate even after a hundred years of investigation. Obviously, not all of the interpretations can be correct, but it has been difficult to resolve these issues through the use of archaeological data alone. Furthermore, all of the various interpretations of platform mound function are essentially permutations of only two basic models. These are the "elite residence" and nonresidential "ceremonial specialization" models for mound use (Jacobs and Rice 1997), or what Howard (1992: 69) has termed the "functional duality" in platform mound reconstructions. A third model combines the two and suggests that the mounds were both public places of worship and priestly residences. These theoretical orientations can be generally traced to work undertaken around the turn of the century by two men: Frank Hamilton Cushing at Pueblo Grande and later Los Muertos and J. Walter Fewkes at Casa Grande. Therefore, this basic duality, with minor variations, has remained relatively unaltered during this long period of platform mound research.

The confusion that surrounds the prehistoric use and function of platform mounds in the Southwest is at least partly due to a lack of ethnographic information on which archaeological models can be based. Without documentation of the range of ethnographic behavioral possibilities, archaeological interpretations have been essentially unlimited. To at least partially rectify this problem and to achieve more insight into platform mound use in the Tonto Basin, in the following chapter I describe the characteristics of seven historic mound-building groups in other regions of the world.

CHAPTER TWO

Accounts of Historic Groups with Platform Mounds

To better understand the social requirements that are presumed necessary to build platform mounds in prehistoric times, I examined seven historic groups that have been documented by ethnographers and ethnohistorians. Groups selected for analysis included only those that could be categorized as "middle-range" societies, which essentially subsumes the evolutionary stages of "tribe" and "chiefdom" (Bayman 1994; Feinman and Neitzel 1984; Upham 1987). I chose middle-range societies to avoid analyzing groups that were either far below (such as "bands") or far above (such as "states") the level of social organization present among the mound builders in the prehistoric Southwest. Actually, no "band" level mound-using groups were identified in the course of this research.

Of the seven analyzed groups, four are from the Pacific Ocean region, two are from the southeastern United States, and one is from South America. The case study approach used in this analysis is not meant to be inclusive or statistically representative. I identified additional mound-using groups that are not discussed; many of them have little substantive information and an unknown number of others undoubtedly exist. Of the more than 30 groups with mounds examined in selecting this sample, however, there was no evidence that other middle-range mound-using groups had attributes significantly different from those discussed here.

The ethnographic and ethnohistoric accounts describe extreme variability in groups who built mounds: they encompass many different kinds of subsistence activities, descent systems, residence rules, religious practices, and types of social organization. The number of individuals in these groups and their ethnic composition are also highly diverse and the form and size of the mounds themselves vary widely, both within and between groups. Mounds are more similar within a region than between regions, but even this relatively simple generalization has analytical and interpretative problems.

Following a brief discussion of methods, I present detailed descriptive data for each of the seven groups. A comprehensive level of detail is necessary to enable cross-cultural comparisons and to critically evaluate the results of this research. In Chapter 3, I discuss the societal attributes held in common by the analyzed groups that may clarify how the prehistoric mounds were used.

ANALYTICAL METHODS

The Human Relations Area Files, commonly known as HRAF, is an unparalleled data base, particularly for initial exploration of specific cultural traits across large geographic and cultural areas. Within each defined area, up to 631 cultural variables classed into 79 categories have been coded by a team of researchers (Murdock and others 1971: xx). Despite some subjectivity and no specific code for platform mounds, the methods used in compiling the HRAF are sound, and I used these Files to locate sources of material pertaining to groups who built platform mounds.

To cover all possible codes that might lead to information on platform mound structures, I made an initial search through the following categories (with their HRAF code): Monuments (211); Construction (331); Earth Moving (332); Architecture (341); Dwellings (342); Outbuildings (343); Public Structures (344); Religious and Educational Structures (346); Miscellaneous Structures (349); Maintenance of Nondomestic Buildings (358); Settlement Patterns (361); and Housing (362). These categories revealed more than 1,500 potential sources from the seven primary HRAF regions. As one example, nearly 140 groups had some sort of information on religious or educational structures (code 346) whose nature (whether or not they were platform mounds) remained unknown without looking at approximately 700 sources, primarily to confirm that the majority were not platform mounds. Consequently, the geographical search was limited to three primary regions known to have ethnographic or ethnohistoric information on mound-using groups: the Pacific Ocean region, South America (including Central America), and North America.

Once groups were identified as possibly building features like platform mounds, I examined the literature pertaining to the specific group and to the general geographic or cultural area. Groups with insufficient information or with a sociopolitical level not compatible with middle-range societies were excluded. This selection process eliminated many of the more complex Mesoamerican and South American mound-using societies familiar to anthropologists, as well as groups from Southeast Asia. In general, the goal was to secure from each region a sample of middle-range groups using platform mounds that included various types of social organization.

For each group in the sample, I recorded, insofar as possible, a standard set of characteristics (Table 2.1). The quantity and quality of data varied; information was not always available for each category from every group. More traits were available from groups in the Pacific region and South America than from elsewhere, mainly because anthropologists had studied these groups while they were still using platform mounds or had used them within living memory. Although most of these investigations had been undertaken in the past century using relatively modern anthropological methods, some of the research was still problematic because cultural anthropologists did not record in detail the kinds of information most useful to archaeologists. In particular, metric measurements on mound and platform size and observations pertaining to the organization and effort expended in mound construction were lacking for almost all groups in the sample. Information on material culture in general was scarce. Where available, archaeological sources mitigated a few of these problems.

The Pacific Ocean area probably has the largest number of mound-building groups, if both house mounds (including large community house mounds) and temple mounds are considered. Most island groups in the Pacific are related to some degree, originating via trans-Pacific migration from a few common source areas. Because of the wide range of variation in social organization and the fact that archaeological data indicate significantly early settlement of many of the islands, these groups may be viewed as independent cases for analysis. The four groups from this area were selected primarily on the basis of available information and because they represent several different types of social and political systems: analyzed groups include the island societies of Ifaluk, Yap, Samoa, and Marquesa. Hawaii and Tonga, perhaps the two most well-known Pacific region mound-building groups, are considered as supplementary information but not used directly because

Table 2.1. Categories of Information Recorded for Historic Groups with Platform Mounds

Environment
  1. Description of environmental setting

Demography
  1. Population size and composition
  2. Presence, nature of immigrant groups
  3. Evidence for seasonal or permanent settlement

Subsistence
  1. General subsistence practices, subsistence technology
  2. Nature, composition of subsistence group
  3. Evidence for food redistribution
  4. Evidence for feasting

Social and Political Organization
  1. Type, nature of social organization and kinship system
  2. Nature of political system, leadership
  3. Evidence for ranking or social stratification

Religion
  1. Nature of religious, ritual system
  2. Mortuary practices
  3. Material evidence for ritual system

Architecture, excluding platform mounds
  1. Architectural nature of domestic structures
  2. Presence, nature of other nondomestic structures
  3. General nature of settlement pattern, village layout

Platform Mound Architecture
  1. Architectural nature of platform mound
  2. Function, use of mound
  3. Social group associated with mound
  4. Construction of mound (how, who, labor organization and estimates)
  5. Material culture associated with mound
  6. Other cultural features associated with mound

their social organization appears to be more complex than that of most groups in the prehistoric Southwest.

Descriptions of the Mapuche, a South American group in south-central Chile, are particularly informative. Not only are the Mapuche still using platform mounds, some of which were constructed in living memory, but they were studied by the archaeologist Tom Dillehay as part of an ethnoarchaeological analysis focusing in part on mound use. Recent ethnographic observations on the Mapuche are also available.

Information on platform mound use in the southeastern United States is largely from ethnohistoric sources. Southeastern groups were no longer using platform mounds by the time anthropologists studied them in the early 1900s. Ethnohistoric accounts, although fascinating, can leave much to be desired in terms of detail and sometimes veracity. The discussion of these groups largely relies on secondary analyses of ethnohistoric accounts, although I examined some original accounts as well. Even though the Southeast is the closest area in terms of both cultural and biological affinity to the American Southwest, it unfortunately has the weakest data base. The two groups I review, the Choctaw and Natchez, encompass different forms of Southeast social organization.

THE PACIFIC OCEAN REGION

The Pacific Ocean region, covering a third of the earth's surface, contains approximately 25,000 islands. Most of these are extremely small, having an area of less than 250 square kilometers, and are highly variable in landform, natural resources, and agricultural potential (Thomas 1968: 12). A multitude of cultural groups inhabited this region, and after approximately A.D. 1000 some of them began building platform mounds (Herdrich and Clark 1993: 52). Throughout the Pacific region, mounds served as bases for domestic residences, communal houses, temples, and mortuary features. Other mounds were used solely for ceremonial activities without accompanying structures.

Variation in social and political organization, economic systems, the degree of social complexity, and the use of platform mounds, has long been noted throughout the Pacific region. Numerous reasons have been posited to explain this diversity, ranging from the differential productivity of the various island environments (Kirch 1990; Sahlins 1958), to the role of status rivalry (Goldman 1955), to the evolutionary selection of certain adaptive traits (Graves and Ladefoged 1995; Graves and Sweeny 1993). Population density, warfare, migration, and differences in the modes of production have also been suggested as causal mechanisms (Firth 1957; Labby 1976; Lingenfelter 1975; Linton 1939; Sand 1993).

The groups examined in this study span the range of organizational forms, from the primarily undifferentiated but still socially ranked Ifaluk, to the more highly ranked inhabitants of Samoa, to the stratified Yap and Marquesan Islanders. All of these groups used platform mounds, but they built different types of mounds with differing functions.

The Pacific Ocean region can be divided into three smaller geographic subareas, each of which contains populations that in general are more similar to each other than to groups in other areas: Micronesia, Melanesia, and Polynesia. Of the groups selected for examination, the islands of Ifaluk and Yap are in Micronesia, and Samoa and the Marquesas are in Polynesia; Hawaii and Tonga are also in Polynesia (Fig. 2.1). The brief summaries of these cultures presented below are ordered by population size within their particular subarea.

Ifaluk Island

Ifaluk is a small coral atoll situated in the Caroline Islands group of Micronesia. It is approximately 650 km (404 miles) southeast of Yap, with which it had a subordinate tribute relationship. Eight other inhabited atolls are within 200 km (124 miles) of Ifaluk, all of which share a similar culture. The island encompasses approximately 2.6 square kilometers and consists of a central lagoon surrounded by four small coral islets, with a usable land area of only 1.6 square kilometers. The highest point on the atoll is approximately 6 meters above sea level. Subsistence resources include coconuts, taro, breadfruit, banana, and seafood, all of which are plentiful.

At the time of the primary ethnographic study in the late 1940s (Burrows and Spiro 1953), Ifaluk had a population of about 250 inhabitants. The earliest ethnohistoric estimate from 1797 places the population at around 200, but, like many Pacific area islands, it is likely that depopulation through European-introduced disease had already occurred by this time (Burrows and Spiro 1953: 5).

Social organization was household, lineage, and clan based, and descent was matrilineal with matrilocal residence. The clan was the primary named social group; although lineages within clans were recognized, they were not formally named. Clans were ranked, and the heads of the four highest ranked clans (of eight clans total) had chiefly titles, which were actually held by one lineage within each clan (Burrows and Spiro 1953: 138). This title was inherited through primogeniture in the matrilineal line, and usually, if not always, passed on to a male. Although "rank seems to be the most prominent characteristic in native thought," and "is so highly valued and respected that it stands out as one of the master-values of this culture," in reality it conferred very few privileges (Burrows and Spiro 1953: 122, 129, 179). For example, the highest ranked clan had the right to all captured sea turtles (considered to be a delicacy), and the second ranked clan had similar rights for yellow-fin tuna, but even these were distributed beyond the clan if there was a surplus. Some deferential behavior was also accorded to chiefs, although not to a great degree.

Chiefly duty was a part-time occupation and chiefs did not constitute a distinct social class. All property

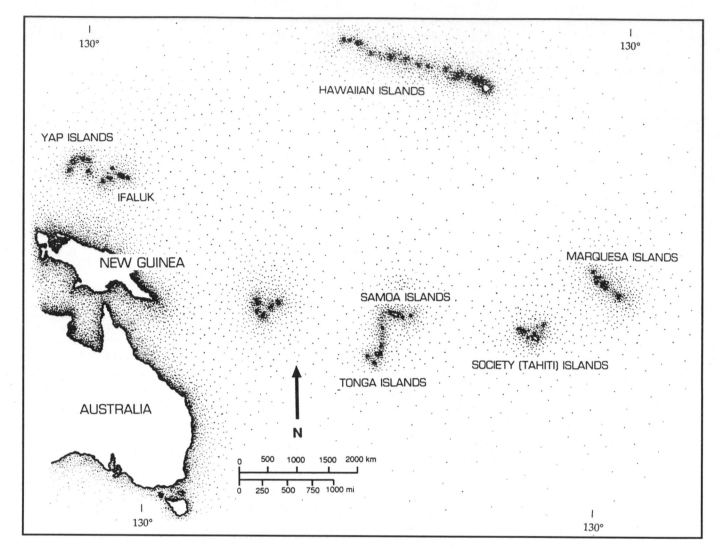

Figure 2.1. Island groups in the Pacific Ocean region
that are analyzed or discussed in this study.

was owned communally by the clan, except for paths or roads, the men's house and canoe house, and the beach between high and low water mark, which were owned by the chiefs. Subsistence, such as fishing or taro cultivation, was a communal pursuit, and food was redistributed among households within the clan. Obtaining sufficient subsistence did not seem to be a problem; apparently labor was the limiting factor (Burrows and Spiro 1953: 51).

The equality of the group was continually stressed by Burrows and Spiro, and they suggested that, unlike many other Pacific island societies, status on Ifaluk was not equated with the possession or expenditure of material goods. Although chiefs did control a body of com-

munal labor, this labor was only used for common welfare and not for chiefly enrichment (Burrows and Spiro 1953: 169–170). Religious specialists, like chiefs, were part-time, and their duties involved both medical and spiritual practices. Neither religious specialists nor chiefs claimed descent from the gods (Burrows and Spiro 1953: 183).

Architecturally, the Ifaluk built domestic houses, cook sheds, canoe houses, men's houses, and menstrual huts. According to ethnohistoric accounts, both domestic residences and men's houses were constructed on coral platforms (Burrows and Spiro 1953). Although the authors did not record information on the size of the house or platform, they did imply that the platforms were quite small. Building a domestic residence was a household undertaking that could be supervised by any adult male. There was no record indicating the chief's house was larger or on a higher platform than the regular domestic residences.

According to Burrows and Spiro (1953: 60), the construction of a men's house was a rare event, and none were built during the six months of their ethnographic research or within living memory. The repair of just a single massive beam of the men's house took nearly a full day's work for almost 45 men (Burrows and Spiro 1953: 67). The construction of an entire men's house, including the underlying coral platform, must have been labor-intensive, involving most members of the clan or community. Considering the fact that men's houses were owned by chiefs, although used by all affiliated men, it is probably safe to assume that they were constructed under chiefly supervision. Neither temple nor burial mounds were recorded and the dead were buried at sea (Burrows and Spiro 1953: 311).

Yap Islands

The Yap Islands consist of four main islands and six minor ones, which, like Ifaluk, are within the Caroline Islands group of Micronesia (Fig. 2.1). The total land area is approximately 96 square kilometers, and the 10 islands form a chain 26 km (16 miles) long by 2 km to 10 km (1.2 to 6 miles) wide. All of the islands are separated by narrow water passages and may be considered as constituting a single land mass (Intoh and Leach 1985: 2).

Yap is classified as a "continental island" (Thomas 1968: 12); it is more rugged and environmentally diverse than the coral atolls such as Ifaluk. The interior of the island contains hills and ridges, some as high as 180 meters. Primary subsistence resources include coconut, taro, breadfruit, banana, Tahitian chestnut, and seafood. The cultivation of taro is the mainstay of the diet. Soils are generally poor and periodic droughts common (Lingenfelter 1975: 7-9); only about half of the available land area is suitable for cultivation (Labby 1976: 13). Small streams constitute the primary source of fresh water, but between February and April the flows of all streams decrease and many become dry.

There are various estimates for the precontact population of Yap, based largely on historic accounts and on the extent of archaeological remains. The earliest recorded European visit was in 1528. After that, contact was infrequent until the late 1800s, by which time the islands had been largely depopulated (Intoh and Leach 1985: 6). Precontact population estimates range from around 25,000 to more than 50,000 inhabitants (Labby 1976: 2). The extreme depopulation experienced by Yap and many other Pacific societies is demonstrated by the first census of the island undertaken in 1899, which recorded 7,808 inhabitants. Yap once had 180 separate villages, of which 90 were still occupied in the early 1980s (Intoh and Leach 1985: 8).

Yap social organization was highly complex and relatively unique among Pacific island groups, perhaps in response to the high population density and resulting pressure on subsistence resources (Labby 1976: 12). The primary social groups were the household, clan, and *tabinaw*, or "landed estate." Clans, of which there were thirty to forty on Yap, were exogamous, with membership conferred through the matrilineal line; each clan traced its descent back to a single original ancestress. Clans did not function in a corporate manner nor confer status nor hold rights to land. They included persons of all social classes, ranks, and statuses and were important primarily as a source of social identity (Labby 1976: 15).

Of the social groups, the *tabinaw* estate was the most important, because it was the land-holding body, passed on patrilineally via primogeniture. Residence was patrilocal, with males staying on the estate and women marrying out. Previously, all land on Yap was owned by the various estates, which were focused around a raised stone house platform (*dayif*) where the head of the estate and his family lived (Labby 1976: 15). The estates were ranked, and certain ones had chiefly titles (Lingenfelter 1975: 93). Membership in a particular estate not only supplied a place to live and means for subsistence but also provided the primary source of rank and status.

The Yap were stratified into nine hierarchical levels roughly corresponding to four basic social divisions: chiefs, nobles, commoners (or servants), and serfs (Intoh and Leach 1985: 8). The most critical distinction was between those who owned land (*pilung*), which included the chiefly and noble classes, and those who did not (*pimilingay*), which included the commoner and serf classes. Members of the *pimilingay* functioned as servants for the higher classes and lived on the estates of the *pilung* in tenant villages (Labby 1976: 85). The relationship between the lower and chiefly classes was legitimized through religion, particularly through the observance of taboo restrictions by the serfs. Breaking taboos was grounds for punishment by the estate head, sometimes resulting in the death of the offending serf (Lingenfelter 1975: 158–159).

The disparity in wealth and power between the higher and lower classes was extreme and was perhaps most obvious in the form of differential access to resources, particularly good agricultural land for taro cultivation, the primary subsistence food. All Yap villages were centered around taro plots, which were cultivated by village-level communal labor under the control of the village chief (Lingenfelter 1975: 87). Because Yap does not have an abundance of rainfall and swampy areas needed for taro to grow, irrigation was required to keep the soil continually moist, and taro cultivation was labor intensive. Land was distributed within the village plot by estate, and the quality of the land was directly correlated with rank, with the best land being owned by those of the highest rank (Lingenfelter 1975: 97).

Each village had an advisory council made up of the speakers of the leading estates in the village. The high chief, as "executive head of the village," was expected to work with the council (Lingenfelter 1975: 100). As in many small-scale societies, discussion, persuasion, and compromise were the primary means by which decisions were made. Still, it was acknowledged that the highest-ranking chief in a village had the right to life and death over the other villagers, and each estate head had this right over his *pimilingay* (Lingenfelter 1975: 110).

The village chiefs, then, were the social, ceremonial, and economic leaders of the community. Only the chiefs had the resources to hold ceremonial feasts, arrange trade alliances, or pay the priests for religious ceremonies. Chiefs had the right to demand tribute, either as food or labor, from the *pimilingay* villages on their estates, but this tribute was then redistributed in various forms back to the villagers. The high chiefs of two Yap villages also received tribute from a number of atolls in the Caroline Islands, including the island of Ifaluk discussed above, approximately 650 km (404 miles) to the southeast. Tribute from all areas, both within and outside of Yap, was extremely important to the chiefs and served as a basis for their power. "Chiefs used collection and distribution of tribute as a trading mechanism, shifting goods from areas of plenty to areas of scarcity. In the process of this exchange, the chiefs gained and maintained political obligations and power, particularly through demonstrations of generosity and the concomitant obligations of reciprocity" (Lingenfelter 1975: 153).

Yap religion centered around worship of lineage ancestors (Lingenfelter 1975: 102–104), although little is actually known about traditional practices (Labby 1976: 9). Ancestors who had lived on and worked the estate

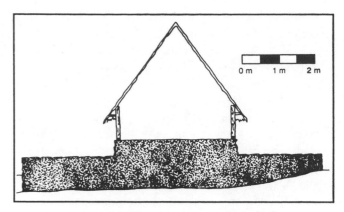

Figure 2.2. Yap community structure (after Morgan 1988: 53). Scale is approximate.

land were believed to remain there as spirits after death. The role of the priest, like that of chief, appears to have been a full-time occupation, and priests as a class were internally ranked. Priests were from the higher classes, and the highest-ranked priest was accorded the title of "ancient voice" or sitting-chief. Like the village chief, the sitting-chief was the head of an estate and had authority over lands. The priests were subordinate to the chiefly class and neither chiefs nor priests claimed direct descent from the gods (Lingenfelter 1975: 104).

The Yap built several different kinds of architectural features, including young men's community houses, old men's community houses, dwelling houses (including separate cook houses), stone-paved sitting platforms, and canoe houses. All of them, with the exception of the canoe house, were built on stone platforms (Fig. 2.2), and some grave plots were also marked by large stone platforms (Intoh and Leach 1985: 10, 21). Differences in the size and form of structures existed between high- and low-ranking villages, but Intoh and Leach (1985: 14) did not quantify that information.

Ethnohistoric sources indicate that house platforms ranged in height from 0.75 m to sometimes more than 2 m; most are said to be around 1 m. The platforms were hexagonal, with a rubble-filled interior (Furness 1910: 22; Salesius 1907: 147). There are no specific observations on whether chiefs' houses were larger or on higher platforms than others, but size differences are considered likely.

Old men's community houses (*pebaey*) were essentially similar in form to the domestic residences, although significantly larger; one ethnohistoric source estimates that they were between five and eight times larger than an ordinary family dwelling (Salesius 1907: 147).

[The *pebaey*] is set upon a large stone platform with stone backrests placed at strategic places for sitting purposes. . . . On the sitting platform backrests for the chiefs are placed around a stone table called a *rarow*, which is used for distribution of fish and other items for the chiefs. . . . Directly in front of the building is the dance ground and show place. . . . Around the dance ground are a series of sitting platforms from which village people and guests from other settlements watch the dances (Lingenfelter 1975: 111–112).

Building a *pebaey* required a large amount of organized communal labor, most likely under the direction of the chief or his representative. Müller (1917: 153) reported that the construction of one large community structure went on for about 10 years without being completed. Certain taboos were followed during house building, one being abstinence from sexual activities by both the builder and the owner. When a community house was built, it was the chief who abstained from sexual activity (Müller 1917: 153). The *pebaey* served as a learning center for the young and as a central point for food redistribution. Lingenfelter (1975: 81) further noted:

All important political activities center in the men's house. . . . Collection and distribution of economic goods occur [there]. For lower-ranking villages who take tribute to higher-ranking villages, the collection is made at their community center, transported to the village of higher rank, and distributed from its men's house. Fishing catches in particular are distributed at the house, according to the rank and privileges of the members present. Fish are generally placed on the special stone table and the chiefs direct the distribution. Those fish pushed off the table onto the ground are distributed to the people of the village, while those left on the table are for the chiefs.

The final category of mounded structures includes *teliw* (sacred places) and shrines. Shrines, which were associated with specific events or gods in the mythology of Yap, were generally small, mounded piles of stone or small miniature hexagonal platforms, no more than a meter high. *Teliw* were houses for priests built on stone platforms that contained within them artifacts dedicated to the ancestors or specific gods (Gifford and Gifford 1959: 152; Lingenfelter 1975: 104). These sites remained sacred places after they were abandoned. Like

chiefs' houses, it is difficult to determine if they were better constructed or had larger or higher platforms than regular domestic residences.

Samoa Islands

The Samoan archipelago consists of ten islands, nine of which are inhabited, arranged in a general east-west line in southwest Polynesia (Fig. 2.1). Samoa is divided politically (and to a certain extent, traditionally) into Western Samoa, an independent nation, and American (or Eastern) Samoa, a territory of the United States. Although the archipelago extends across a distance of approximately 400 km (250 miles), the population is relatively homogeneous, sharing similar cultural, physical, and linguistic traits (Holmes 1987: 25; Mead 1968: 245).

The Samoa Islands are volcanic in origin and therefore relatively rugged with high interior ridges and peaks. Rainfall and fresh water are plentiful. The largest islands are in Western Samoa, two of which have areas of more than 1,000 square kilometers. American Samoa, separated from Western Samoa by about 75 km (47 miles), contains a much smaller land mass, comprising 200 square kilometers. The island of Tutuila makes up its bulk, with an area of 145 square kilometers. The three-island Manu'a group, which includes most of the rest of American Samoa, is 100 km (62 miles) east of Tutuila. The Manu'a group is where Margaret Mead conducted the majority of her research. Ta'u is the largest of the group, measuring 8.4 km long by 4.8 km wide (40 square kilometers), with the highest point in the interior reaching 960 meters above the coastal plain. The other two islands of the Manu'a group are located around 20 km (12 miles) northwest of Ta'u and are extremely small, with areas under 15 square kilometers.

The primary subsistence resources of the Manu'a group, and the Samoan archipelago in general, include taro, coconut, breadfruit, Tahitian chestnut, banana, and seafood. Taro agriculture is by far the most important economic activity (Holmes 1987: 30). Food shortages and starvation are almost nonexistent (Holmes 1987: 34; Mead 1968: 250).

The population of Samoa at the time of European contact is unknown. The archipelago was first noted by Europeans in 1722 and visited sporadically after that, although contact with the natives was rare. Missionizing activity began in 1830, and Turner (1884: 3) reported the population for all of the islands as 35,000 in the mid-1800s. At the time of her fieldwork in the mid-1920s, Mead (1968: 244) estimated a population of

60,000 for the archipelago, with 2,200 in the three-island Manu'a group. Manu'a was selected as the site of her research because it was the most conservative area of Samoa and was believed to be relatively unaffected by missionizing activity.

Social organization in Samoa centered around the household, the lineage (or extended family), and the village. Unlike many other groups in the Pacific region, Samoa did not have clan or tribal organization (Holmes 1987: 38). The household was presided over by the household head, or the *matai*, who held the title of either chief (*ali'i*) or talking chief (*tulafale*). The composition of the household was fluid, ranging in size from 8 to 50 persons from one or more families (Holmes 1987: 38; Mead 1968: 246). Descent was cognatic, being traced through both the mother and the father, and there were no formal postmarital residence rules (Holmes 1987: 39). The *matai* directed the household in its daily activities, including subsistence pursuits, religious practices, and social affairs. Although the *matai* theoretically had the power of life or death over household members, this power was rarely exercised (Mead 1968: 246).

Each village had from 10 to 50 *matai* titles. These were ranked within the village, and three ranks of chief and three ranks of talking chief were recognized (Holmes 1987: 47). The *matai* represented the household in the village council, or *fono*, which was presided over by the high chief and high talking chief, who represented the village in island-wide matters. The village council decided all important community matters and scheduled religious and group economic activities. The talking chiefs were the orators, and the art of oration played a large role in both political and religious affairs, often in a competitive manner. Although consensus was generally reached, opinions of those of higher rank carried more weight in council decisions (Holmes 1987: 49). Personal rank could be raised through achievement, but this elevated rank could not be passed on to one's descendants.

The *matai* title and its rank were usually inherited through the patrilineal line within the household or extended family lineage, and only men could hold titles or participate in political affairs. The holders of chiefly titles, particularly the high chiefs, had a number of duties and obligations outside their role as household heads, such as settling disputes, hosting important visitors, conducting warfare, organizing village-wide activities, and distributing food at meetings and religious festivals. Rank pervaded all aspects of Samoan life. Mead (1973: 28) wrote:

The status of a village depends upon the rank of its high chief, the prestige of a household depends upon the title of its *matai*. . . . the Samoans find rank a never-failing source of interest. They have invented an elaborate courtesy language which must be used to people of rank; complicated etiquette surrounds each rank in society.

This courtesy language, commonly known as the "chief's language," was an important part of the deference paid to chiefs by the common people. Chiefs were also distinguished from commoners by dress and by carrying special ceremonial artifacts such as a fly switch or wooden speaker's staff (Holmes 1987: 45).

The Samoan environment and subsistence system appear to have always supplied a sufficient quantity of foodstuffs: three days of work in the plantations and gardens could supply the average family with enough food for a week (Holmes 1987: 34). The land was owned and worked by the household group under the supervision of the *matai*. Although the *matai* administered and technically had jurisdiction over the land, it could not be disposed of without the consent of the family.

A portion of the harvest was given to the village for use by the high chief, and the family *matai* was expected to use some of the household resources to hold feasts and provide goods for marriage transactions and other ceremonial activities, thereby maintaining family prestige (Holmes 1987: 39). Because of this continual exchange of property, there was no great disparity of wealth, although some households were better off than others (Mead 1968: 255–256). "Reciprocal exchanges of property are an important part of the Manu'an economy and mark all important events in the lifetime of the Manu'an people. . . . wealth is dynamic, and prestige comes through its use, rather than simply its ownership" (Holmes 1987: 36).

Religion was once thought to have been of limited importance in Samoan life (Mead 1968: 266). More recent research, however, demonstrated that the notion of a godless Samoa had been overstated and that religion and ceremony pervaded all aspects of Samoan culture (Holmes 1987: 56–64). The Samoans worshiped a single high god and numerous lesser gods, with every village and family having their own individual deity (Holmes 1987: 56; Mead 1968: 266; Turner 1884: 16–77). What the Samoans did not have were the more typical Polynesian features such as large temples, stone altars, and stone-lined sacred courtyards. Samoan temples physically resembled domestic structures, and the village *fono*, or council house, also served as a temple, as did certain natural areas like sacred groves of trees (Holmes 1987: 58; Turner 1884: 19).

The household *matai* and the high chiefs of the village functioned as ceremonial leaders, although there were also nonchiefly religious specialists who controlled certain spirits or cured the sick (Holmes 1987: 34). The nonchiefly specialists were part-time; the specialty appears to have been inherited within families, but the exact mechanism of inheritance is unknown (Holmes 1987: 34; Turner 1884: 20). Although the gods at times may have possessed the chiefs or other religious specialists, and the spiritual power of the chiefs was acknowledged to have come from the gods, there was little notion that the *matai* was directly descended from the deities.

Architecturally, Samoans built domestic residences (sleep houses), guest houses, cook houses, community houses, and temples (Holmes 1987: 29). Canoe sheds, young men's houses, and "star mounds" were also mentioned in ethnographic and ethnohistorical accounts and in the archaeological literature (Buck 1930: 11; Jennings and Holmer 1980: 98). All these structures, with the possible exception of cook houses and canoe sheds, were built on raised stone or earthen platforms. The wood and thatch structures on top of the platforms were all relatively similar in appearance, described by many as beehive-shaped (Fig. 2.3), but differed in size. Guest houses and community houses, which sometimes were one and the same, were substantially larger than the domestic residences and temples. Houses of chiefs were also larger than the average domestic residence.

Significantly, the ethnographic and ethnohistoric reports indicated that the height of the stone platform (the *paepae*) was directly related to status. Turner (1884: 153), for example, noted that although the floor of regular domestic structures was raised approximately 0.15 m to 0.20 m (6 to 8 inches), a height put by others at 0.30 m to 0.60 m (12 to 24 inches), chiefs houses were raised to a height of more than 1 m (3 feet). Buck (1930: 66), who researched Samoa at about the same time as Mead, wrote: "The height and extent of the house platform depend on the status of the house." And Grattan (1948: 57–58), who visited Samoa some 20 years after Mead, said: "The leading chief of the village is the person entitled to have the terrace of his house highest above ground level." Grattan (1948: 58) further indicated that legal recourse through the Native Land and Titles Court could be taken against "any presumptuous person who raised his house high without proper reason," suggesting that this entitlement was an important and culturally embedded principal of Samoan society. Stone platforms

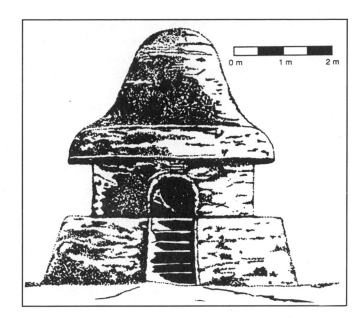

Figure 2.3. Samoan temple mound (after Stair 1897: 226). Scale is approximate.

as high as 2 m have been recorded, with the largest confined exclusively to chiefs' houses. The distinctions between chiefly platforms and those of the commoner classes are also supported by archaeological data (Jennings and Holmer 1980: 94).

Guest houses, communal houses, and chiefly residences required communal labor to build, under the direction of the *matai* or high chief. Construction was apparently always accompanied by ceremonial rites and large feasts (Buck 1930: 90), particularly when the chief married a woman of the noble class. J. B. Stair (1897: 111–112), who was in Samoa for several years in the late 1830s and early 1840s, observed:

> Upon the marriage of a chief with a lady of rank, the site selected on which to build their house was formed into a *fanua-tanu*, or paved ground, by the united labor of the inhabitants of the entire settlement or district. . . . By this means a raised terrace of stones was formed from fifty to seventy feet square, and often many feet in height, on which the house was built. This widespread custom prevailed throughout the whole group, not only in the case of dwelling-houses, but also in sacred edifices or buildings, *fale-aitu*, houses of the gods.

Buck (1930: 69) stated that the stone platforms were raised higher, or, probably more often, had additional terraces added to them, upon the marriage of a chief.

Information on temples is sparse, and some researchers, including Mead (1968: 266), thought that temples did not exist in Samoan culture. Although not directly from Manu'a, there are abundant ethnohistoric accounts indicating that temples were present in at least some parts of Samoa (Stair 1897: 226; Turner 1884: 19, 25, 27, 29–31, 44–46, 49, 53, 55) but that they were structurally similar to domestic residences. Perhaps most interestingly, Stair (1897: 227), who illustrated a temple constructed on top of a stone platform with a stairway extending up to the entrance (reproduced in Fig. 2.3), suggested that the height of the temple platform was directly related to "the amount of respect felt towards the presiding god of the temple by those who erected them." This comment is similar to the association noted above between the height of a platform and the status of a chief, although Stair was the only source that mentioned height in relation to the sacred realm.

Burials were sometimes placed in stone platforms that had previously been used for residential purposes, at least as determined through archaeological remains (Jennings and Holmer 1980: 98). Mead (1930: 49) reported that burials were placed in the earth near residential structures, with chiefly graves marked by large stone piles and commoner graves simply outlined in stone.

Archaeological investigations have also documented the presence of "star mounds" (Jennings and Holmer 1980: 101). These raised earthen or rock mounds varied in height between 0.20 m and 3 m, with anywhere from a single to 11 raylike projections and a surface area generally greater than 50 square meters (Herdrich and Clark 1993: 52). To date, they have only been found in the Samoan archipelago, including both Western and American Samoa; 62 have been recorded in American Samoa alone and this quantity is considered a minimum number (Herdrich and Clark 1993: 55–56). Wood and thatch structures were not constructed on top of star mounds, and Jennings and Holmer (1980) and Herdrich and Clark (1993) argued that these features were constructed by *matais* and used primarily for the chiefly sport of pigeon-snaring. Less certain are other functions they may have had, such as "defensive features and. . . sites for ritual activity related to marriage, healing and warfare" (Herdrich and Clark 1993: 61).

Marquesa Islands

The Marquesas consist of 12 islands in an area of 52,000 square kilometers situated in the easternmost portion of Polynesia (Fig. 2.1). They can be divided into two groups approximately 100 km (62 miles) apart; within each group, the islands are separated by distances of 10 km to 60 km (6 to 37 miles). The islands are volcanic and extremely rugged, with deep-cut interior valleys and surrounding peaks that reach a height of more than 1,000 meters (Ferdon 1993: 1–6). The total land mass is 1,275 square kilometers, making it significantly smaller than the Samoan Islands. The largest islands are over 400 square kilometers in area, but most are under 100 square kilometers and some are quite small, with areas under 25 square kilometers.

The primary subsistence foods are breadfruit, taro, coconuts, bananas, and seafood; breadfruit is by far the most important resource. Taro, the economic mainstay of many Pacific island groups, is not especially important in the Marquesas because dependable rainfall and large areas of irrigable land are lacking. The islands are north of the trade winds and without the seasonal rains that are frequent farther south (Linton 1939: 139). They are influenced by El Niño and La Niña events, both of which have the ability to cause relatively dramatic fluctuations in the climate and precipitation (Ferdon 1993: 4–5). Consequently, the Marquesas are subject to severe and unpredictable droughts, causing periodic crop failures, shortages of drinking water, and even starvation. These droughts may last as long as three years and death through starvation of up to a third of the population has been recorded (Linton 1939: 139). Additionally, despite the tropical location of the islands, there is an absence of nearby coral reefs. The nearest fishing grounds are 15 km to 30 km (9 to 19 miles) from land, making it a relatively time-consuming and often dangerous undertaking (Linton 1939: 139, 141).

Subsistence on the Marquesas, then, was not as easy as it was on some of the other islands examined, such as Samoa and Ifaluk, although in years with adequate precipitation, starvation was not a problem. Breadfruit, the primary foodstuff, does not need to be cultivated, nor does it require much care in general except for the occasional transplanting of trees into orchard areas. In good years, the procurement of sufficient food was not a demanding task, leaving leisure time for other activities. Like the island of Yap, however, good agricultural land was at a premium (Ferdon 1993: 6).

The first record of European contact was in 1595 (Ferdon 1993: 135). The ethnohistoric reports indicated at least eight visits to the Marquesas prior to 1800, but demographic figures are lacking for this period. Based on the numbers of warriors estimated in the late 1700s, Ferdon (1993: 7) proposed a total population at that time of 90,750, using the formula that "each fighting man represented 3.75 individuals in the population."

The Marquesan social system was based primarily on the household, lineage, and tribe; there was no clan organization within the tribe. The household and tribe were the most important social groups. The actual number of tribes is unknown, but most islands seem to have had several, and ethnohistoric accounts indicated that some of the large islands had between eight and ten tribes apiece (Ferdon 1993: 31). Just one island may have contained only a single tribe. Tribes were localized groups whose members shared a common ancestry (Linton 1939: 151). Relations between tribes were hostile, although alliances were sometimes formed through marriage or adoption between ruling families. Tribal population varied, but rarely exceeded 1,000 members (Linton 1939: 150). Ferdon (1993: 31) suggested that the tribes originated from separate migrations to the islands, an idea supported by slight differences in cultural customs between groups and by reports that some of the tribes were not able to fluently speak Marquesan.

The household, rather than the family, was the basic social unit. Households were ranked and the raising of household status was a constant preoccupation of Marquesan life (Linton 1939: 153, 157–158). Like most other Pacific groups, a household gained prestige through the accumulation and particularly the dispensing of wealth. "There was not much prestige . . . in mere hoarding of wealth; it was conserved only to be expended at the time of big ceremonials, when the total wealth and the amount of disbursement at feasts were important factors in determining the relative prestige of various households" (Linton 1939: 153).

The primary means of accumulating wealth was through manpower; that is, the larger the number of males in the household, the greater the amount of goods manufactured, food procured, and general work undertaken (Linton 1939: 153). It was the job of the household head to attract as many unattached males to his household as he could. According to the early ethnographic accounts, attracting males was primarily achieved through the sexual attractiveness of the household head's wife, and the households of all but the lowest classes were polyandrous, generally consisting of the household head, a group of other men who were sometimes called "secondary husbands," and a single wife (Handy 1923; Linton 1939: 158). Considering the fact that true polyandry is notably rare in the ethnographic record, it is possible that this relationship was misinterpreted by the early ethnographers and that the "secondary husbands" were in fact unattached males participating in a patron-client relationship with the household head.

Linton (1939: 150) stated that the household and its accompanying social rank were inherited through primogeniture regardless of sex or line of descent. Although Linton cited several examples of succession by the eldest female, in most cases it was the eldest male. In the chiefly classes, land and rank appeared to have been inherited patrilineally through primogeniture, but again, there were exceptions (Ferdon 1993: 33). Residence was patrilocal in the sense that the wife always moved to the husband's household if he was the head of an estate. Younger brothers of the estate inheritor either established their own households, sometimes on their elder brother's property if the estate was wealthy enough, or became secondary husbands on other estates.

Marquesan society was stratified and was divided into two primary categories: a commoner group and a taboo (or noble) group, with each internally ranked (Ferdon 1993: 26). Tribal organization centered around the high chief, who was the highest ranking member and who served as both administrator and symbol of the tribe (Linton 1939: 159). A number of lesser chiefs were also present, perhaps the heads of prominent lineages or districts within the tribe, but this is not entirely clear (Ferdon 1993: 31). The high chief's household was similar to others within the taboo group except it was considerably larger with a much greater estate and with a *tohua*, a large arena that was used for feasting, dancing, and other ceremonies (Handy 1923: 43). The chief's household included several wives, a large number of secondary husbands, and permanently attached craftsmen, messengers, executives, and servants (Linton 1939: 160).

Chiefly power came largely through the control of land and tenant labor and through largesse in gift exchange and the distribution of crafts and foodstuffs at ceremonial feasts and other religious activities. Although the chief was believed to be protected by the spirits of his dead ancestors, his rank and power did not stem from direct godly descent (Ferdon 1993: 32). Unlike the less socially differentiated Samoans with their elaborate "chief's language," acts of deference and obeisance were apparently only granted to the chief at ritual ceremonies or on other formal occasions.

Tenants of the chiefly and noble classes were expected to pay up to 25 percent of what they raised in exchange for use of the land; this percentage could be adjusted in lean years. Chiefs and nobles could not force tribute from anyone not living on their land. Part of the high chief's power stemmed from his role in organizing trading expeditions with members of other tribes and other islands. These expeditions often involved hundreds of men and were both economic and social affairs.

> Although a few objects might be brought for personal trade, the main load of the tribe's specialty was owned by the chief, and private individuals could not use it for trade purposes. Trade was organized by the chief, but at the close of the transaction, the goods would be prorated to all members of the tribe. . . . Gift exchange was as essential to social prestige as the giving of feasts (Linton 1939: 147).

The taboo category was a "socioreligious group," distinguished, as its name implies, by the observance of certain taboos and religious rites that commoners did not have to follow (Ferdon 1993: 27). Membership was open only to socially prominent men. Besides the chiefs, other members included the priests, the chief warrior, and heads of landed estates. Small landholders, master craftsmen, and important or "skilled" warriors were also part of the taboo group, but of lower rank (Linton 1939: 161–162). Members of this group could be distinguished from commoners by both dress and by the nature of their tattoos, and specific tattoo designs indicated internal position and rank within the taboo group (Ferdon 1993: 13–14).

The commoner class included all women, landless tenants, servants, and, with a few exceptions, secondary husbands (Ferdon 1993: 26–27). The basic distinction was between landholding and nonlandholding groups, with servants and landless tenants at the bottom of the social order. Because they were free to leave their employer, even the high chief, whenever they desired, servants and tenants were not slaves, but they could be put to death for such simple transgressions as stealing fruit or allowing a noble child to be hurt while in their care (Ferdon 1993: 30–31).

Priests were full-time specialists who generally came from the class of major landholders. The two primary rankings were ceremonial priests and inspirational priests (*tau'a*). Ceremonial priests, who were always male, were "specialists in dealing with supernatural things" (Linton 1939: 161). They were not divinely inspired but instead were considered to be skilled craftsmen. The position was hereditary, and generally passed from father to son.

Inspirational priests could be either male or female, although usually male, and they were most often members of the high chief's immediate family, such as a younger brother of the high chief (Linton 1939: 160).

They received their vocation directly from the deities and controlled supernatural powers. Because their power was divinely sanctioned, inspirational priests were ranked higher than ceremonial priests and commanded real authority within the tribe, particularly when possessed. At such times their power was greater than that of even the high chiefs, and they literally held the right of life or death over all other tribal members. In times of extreme famine, for example, it was the inspirational priest who designated which tribal members were to be killed and eaten (Linton 1939: 142).

The Marquesan religious system was highly organized and primarily focused around the deification of dead tribal leaders and worship of creation gods and gods of the craft trades (Ferdon 1993: 38–39; Linton 1939: 182). A form of ancestor worship was practiced, signified by keeping the skulls of dead chiefs and inspirational priests in tribal temples and the skulls of dead household heads in family shrines, often within the house itself (Linton 1939: 186).

The Marquesan subsistence economy was dependent almost entirely on tree crops, particularly breadfruit, but also coconuts and bananas (Linton 1939: 139). The cultivation of taro was a secondary resource. Tree crops required little, if any, care, and during good years with sufficient rainfall, foodstuffs were plentiful. At those times, four breadfruit crops were harvested, the first of which (the first fruits) was undertaken communally with accompanying ritual. Because of the unpredictability of rainfall, nearly all of this first breadfruit crop was stored in large communal stone-lined pits that were only opened in times of famine. The second through fourth crops were gathered by individual household groups and stored within household pits.

Even with these precautions, famine and starvation were real possibilities, because droughts could last as long as three years, exhausting the supply of stored food. Animal protein was in relatively short supply because of the lack of fish-bearing coral reefs surrounding the islands. "The fear of famine resulted in tremendous value being placed on food. . . . Every form of social advancement was linked with some ceremony involving a feast" (Linton 1939: 143–144).

The concept of property rights was especially strongly developed in the Marquesas, and all trees, crops, and gardens were individually owned by the heads of estates and inherited by their successors (Linton 1939: 140). Even so, there was recognition of the superior right of the group over the individual, and one of the roles of the high chief was to administer the land for the benefit of all.

Figure 2.4. Marquesan residential platform mound (after Suggs 1965: 130). Scale is approximate.

Architecturally, the Marquesans built several different types of structures. The typical household estate, which usually had been in the family for generations, consisted of structures of varying functions, garden plots, and additional trees and cultigens spread throughout the island, representing a considerable outlay of labor (Linton 1939: 154). Noble estates contained sleeping houses, separate cooking and eating houses, storehouses, a taboo house for the men, and sometimes a household temple (me'ae), along with a fenced garden area (Handy 1923: 43). Most, although not all, Marquesan dwellings were built on stone platforms (Fig. 2.4), including the sleeping house and the household temple, if one was present. A new stone platform for a sleeping house was constructed for the eldest son when he reached puberty and was ready to take a wife, and the oldest estates had numerous platforms, some occupied and some abandoned. It is unclear whether the taboo house, cook house, and storage house were also constructed on stone platforms.

There is little ethnohistoric information on platform height for residential dwellings, but from an early drawing illustrated in Ferdon (1993: 25), the platform appears to be approximately 1.0 m to 1.5 m high. Handy (1923: 152), based on his ethnographic work, recorded platform height as between 1.5 m and 3.0 m, and Linton (1923: 272) stated that the average was around 1.0 m with the most massive reaching 2.5 m. The platforms were constructed by master craftsmen and built by laying out a row of rocks in the platform outline, filling in the interior space with earth and rocks, and repeating the process for each successive course until the desired height was reached (Handy 1923: 152; Linton 1923: 273).

As in Samoa, the size of the stone platform was directly related to the status of the household and its household head.

The house, which was quite perishable in itself, was erected on a stone foundation; the larger the stone used, the greater the prestige of the family. The house platforms of prominent households contain rocks weighing two or three tons, which were worked into platform walls and often had to be lifted by sheer man power to an elevation of four or five feet above the ground. The size of the stone thus advertised to all the world the number of men that the household could call upon to help in its house-building (Linton 1939: 153).

Platform surfaces were sometimes paved with dressed and fitted stone masonry, which, in some cases, extended several feet in front of the building. The platform in front of the houses was said to have been used on occasion as an area for feasting (Ferdon 1993: 66).

All house construction was accompanied by ritual and feasting (Ferdon 1993: 42). The superstructure on top of the platform was rectangular in plan, and ranged in width from approximately 2 m to 4 m and in length from 3 m to 8 m. One chief's house visited prior to 1800 was estimated to have a width of 6 m and a length of around 25 m (Ferdon 1993: 21). The house was on the rear half of the platform, and both the platform and house were sometimes decorated with ornamental stone work and wood carvings (Linton 1923: 285). Linton (1939: 157) observed, "the Marquesans spent the greater part of their time building house platforms" because "a household which had not built its own house had no social status."

The most impressive architectural feature was the *tohua*, which was an arena for public viewing of social and ceremonial activities and for the gathering of tribal warriors in times of danger (Ferdon 1993: 67). The building of a *tohua* involved a large amount of organized labor: measurements given by Linton (1939: 151) indicated that these features were often 90 m to 120 m long by 12 m to 15 m wide and rose up 6 m high on the lower side. Surrounding the *tohua* were a number of raised platforms for viewing, and the platform of the high chief's residence sometimes enclosed one end (Ferdon 1993: 67).

Building a *tohua* was a ceremonial affair, which might last as long as six months (Ferdon 1993: 85). It was constructed by the entire tribe, under the direction of the chief and master craftsmen, and, although used by the lineage or tribe, was considered to be part of the chief's personal estate. New *tohuas* were generally built for the eldest son of the head chief, thereby raising the status of the chief's family, or as part of important ceremonies, such as memorial celebrations for the dead (Handy 1923: 205; Linton 1939: 152). The sheer size of these features is indicated by the fact that they sometimes held as many as 10,000 people from numerous tribes (Ferdon 1993: 65–66).

Other structures built by the Marquesans included *me'ae*, or temples, with a number of different features. Within the *ma'ae* category were both household and tribal temples, as well as sacrificial temples and funerary preparation areas, all built on stone platforms. The construction of tribal temples, although carried out only by the priests and their assistants, required materials gathered by all members of the tribe. Human sacrifice often accompanied this construction (Handy 1923: 231–232).

THE MAPUCHE OF SOUTH AMERICA

The Mapuche are located in south-central Chile (Fig. 2.5), between the Biobio River in the north and the Rio Bueno in the south. Their territory, once encompassing around 30,000 square kilometers, includes three geographic zones: the Pacific Ocean coastal strip, the Central Valley, and the foothills of the Andes (Dillehay 1990: 231; Faron 1986: 1). The Mapuche live within a cool, temperate rainforest environment, with snowfall and colder temperatures increasing with elevation. Subsistence is based primarily on agriculture, animal husbandry, and fishing, the proportion of each depending on the environmental zone (Stuchlik 1976: 13).

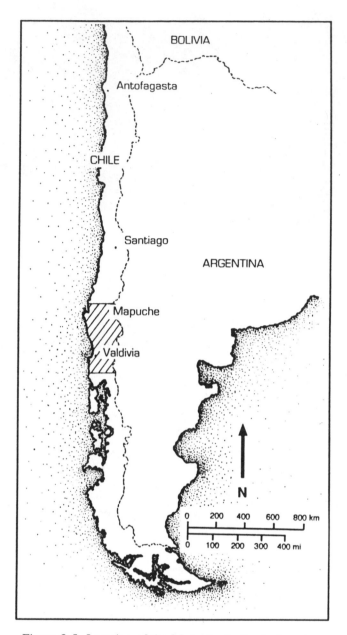

Figure 2.5. Location of the Mapuche in South America.

The Mapuche have also been called the Araucanians, and this name appears in most ethnohistoric and early ethnographic accounts. Beginning with the Inka in the fourteenth century, followed by the Spanish in the sixteenth century, the Mapuche violently resisted all intrusions into their territory by outside groups. Armed resistance by the Mapuche continued well into the nineteenth century, and they were one of the last native Chilean groups pacified, finally confined to reservations in 1884. Their present lands are within their former territory, although significantly reduced, extending over an area of about 6,500 square kilometers (Faron 1986: 12–

13). Within this territory are more than 3,000 small, separate Mapuche reservations (Stuchlik 1976: 16). On a number of them, particularly in the more rural areas, the Mapuche have maintained their traditional lifestyle and religious practices (Dillehay 1990: 225). From early ethnohistoric reports, the Mapuche may have numbered around 500,000 at the time of Spanish contact (Faron 1986: 10). By the end of the nineteenth century, European-introduced disease, continuous warfare, and the migration of many Mapuche into Argentina to escape slavery had reduced the Chilean population to around 100,000.

Social organization was based on the household, lineage, community (or *trokinche*), and tribe. The nuclear or extended family household was the primary economic unit. Mapuche houses were situated near their agricultural fields and consisted of pole and thatched huts in the Central Valley and wood plank huts in the higher uplands (Bennett 1949: 10; Faron 1986: 2; Stuchlik 1976: 13). The houses almost always contained a single room and were built directly on the ground; house platforms were not constructed.

The lineage was perhaps the most important social group. Today they are localized by reservation, with each having from one to several lineages. Three or more lineages that were consanguineously related and residentially contiguous formed a *trokinche*, which was the political and religious community of the Mapuche (Dillehay 1990: 227, 1992: 388–389). It is unclear if lineage and *trokinche* groups were localized in the past, although it is likely (Dillehay 1990: 225). Descent and inheritance were patrilineal and residence was patrilocal. Lineages were exogamous, but marriage to members of other lineages within the *trokinche* community was encouraged. Lineage descent was traced back to a male founder of the lineage and after death lineage members became ancestral spirits (Faron 1986: 22). Lineage size varied: Faron (1986: 22) thought 250 members to be an average number, with some much smaller and some considerably larger. *Trokinche* size ranged from 300 to 8,000 members (Dillehay 1990: 227).

Each lineage was ruled by a chief (*lonko*). Beneath the chief were a number of lesser ranked sublineages, each ruled by an elder headman (Faron 1986: 26–27, 59–60). The title of chief was inherited patrilineally, generally by the eldest male child. Although there is some question about how much authority a chief had prior to reservation settlement (Faron 1986: 23, 57–58), there is agreement that the Mapuche were a ranked society (Dillehay 1990: 225).

Chiefly authority was not absolute; it was confined entirely to the lineage and based more on persuasive abilities than on autocratic power (Dillehay 1990: 226; Faron 1986: 57). A chief's job was to uphold the social order, settle disputes, and to organize defensive systems and war parties (Stuchlik 1976: 17). Chiefs also organized communal labor on patrilineage lands (Faron 1986: 19–20). Redistribution of resources was another important chiefly function: "A chief's authority is not based on his ability to accumulate wealth, but on his ability to regulate its redistribution through ceremony and marriage alliance, and to serve as steward of lineage land use inheritance rights" (Dillehay 1990: 226). Whether or not chiefs occupied larger residential structures than other members of the lineage is unknown, although there are indications that they were moderately wealthier; chiefs usually had a greater total number of household structures because they practiced polygamy (Dillehay 1992: 396).

Most chiefs also held the role of *ñillatufe*, or ceremonial priest and, with the heads of the sublineages, were responsible for scheduling, planning, and conducting the annual agricultural fertility ceremonies (*nguillatun*), normally held by a *trokinche* twice a year in the planting and harvest seasons (Dillehay 1990: 227; Faron 1986: 100). In this ceremonial position, the chiefs played significant roles in death and burial rites (*awn*), with their associated platform mound building activities.

Chiefly power apparently increased with the formation of the reservation system in the late nineteenth century (Faron 1986: 57–60). Recognition of the authority of the chief by the Chilean government resulted in the legalization of land ownership in the name of the chief instead of the lineage. Although Faron (1986: 58) claimed that at this time the chiefs also began to collect tribute in the form of gifts and labor from their lineage members, it is unclear if this practice started only after reservations were established or whether some form of gift tribute and labor service was in place prior to this time (see Dillehay 1992: 396). Faron (1986: 58) noted of this period:

> Chiefs came to have life and death powers over their constituents. Social grievances were usually framed in terms of witchcraft and witches were dismembered and burned under the most adverse conditions. Otherwise, they, along with other trouble-makers, were evicted from the reservation precincts.

Regardless of what practices occurred before or after the formation of reservations, the transference of land rights from the corporate lineage to the chief appears to have been a significant factor in solidifying chiefly power.

Mapuche religion was polytheistic, with deities having tribal, regional, and lineage specific importance. The worship of ancestral spirits, particularly former chiefs, was central to Mapuche religious practices (Faron 1986: 67), and worshipping of chiefly ancestors suggests that the power of the chiefs was not limited to the reservation period. There is no indication that the chiefs considered themselves directly descended from the deities or received supernatural power from them. The shaman, as distinct from the chiefly ceremonial priest, also played a central role in Mapuche religion. Shamans could be either male or female. Besides curing the sick and conducting certain ceremonial rites, shamans held positions of authority residing in their knowledge of genealogy and particularly of cultural rules and customs (Dillehay 1990: 226). Being a shaman was primarily a full-time specialty; there is no indication that the role was inherited.

Dillehay (1990, 1992) noted that chiefly power was consolidated through community-wide participation in public ceremony and the construction of monumental architecture. The Mapuche engaged in more than 20 different yearly ceremonies, all or most of which were coordinated and scheduled by the chiefs in their role as ceremonial priests (Dillehay 1990: 227, 236–238). The three most important ceremonies that involved construction of some type of public architecture were the *nguillatun* (fertility), *awn* (burial), and *cueltun* (mound construction).

The *nguillatun*, or agricultural fertility rite, was the most important community-wide ceremony and the primary factor in group identification and integration (Dillehay 1990: 227). This two- to six-day affair occurred twice a year, usually around the full moon in the planting and harvesting seasons. The ceremony was sponsored by the *trokinche* community and was planned by the ceremonial priest-chiefs and elders of the member lineages. The event was held at a shared ceremonial field, and responsibility for hosting the event rotated among the lineages. It was attended by members of the host *trokinche*, and chiefs or household members also invited potential marriage and trade partners from other lineages (Dillehay 1990: 227). Through this system, alliances were created with other lineages.

The *nguillatun* ceremonial fields were permanently designated sacred areas that were uniform throughout Mapuche territory (Dillehay 1990: 227; Faron 1986: 100). The fields were U-shaped or semicircular and

ranged from approximately 60 m to 500 m long; the various lineage groups were clustered in contiguous huts along the sides of the field. The east end was always open and usually faced a stream or a lake. In the center of the field was an altar, often decorated with symbolic motifs, where shamans conducted the rites of the ceremony. The standardized nature of the fields and ceremonies served to reinforce Mapuche identity and tribal integration (Dillehay 1990: 228, 230).

Unlike the *nguillatun*, which was a multilineage affair containing both religious and social components, funerals (*awn*) and platform mound construction (*cueltun*) were attended only by members of the associated lineage and served to link the deceased with lineage ancestors. Although there were several different types of Mapuche tombs, including urns, stone-slab coffins, and log chambers, platform mounds were constructed only for the burial of chiefs, shamans, and, occasionally, wealthy men (Dillehay 1990: 230).

Platform mounds have had a long tradition among the Mapuche, probably beginning in the twelfth or thirteenth century. Dillehay (1990: 231) estimated that approximately 100 to 150 prehistoric and historic mounds were in the traditional tribal territory of about 30,000 square kilometers. They occurred as isolates or in clusters of 8 to 12 mounds and averaged 5 m in height and 20 m in diameter; the largest were approximately 12 m high and 35 m in diameter.

Platform mounds are still being used in the Lumaco Valley and these features have been a primary focus of Dillehay's ethnoarchaeological research. The Lumaco Valley encompasses approximately 8 square kilometers and contains 14 paired or individual mounds. Oral tradition, ceramics, and genealogical accounts indicate that the mounds contain the burial remains of a 300–to–400–year sequence of chiefs of a single localized patrilineage (Dillehay 1990: 231). Through ethnographic interviews and the use of historic documents, Dillehay has reconstructed three phases of mound building, curation, and abandonment. Because of the importance of these processes, representing some of the only recorded ethnographic data on mound construction and associated ceremonial use, Dillehay (1990: 231–233) is quoted extensively:

First, the deceased is placed in a shallow *eltun* grave and covered with soil. Second, after one year, the grave becomes lineage architectural property and is maintained and eventually built up by periodic soil capping, or *cueltun*, rites. These rites are administered by a corporate social group, headed by a shaman and made up of all the chief's consanguineal and affinal relatives. During this rite, shamans and relatives dance around the tomb, perform animal sacrifice and bloodletting rituals on it, and cap it with soil layers to symbolically lift the spirit of the corpse into the upper [ancestral] world. . . . Third, upon the death of the next lineage ruler, or successor of the interred chief, the *awn-cueltun* cycle is repeated at a new grave site. . . . the old mound becomes a public historic monument and joins the growing family, or suite, of earthen structures stretching along the bluffline. This sequential construction of mounds continues as long as the local patrilineage is politically secure and territorially stable in the same area.

Significantly, unlike some of the Pacific groups discussed, mound size was not directly associated with chiefly status. Instead, it was related to the number of people in the deceased chief's lineage and the length of the rule of his successor. Until the successor died and a new mound was established, the old mound was visited by lineage members every four to eight years and recapped, with each lineage member placing a container (basket, bucket, bottle) of dirt on top of the mound. Therefore, the longer the reign of the successor, the greater the number of capping episodes; the larger the size of the kin group, the greater the quantity of dirt associated with each episode.

Chiefs were buried with various grave goods, the number and type of which were directly related to the personal wealth of the chief and associated patrilineage (Dillehay 1992: 403). Although mound size was not directly related to status, the quantity and quality of grave goods may have been indicative of social position.

Along with their religious, integrative, and identity-reinforcing functions, mounds and other forms of permanent ceremonial architecture also served as territorial markers for Mapuche lineage land claims. "Lineage claims are legitimized 1) by referring to long-term occupation in a particular area; 2) by marking territories with lineage architecture . . . ; and 3) by transforming chiefs from land stewards to land patrons, and upon their death, from local lineage ancestors to special regional ancestors" (Dillehay 1990: 224–225).

The third form of Mapuche ceremonial architecture discussed here is the *nache-cuel*. It was constructed around 1900 and was the last mound built in the Lumaco cluster; it is still in use today. The *nache-cuel* consists of both a burial mound and a *nguillatun* cere-

monial field, and it represents the combining of what were once two functionally separate ritual architectural forms. In a sense, the *nache-cuel* site may be considered as the latest, and possibly the final, stage in a 400–year developmental process.

Dillehay (1990: 236) posited that this feature originated through the rise in power of a single lineage in the Lumaco Valley, perhaps initiated in part by the accumulation of land and power by the chiefs of the Lumaco patrilineage through the Chilean government's native land policy. The chiefs of this patrilineage, exercising their personal abilities in negotiating advantageous trade and marriage alliances, were then able to extend their influence beyond the domain of their own descent group. Once this power had been established, it continued through the control of "two highly valued and integrated commodities that were, and still are, much in demand—*time and scheduling of public events*" (Dillehay 1990: 226, emphasis in original).

Scheduling of ceremonial activities was critical because most events, including the *nguillatun*, occurred during the six-month agricultural season. The majority of adults spent around 31 days during this time preparing for or participating in ceremonial affairs, which calculates to about 15 percent of the available time per adult. By controlling the scheduling of ceremonial events, the Lumaco chiefs could also regulate alliance formations, trade and exchange, and the selection of marriage partners, particularly with desirable nonlocal groups (Dillehay 1990: 237–238).

The ceremonial architecture of the *nache-cuel* site reflects this change in ceremonial emphasis. The platform mound is located at the base of the U-shaped field, and the focus of the ceremony, instead of being directed toward the central altar of the *trokinche* lineages, is directed toward the ancestral mound of the dominant chiefly lineage. Dillehay (1990: 238) wrote: "the locus of activity and power . . . at the *nache-cuel* site . . . is the top of the mound where most activity takes place, including animal sacrifice and bloodletting rites in the name of celestial ancestors and deities." The mound was also in the best position for displaying the chiefs and the principal men of the lineage and it afforded the most commanding view of surrounding activities.

THE SOUTHEASTERN UNITED STATES

The Southeastern Culture Area, as traditionally defined by anthropologists, includes all or part of the states of North Carolina, South Carolina, Georgia, Flor-

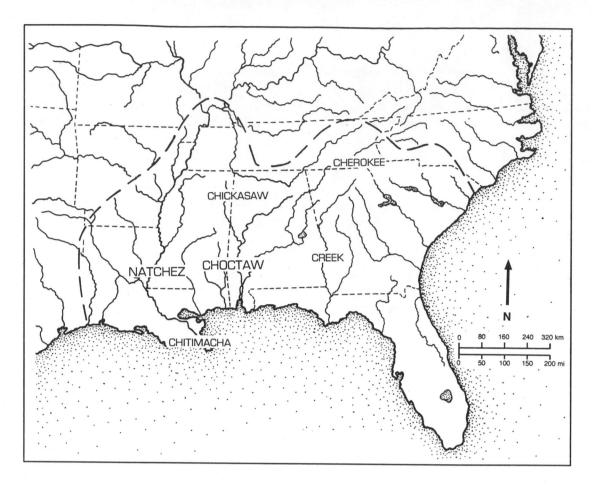

Figure 2.6. The southeastern United States, showing the location of the Choctaw, Natchez, and selected surrounding groups.

ida, Alabama, Tennessee, Mississippi, Arkansas, and Louisiana (Fig. 2.6). Portions of the states of Missouri, Illinois, and Kentucky that border the Mississippi River are also included by some (Hudson 1976: 5), whereas others have included parts of Texas, Virginia, and West Virginia (Swanton 1946: 1–2). Drawing boundaries around ethnographic culture areas is inherently risky because deviations always occur, but in general Native American groups in this area shared a number of cultural and social traits, brought on, at least in part, by the more-or-less uniform nature of the woodland environment (Hudson 1976: 11).

The characterization of native groups in the Southeast as similar is not limited to anthropologists. It was first noted by the early European explorers of the region, such as members of the de Soto entrada, who encountered a greater number of Southeastern groups than any other early expedition. Upon landing in northern Florida in 1539, de Soto and his party spent more than four years traversing 5,600 km (3,480 miles) of the Southeast and only noted major cultural differences when reaching Caddoan groups in western Arkansas and eastern Texas (Hudson 1976: 10, 1994: 99).

Almost without exception, Southeastern groups traced descent through the matrilineal line and followed matrilocal residence rules (Anderson 1994: 84–85, 87; Hudson 1976: 185). They lived in sedentary villages in similar types of small, circular or square mud-plastered structures (Swanton 1946: 806). Nearly all Southeastern peoples were farmers and subsistence was based mainly on corn agriculture, with the additional cultivation of beans, tobacco, and a variety of pumpkins and squashes (Swanton 1946: 289). Gathering wild foodstuffs, hunting, and, to a certain extent, fishing, supplemented the diet, with emphasis varying by region. Most groups also celebrated some form of the Green Corn ceremony (or Busk), a "rite of thanksgiving" feast held with the ripening of the late corn crop (Hudson 1976: 367).

Like the Pacific area cultures discussed above, which on the surface also appear similar, there are a number of important differences among Southeastern groups. For one, five distinct language families have been identified in the Southeast, with a number of language isolates (Hudson 1976: 23; Swanton 1946: 10, 800–801). For another, although the Southeast can be generally characterized as having a uniform environment, there is

[34]

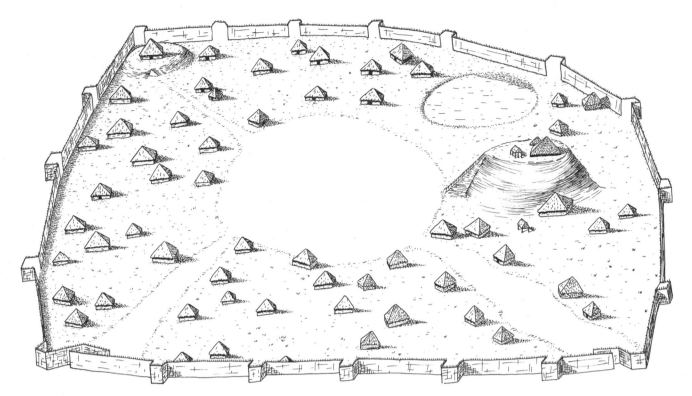

Figure 2.7. Example of a Southeastern platform mound community inhabited by
the Toqua of Tennessee around A.D. 1500 (after Nabokov and Easton 1989: 94).
Of interest is the spatial arrangement of mounds in the upper left and right-center.

a great deal of local variation that influenced the par-
ticulars of subsistence, settlement, and social systems
(Scarry 1994: 23–26). Other significant differences
among Southeastern groups occur in the types of social
and political organization, in religious practices, and in
the degree of social differentiation; variations also
appear in the construction of public architecture, including platform mounds.

The Southeast contained a relatively large number of
groups with platform mounds that are known from both
archaeological and ethnohistoric research (Fig. 2.7).
Ethnohistoric groups who apparently built mounds in
the Southeast include the Apalachee, Caui, Chica,
Chitimacha, Choctaw, Cofitachequi, Coosa, Natchez,
Oċute, Pacaha (or Capaha), Taensa, Tastaluca, Timu-
cua, Toqua, and Tunica (Anderson 1994; Blitz 1993;
Hudson 1976; Hudson and Tesser 1994; Swanton 1911,
1946; Thomas 1894). There is some evidence that the
Cherokee, Chickasaw, Creek, and Shawnee also built
mounds (Swanton 1946: 636; Thomas 1894: 718), and
there are undoubtedly a number of other mound-using
groups not recorded.

These groups ranged over an area of about 233,000
square kilometers (Hudson 1976, Map 1, and 1994,
Fig. 1). Many populations who did not use mounds also
lived in this area, but the number and geographical ex-

tent of known mound-building peoples are impressive.
The distribution of prehistoric platform mounds may
have been even wider. Construction of platform mounds
began as early as 3500 B.C. (Saunders and Allen 1994;
Saunders and others 1997) and they were relatively
common by 100 B.C. (Lindauer and Blitz 1997), but
most of them were built after A.D. 1000 when mounds
became "ubiquitous" (Blitz 1993: 70). They probably
continued in use in the Southeast until the early-to-mid
nineteenth century. In contrast, platform mounds in the
American Southwest were largely confined to a 45,000-
square-kilometer area in the Sonoran Desert and were
built primarily between A.D. 1200 and 1450, although
several mounds date to the A.D. 900s and a few may
date as early as the A.D. 700s (Doelle and others 1995:
386).

Why some Southeastern groups developed complex
social systems and others did not is a central question in
archaeology and anthropology, and one still unresolved
(Scarry 1994: 23). Numerous reasons have been suggested to explain the rise of the powerful Mississippi
period (post–A.D. 1000) chiefdoms documented by the
Spanish in the sixteenth century: environmental diversity (Scarry 1994: 23–26, 1996: 217–219), the intensification of corn agriculture and the need for communal
food storage (Blitz 1993: 179–180), the control of food

surplus (Blitz 1993: 23; Scarry 1994: 30), the establishment of a prestige goods economy and tribute system (Steponaitus 1978: 420), and changes in the nature of the political hierarchy (Anderson 1994: 105, 1996). Population pressure, competition for resources, warfare, exchange, and religion, particularly the practice of what has been called the Southeast Ceremonial Complex, have also been cited as possible causal mechanisms in the differentiation of Southeastern societies (Anderson 1994, 1996; Hally 1996b; Peebles and Kus 1977; Scarry 1994; Steponaitus 1986).

To better explore the relationship of some of these social factors to platform mound construction, I examined two Southeastern groups. The groups selected exhibited some of the different organizational forms that existed in the Southeast, including the primarily undifferentiated but still ranked Choctaw and the stratified Natchez (Fig. 2.6). Platform mounds were built by both of these groups, although the mounds differed in their nature and function.

Ethnohistoric sources provide most of the information on Southeastern groups because by the time anthropologists began to formally study these cultures in the early twentieth century most of them had been so radically altered by European contact and subsequent colonial settlement that they little resembled their mound-using ancestors. Mound construction in the Southeast probably ended by the mid-1800s, if not earlier, except small funerary mounds may have been used for a longer period. By the early twentieth century some groups had been so decimated by disease, slavery, and warfare that they had literally ceased to exist as defined cultures (Hudson 1976: 436). The ethnohistoric accounts, then, offer the only available observations on the social and political organization of these groups when they were still building and using platform mounds.

Fortunately, some of the Spanish explorers of the early-to-mid sixteenth century and the French and British of the late seventeenth and eighteenth centuries kept chronicles of their visits. These records vary greatly in their nature and level of observational detail, but some are quite meticulous, often recounting day-to-day events. The most important accounts, and some of the earliest, are those from the Spanish entrada of Hernando de Soto (Hudson 1994; Lewis 1990; Milanich and Hudson 1993). De Soto, who had been second in command to Pizarro in his conquest of the Inka, led an expedition to the Southeast in a quest for new sources of riches, particularly gold, silver, and pearls. Landing near Tampa Bay, Florida, in May of 1539, de Soto and his party of more than 600 men, 100 servants, and numerous horses,

mules, hogs, and dogs, spent the next three years wandering throughout the interior of the Southeast (Anderson 1994: 59; see Hudson 1994, Fig. 1). De Soto never discovered the riches he sought, although just about every native group he encountered assured him that fantastic treasures could be found with the next group down the way. De Soto himself died in May of 1542, possibly in the territory of the Natchez-related Taensa of Arkansas (Swanton 1911: 257), and it was not until 1543 that the 300 survivors of the expedition made their way by boat down the Mississippi River to the Gulf of Mexico and eventually to Spanish territory in Mexico (Hudson 1994). There are four surviving accounts of this entrada, which were written during the expedition, immediately after, or more than 50 years later.

Other notable Spanish sources include the Narváez expedition of 1528, particularly the account of Cabeza de Vaca. One of the only survivors of an original group of about 300 men, he wandered for eight years throughout the Southeast and Texas, eventually making his way to Mexico (Hodge 1990; Hoffman 1994). Another source is from the 1566 to 1568 expedition of Juan Pardo, who some 20 years later visited some of the same groups as de Soto, thus providing a limited temporal comparison (Hudson 1990). Later French sources, which provide much of the data on the Natchez, include accounts by the soldier Iberville, who established a colony on the lower Mississippi River at Biloxi Bay in 1699, and by the missionaries Le Petit and Le Page du Pratz, both of whom spent several years in the early 1700s along the lower Mississippi (Hudson 1976; Swanton 1911, 1946). Comments on the Choctaw come from later British or American naturalists and explorers, including James Adair, Lieutenant Henry Timberlake, and William Bartram, all of whom were in the Southeast in the mid-to-late 1700s (Hudson 1976: 11; Swanton 1922, 1946). De Soto also passed through Choctaw territory, evidently burning a number of villages as he went, but he recorded little substantive information (Hudson 1976: 114; Swanton 1946: 121).

As with many ethnohistoric reports, there are problems with all of these accounts because they are biased by the particular subjective view of the recorder. Soldiers, for example, tended to record events of military interest, and battles, weapons, and defensive fortifications are described in detail. Missionaries, on the other hand, generally focused on religious aspects: not so much on the native religion, which was "devil-based," as on their efforts to convert the heathen to Christianity. As a result, material of interest for this analysis, such as methods of platform mound construction, the time and labor necessary to construct a mound, or the social makeup and leadership of the construction group, are often unrecorded. The fact that many ethnohistoric accounts are synchronic and based on observations of a relatively short duration (Drennan and Uribe 1987: viii) compounds the problem: information on platform mound construction may not be available simply because no mounds were built during the short stay of the observer.

The veracity of many accounts may be questioned, particularly those written many years after the recorded event. Also, there are often conflicting views when two or more accounts describe the same event, particularly for quantitative measures such as time, physical space, and population. A degree of exaggeration is common because many of these accounts were written for consumption by the popular European market, hungry for tales of bloodthirsty savages and deviant practices.

As a result, information on the Southeastern groups is far less detailed than for the Pacific and South American areas previously described. Observations for many of the categories in Table 2.1 were sometimes insufficient or unavailable, even though reporting on the two groups examined was some of the best from the Southeast. When pertinent facts were available, they were sometimes ambiguous and therefore open to interpretation, with some disagreement among the various sources. These drawbacks are unfortunate because, of the three areas examined, groups in the Southeast have the closest biological and cultural affinity to those of the American Southwest. Even so, the Southeastern data are important and worth consideration, representing the only eyewitness accounts of platform mound use in the New World north of Mexico.

Choctaw

The Choctaw are a Muskogean-speaking tribe who, at the time of European contact and during the early historic period, inhabited the region now defined by the states of Mississippi and western Alabama (Fig. 2.6). They are closely related to the Creek and Chickasaw, whose territories were contiguous with the Choctaw on the east and north, respectively. Swanton (1946: 123) estimated that the Choctaw numbered about 15,000 in 1650 and that the population probably fluctuated between 15,000 and 20,000, making them the largest tribe in the Southeast after the Cherokee (see also Galloway 1995: 357). In 1675 Bishop Calderón wrote of "the great and extensive province of the Chacta which includes 107 villages" (in Swanton 1946: 121).

Like most other Southeastern tribes, the Choctaw were matrilineal with matrilocal residence. Polygyny and the sororate were evidently common, although information on these practices is limited (Swanton 1946: 706–707). The primary social group was the household, followed by the moiety and then the *okla* and the tribe (Galloway 1995). Clans were probably present (Blitz 1993: 11; Debo 1934: 15); Swanton (1946: 655) stated that the Choctaw had small group divisions, which he called "house groups," similar to clans but without totemic names.

House groups were organized into exogamous moieties (Hudson 1976: 237). According to one early source, the name for one of the moieties was "captives" or "slaves," although later sources claimed that the name for this moiety was "their own people" or "divided people" or "friends" (Swanton 1946: 662-663). The other moiety was called "chiefs." These names at least intimate the possibility of ranked divisions.

The Choctaw were ruled by a chief or by several chiefs, but the exact nature of this role and the amount of power the chief had is unclear. Each of the three or four main Choctaw divisions, which were apparently localized, seems to have had a chief, and a few early accounts speak, indecisively, of a head chief of the entire Choctaw (Debo 1934: 20). Each localized division constituted an *okla*, which was the political, social, economic, and ceremonial group of the Choctaw, led by a civil chief, a war chief, religious leaders, and a council of elders (Blitz 1993: 11). Swanton (1946: 653, 662, 817) noted that in comparison with stratified groups like the Natchez, Choctaw chiefs had very little authority and that the Choctaw, like the closely related Chickasaw, were largely democratic. Considering the autocratic power of Natchez chiefs, described below, this comparison does not necessarily mean that the authority of Choctaw chiefs was negligible.

There is no clear record of the means of chiefly succession. Swanton (1946: 653) thought that inheritance counted little, based on the fact that "the greatest of all Choctaw chiefs, Pushmataha, was of such obscure origin that it was a matter of comment." Therefore, to Swanton, Choctaw chiefs were "self-made men," implying that rank and status were achieved rather than ascribed. The Choctaw also appear to have had specialized war chiefs or war leaders, whose role was similarly based on achievement and, particularly, on prowess in battle (Swanton 1946: 697).

An alternative interpretation to the statement that his origin "was a matter of comment" may be that Pushmataha was the exception rather than the rule. The fact that chiefs were treated differently from the common people in mortuary rites (described below), along with the possibility that the moieties were ranked, indicate that Choctaw society may not have been as undifferentiated as Swanton maintained and that ranking was an important part of the social system (see also Blitz 1993: 12). With the large population size, 15,000 people, some form of hierarchical organization seems likely. Furthermore, the presence of at least four divisions of Choctaw, each with head chiefs, means that matrilineages may have played a larger and more formal role than recognized and, if so, it is possible that rank was inherited through this group. More recently Anderson (1994: 75) observed that Swanton had a tendency "to minimize the authority of Southeastern chiefs." It is likely the Choctaw were a ranked society, but one that may not have engaged in a high level of social differentiation.

Economically, the Choctaw were primarily corn agriculturists who raised enough surplus to trade with neighboring groups (Swanton 1946: 817). Hunting of small game during the summer and large game from winter camps supplemented the diet.

Little is known about the Choctaw religious system, but some accounts do describe a five-day Green Corn ceremony and social or semisocial dances with masked participants (Swanton 1946: 777–778). There appear to have been two classes of medicine men: one controlled supernatural powers and had the gift of prophecy, the other primarily healed the sick. There is no record of whether religious specialists were full or part-time.

Architecturally, each Choctaw family had a winter (cold weather) and summer (warm weather) residence and sometimes a storage structure, all typically arranged in a cluster (Hudson 1976: 213). Some villages were surrounded by palisades, but descriptions of them are lacking. Swanton (1946: 637) postulated that larger communal buildings were present but not recorded because of their inconspicuous nature when compared to the neighboring Creek. Each town did have one or several mortuary charnel houses. James Adair observed around 1770 that at least some charnel houses were adorned with carved images (Swanton 1946: 613).

Choctaw mortuary rites, which involved mound building, are one of the few activities with a reasonable amount of information. "The ancient Choctaw mortuary customs were quite different [from those of the Creek and Chickasaw] and of such striking character that they have been often described, though these descriptions do not agree in all details" (Swanton 1946: 725). There is enough concordance, however, that the general outline of the process is clear.

When a person died, the body was laid out on a scaffold near the house with food and other personal property and was allowed to decay. The house of the deceased was then burned "along with the provisions it contained or the [provisions] were sold at a low price" (Swanton 1946: 725). As recounted by William Bartram, a trained naturalist who toured the Southeast between 1773–1777:

> As soon as a person is dead they erect a scaffold eighteen or twenty feet high, in a grove adjacent to the town, where they lay the corpse, lightly covered with a mantle; here it is suffered to remain, visited and protected by the friends and relations, until the flesh becomes putrid, so as easily to part from the bones, then undertakers, who make it their business, carefully strip the flesh from the bones . . . [and] having provided a curiously wrought chest or coffin . . . they place all the bones therein, which is deposited in the bone house, a building erected for that purpose in every town. And when this house is full a general solemn funeral takes place. Where the nearest kindred or friends of the deceased . . . take up the respective coffins, and following one another in order of seniority . . . slowly proceeding to the place of general internment, where they place the coffins in order, forming a pyramid, and lastly cover all with earth, which raises a conical hill or mount. When they return to town in order of solemn procession, concluding the day with a festival, which is called the feast of the dead (in Thomas 1894: 656).

The undertakers mentioned by Bartram, who elsewhere are called "buzzard men" or "buzzard pickers," were a class of mortuary specialists responsible for the care of the dead in the charnel houses and particularly for removal of the putrefied flesh once the body had decayed. For this purpose they grew their fingernails long, which, besides being functionally useful, was a symbol of their role (Swanton 1946: 817). Buzzard men may have functioned as full-time ritual specialists.

Unfortunately, there are no reliable ethnohistoric records on the size of the burial mounds. One account stated that they were "several feet high" (Thomas 1894: 677). Some mounds contained the remains of numerous bodies, each within an individual coffin, and several observers called them "pyramids," indicating that size was variable and mounds could have been relatively large. Descriptive archaeological information on Choctaw mounds is also scarce (Galloway 1995: 10–12). The large platform mound at Nanih Waiya, measuring 12 m to 15 m high and covering almost an acre (0.4 ha) at its base, was believed by the Choctaw to represent their ancestral home, but the site was already abandoned by the time James Adair visited it in 1775 (Debo 1934: 1). The Nanih Waiya mound was not a burial mound, but several small burial mounds surrounded it (Galloway 1995: 300, 333), raising the possibility that in the past the Choctaw or their ancestors had different kinds of mounds with various functions, some of which served as platforms. Unfortunately, the site has been largely destroyed through agricultural activities and the location of archaeological collections made in the early 1900s is unknown (Galloway 1995: 11).

Swanton (1946: 726) provided additional information, primarily from Adair, that indicated that deceased chiefs were treated differently and that their defleshed bones were placed in special charnel houses separate from the remains of the common people (Galloway 1995: 300). There is no report on whether chiefs were then buried communally with commoners in the same mound or were interred in their own mound. That differential burial practices might have occurred among the Choctaw was revealed by other accounts, which stated that, "the burial mound might be added to on several different occasions, and according to one informant, the bone house was covered over in situ after it had become full" (Swanton 1946: 726). All accounts agreed that the mortuary rites were accompanied by feasts, both at the time of burial and on an annual basis (Blitz 1993: 72; Swanton 1946: 726).

Natchez

The Natchez are one of the best documented groups in the Southeast. At the time of European contact, they were situated in southwestern Mississippi, primarily along the eastern bank of the Mississippi River (Fig. 2.6). Although the Natchez were not directly visited by the de Soto expedition, de Soto was told by neighboring groups that the lord of the Natchez province (the chief Quigaltam) "was the greatest of that country" (Lewis 1990: 229). According to Swanton (1911: 2, 45; 1946: 161), the Natchez formed the largest tribe on the lower Mississippi, with an estimated population in 1650 of 4,000 people settled in about 10 villages. This figure accords relatively well with an estimate made in 1686 of 1,500 warriors (Swanton 1946: 160), or a total population of 5,625 using Ferdon's (1993: 7) formula. The Natchez language is one of four language isolates identified in the Southeast (Hudson 1976: 23).

Like other Southeastern groups, the Natchez were matrilineal. Residence rules, however, depended on class; commoners were matrilocal but the ruling class was patrilocal. According to the ethnohistoric records, the Natchez were stratified, and early accounts list four class divisions, from highest to lowest rank, of Suns, Nobles, Honored People, and Stinkards (Swanton 1911: 107). Although the small size of the population raises doubts whether the Natchez were truly stratified or just highly ranked, the common practice of human sacrifice indicates that some degree of coercive force was present.

The Suns were the ruling class, and secondary officers and war leaders came from the Noble class. Honored People were also considered to be of the noble class, but lower ranked than Nobles themselves. Stinkards were the common people, who comprised the great majority of the population. Social differentiation was so extreme that members of the Sun class were considered to be direct descendants of the deities (Swanton 1911: 93).

Class, and rank within class, were hereditary, passed on through the female line. Succession to the title of "Great Sun," the chief of all Natchez, was by primogeniture, and generally went to the eldest son of the reigning Great Sun's sister or other closely related female relative (Hudson 1976: 207; Swanton 1911: 106). The authority of the Sun class, and particularly the Great Sun, was absolute, even though the Suns were the smallest of the four classes by a notably wide margin. Swanton (1911: 107) wrote: "La Harpe states that in 1700 there were 17 Suns, but it is not clear whether he includes only those in the Great Village or the entire number, and whether the Suns of both sexes are referred to. Le Petit [in 1720] gives 11 Suns." Even if there were 50 Suns, which is probably the maximum number possible considering the above estimates, they would have represented only a small fraction of the estimated 4,000 to 5,600 total population.

The authority of Sun class members is demonstrated by their power of life and death over the lower classes and by the high degree of deference paid to them, particularly by the Stinkards, but also by the lower ranked noble classes (Swanton 1911: 93, 1946: 650). The Great Sun was carried on a litter, always addressed in a ceremonially deferential manner, and persons of other classes could not "eat with the Suns nor touch the vessels out of which they ate" (Hudson 1976: 209).

The Sun class was not endogamous, but instead Suns took husbands and wives from the Stinkard class. Members of the Noble and Honored Person classes also had to take Stinkard wives (Hudson 1976: 207). The sororate was practiced and polygyny was common, particularly among the higher classes who could most afford it. According to the early sources, Sun marriage to commoners was practiced because of the Natchez rule that upon the death of a Sun, "it was necessary that the wife or husband be killed in order to accompany the deceased" (Swanton 1946: 661–662). More recently, Anderson (1994: 87) noted that the marrying of Sun women to commoners also lessened the influence of outsiders and reduced threats by male rivals to chiefly power.

The death of a Sun mandated human sacrifice, the number depending on the rank of the deceased. Although one account stated that up to 100 people were sacrificed, which is probably an exaggeration, the sacrifice of 10 to 40 individuals was apparently common. Du Pratz reported that upon the death of a woman Sun in the early 1700s, at least 12 children and 15 adults, including her husband, were sacrificed (Swanton 1911: 141–142). Sacrifices were regarded as a mark of honor for the families of the victims and the victims themselves made the cords by which they were strangled.

Even with the god-given authority apparently held by the Sun class, and particularly the Great Sun, Swanton (1946: 650) noted that personal ability, experience, and age played a role in the attainment of at least some of that power. The Great Sun had an advisory council that included other members of the Sun class and, in particular, the Sun chiefs of the other Natchez towns. It is unclear what role the council actually played, and Hudson (1976: 210) remarked that it was difficult to determine how much power in fact the Great Sun had. Still, the ethnohistoric accounts clearly indicated that the Suns, and especially the Great Sun, wielded a significant degree of authority.

The economic system was based largely on corn agriculture, and the Natchez were second only to the Choctaw in their dependence on farming (Swanton 1911: 73–79, 1946: 818). Fishing, hunting, and gathering contributed to their subsistence. Tribute was collected by the Suns from the commoner class, and apparently from the other noble classes as well, and was paid both in food and in labor (Hudson 1976: 209; Swanton 1911: 97).

Food collected through tribute was redistributed to all classes in the form of feasts and other ceremonial events, and feasts were times when tribute was collected (Swanton 1911: 110). Feasts occurred on a monthly basis or 13 times a year (Blitz 1993: 22). They were celebrated in each village, but some of the larger feasts, such as that of the harvest or Green Corn, were attended by residents of several or all villages. The ethno-

historic accounts indicated that feasts could last from one to as many as ten days (Swanton 1911: 121–122).

Natchez religion was centered on worship of the sun and a number of minor deities. Members of the Sun class were considered to be direct descendants of the sun god; they therefore "had a divine right to the unusual honors and regard lavished upon [them], while as head of the Sun people, the great chief was the representative of the deity on earth and was to be treated accordingly" (Swanton 1911: 174). The religion mandated that a perpetual fire be kept burning in the temple; it was tended on a full time basis by specialized priests (Swanton 1946: 779). The Sun class conducted all ceremonies and priestly functions, and the Great Sun was the head priest.

The Natchez constructed several types of residential structures, food storage granaries, and platform mounds. Houses of the common people were similar to those throughout the Southeast: square, low, and without windows, measuring about 4.6 m on a side (Swanton 1911: 59). The house of the Great Sun was constructed on top of a platform mound (Fig. 2.8) and situated in a plaza or large cleared area opposite the temple, which was also on a platform mound. Du Pratz gave the height of the Great Sun's house mound as close to 8 feet (2.4 m) and the dimensions of the house itself as about 30 feet (9.1 m) square, or roughly two times larger than the domestic structures of the other classes. Iberville, who, like Du Pratz, visited the Natchez in the early 1700s, stated, "We repaired to [the cabin of the Great Sun], which is raised to a height of 10 feet [3.1 m] on earth brought thither, and is 25 feet [7.6 m] wide and 45 feet [13.7 m] long. . . . Before that of the chief is the temple mound, which has a circular shape, a little oval, and bounds an open space about 250 paces wide and 300 long" (in Swanton 1946: 638). For the most part, these estimates were confirmed through the archaeological excavation of the village of the Great Sun, called the Fatherland site, in the early 1960s by Robert Neitzel (1965) for the Mississippi State Historical Museum. Interestingly, Neitzel found three platform mounds instead of the two described in the historic accounts. He was able to determine that Mound B was the chief's mound and Mound C was the temple mound, although both had undergone considerable erosion since their occupation in the early 1700s and little evidence remained of the structures on their tops. The function of Mound A was not determined (Neitzel 1965: 64).

Unfortunately, the historic accounts do not provide information on the nature of the social groups that constructed these features, although it can be assumed that

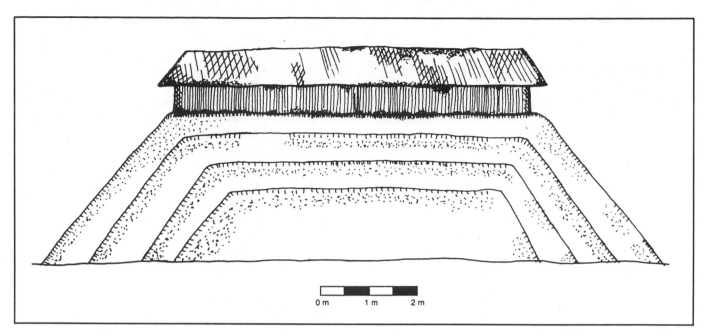

Figure 2.8. Reconstruction of the residential platform mound of the Natchez Great Sun Chief (after Nabokov and Easton 1989: 97). Remodeling episodes are marked by strata in the mound. The size of the mound and the structure on top have been modified from Nabokov and Easton to more accurately reflect the historic accounts. Scale is approximate.

they were communally built under the direction of members of the Sun class, if not the Great Sun himself. There are no details on the interior of the Great Sun's house, but apparently it served both as the chiefly residence and as a place for group ceremonies and other meetings.

Significantly, Le Petit stated that, "When the great chief dies they demolish his cabin and then raise a new mound, on which they build the cabin of him who is to replace him in his dignity, for he never lodges in that of his predecessor" (in Swanton 1911: 103). The validity of this account is unknown, because Le Petit and the other French observers apparently never witnessed, or at least never described, the death of a Great Sun (Neitzel 1965: 84). However, documented in detail in numerous accounts was the death of the Great Son's brother and head war chief, the Tattooed-Serpent (Swanton 1911: 143–157, 1946: 728).

The possibility that a new mound was constructed (or the existing one extensively remodeled) with each chiefly succession is supported by the presence of numerous, often identical, mounds at some prehistoric Southeastern sites (Blitz 1993; Hally 1996a, 1996b: 94–97; Thomas 1894: 653) and limited ethnohistoric reports from other groups (Anderson 1994: 87). Archaeological evidence from the Fatherland site indicates successive building episodes in Mound B, the chief's mound. Specifically, Neitzel (1965: 16, 64–67) documented four mound construction stages, each capped

with the remains of a burned structure, that probably represent the domiciles of earlier leaders.

Aside from having a larger residence on top of a platform mound, the only material status marker that distinguished the Great Sun from other Natchez was an elaborate feather headdress that had the "same shape as the crown of a Plains Indian war bonnet" (Hudson 1976: 209–210). Otherwise the chiefs dressed for the most part like the other Natchez (Du Pratz in Swanton 1911: 52). The chiefs may have possessed other artifacts like beautifully woven mats or special pipes that commoners did not have (Swanton 1911: 61, 349), but in general the ethnohistoric observations agreed in the overall lack of obvious class distinctions in dress, ornament, and material possessions. Elaborate facial and body tattooing may have been a right only of warriors and other members of the noble classes (Swanton 1911: 56).

There are good descriptions from a number of sources on the interior layout of Natchez temples, and they have been used by archaeologists to aid in reconstructing prehistoric platform mounds (Blitz 1993: 88; Neitzel 1965). Although these accounts differ somewhat in specific detail, suggesting to Swanton (1911: 164) that the interiors of the temple periodically changed, they are similar in their basic outline. Swanton (1911: 164) compiled various accounts as follows.

The door was to the east, toward the square, and on the roof were three birds carved out of wood facing in the same direction. One of these was at each end and one in the middle. . . . According to Du Pratz, the southern third of the building was cut off by an inside partition which communicated only with the larger space. . . . In the middle of the building or of the larger room burned, or rather smoldered, the eternal fire, which was fed continually by three logs shoved into it endwise from as many directions. Directly back of this was a low table or platform. . . . On this Charlevoix saw nothing, but Du Pratz states that it bore a basket containing the bones of the last Great Sun.

The temple played a central role in Natchez life. The Great Sun and his wife or wives came every morning to pay their respects, and the first fruits of the harvest were brought there (Swanton 1946: 779–780). Within the inner sanctum, in the partitioned-off southern third of the temple, was a stone idol, "into which the founder of the rites of the Natchez nation and the progenitor of the royal family had metamorphosed himself" (Swanton 1911: 165).

The power of the temple and the theocratic nature of the Natchez religion is particularly well illustrated by the account of Iberville, who in 1700 observed the lightning-caused burning of the Taensa temple. The Taensa were situated just upriver from the Natchez and are believed to have been closely related (Swanton 1911: 9). In fact, the customs, architecture, and language of the Taensa and Natchez were so similar that early accounts often confused the two groups. Iberville stated:

The 16th and 17th [of March 1700] it rained and thundered much; the night of the 16th to the 17th a thunderbolt fell on the temple of the Taensas and set fire to it, which burned it entirely. These savages, to appease the spirit, who they said was angry, threw five little children in swaddling clothes into the fire of the temple. They would have thrown in many others had not three Frenchmen run hither and prevented them. An old man of about 65 years, who appeared to be the principal priest, was near the fire, crying in a loud voice: "Women, bring your children to sacrifice them to the Spirit in order to appease him," a thing which five of these women did, bringing him their children, whom he took and threw into the midst of the flames. The action of these women was regarded by them as one of the finest one could make . . . .(in Swanton 1911: 266–267).

The temple also played an important role in Natchez mortuary practices, particularly for those of the Sun class. Like the charnel houses of the Choctaw, the temple served as a mortuary repository, in this case for the bones of the Suns (Neitzel 1965; Swanton 1911: 164). The records do not indicate if the bones were eventually taken from the temple and buried in a separate funerary mound. The burials of lower class persons were not well documented, but Swanton (1946: 819) stated, without giving sources, that "Commoners seem to have been buried in the earth somewhat after the Chickasaw and Creek manner, but bodies of chiefs and nobles were buried in or near the temple, the bones being later exhumed and placed in hampers in that building." Probably specialized funerary mounds were not constructed for either the commoner or noble classes, but the Suns, or at least the highest ranking members, were buried in the temple mound. Burial of high-ranking Natchez in the temple mound is strongly supported by the archaeological evidence (Neitzel 1965: 83–84).

MOUND VARIABILITY

Ethnographic and ethnohistoric information from mound-using groups indicates that platform mounds occurred in many different cultures across a range of environments, in different types of social, political, and economic systems, and for a wide variety of reasons, both within and between regions. Because of the small number of analyzed cases, the extent of this variability has just been sampled; in reality, the full range of behaviors associated with groups worldwide who used platform mounds would probably educe more insights applicable to archaeological situations. The high degree of mound variability is commonly unrecognized in archaeological investigations, particularly on an intraregional level, and similar functions are often posited for all mounds and all mound-using groups in a specific area.

For each historic group, I recorded observations from numerous sources on environment, population size, social and political organization, economic systems, religious practices, and types and functions of platform mounds. A number of attributes can now be comparatively considered in relation to prehistoric platform mound construction and use. Although some of these results are intuitively obvious and have been suggested by others prior to this investigation, this is the first time a meaningful cross-cultural data base has been assembled to examine these factors on more than a cursory level.

CHAPTER THREE

Societal Attributes of Historic Groups with Platform Mounds

Ethnographic and ethnohistoric accounts indicated that groups that built and used platform mounds shared four primary characteristics: (1) leadership by a designated chief or headman; (2) a system of individual and group ranking or stratification; (3) inheritance of rank or class; and (4) structured resource redistribution and feasting (Table 3.1). These attributes occurred in all the groups examined with platform mounds, including groups not specifically discussed in the preceding chapter, and the relationships are strong.

Table 3.1 shows that there are a number of group attributes that were not correlated with mound-building groups and that platform mounds occurred within a wide spectrum of cultural practices. This "negative evidence" is equally important when using these traits to understand and reconstruct prehistoric platform mound-using societies. For example, the nature of the descent system, marriage practices, and postmarital residence rules had no bearing on whether or not a group built a platform mound. Features like tribute collection or the presence of clans or full- or part-time religious specialists were also probably not important. Mound-building groups inhabited many different environments, had varying population sizes, and exhibited numerous types of social organization. In fact, considering the range of variation that existed in these groups, it is apparent that there were many more attributes *not* patterned with respect to mound use than attributes that were positively related. Although this aspect in itself is not surprising, a cross-cultural view is particularly useful in illuminating the nature of group similarities and differences.

PLATFORM MOUND FUNCTION AND CONSTRUCTION

Ethnographic reports detailed surprising variability in mound function at both an intragroup and intergroup level. For the seven groups examined, mounds were used as general domestic residences (Ifaluk, Yap, Samoa, and Marquesa), chiefly residences (Yap, Samoa, Marquesa, and Natchez), community meeting areas (Ifaluk, Yap, Samoa, Marquesa, and Mapuche), temples (Yap, Samoa, Marquesa, and Natchez), burial features (Yap, Marquesa, Mapuche, and Choctaw), charnel houses (Natchez, and possibly Choctaw), arenas for staging or viewing public ceremonies (Marquesa and Mapuche), areas for food redistribution (Yap, Marquesa, and possibly Natchez), and hunting platforms for chiefly sport (Samoa). Ethnohistoric accounts of groups in Hawaii and Tonga (Kirch 1990; Kolb 1994) and in the southeastern United States (Anderson 1994; Blitz 1993; DePratter 1994; Hally 1994) indicated a similar wide range of functions.

Almost all platform mounds can be classified into four basic types: residential mounds, temple mounds, funerary mounds, and community mounds. These categories may be further subdivided based on the size of the mound, the amount of energy expended in mound construction, and whether construction required household or suprahousehold labor. Using these criteria, small, household-constructed residential mounds, such as those located on Ifaluk where there was little social differentiation, can be distinguished from large, community-constructed residential mounds generally occupied by chiefs or lineage heads, such as those of Yap, Marquesa, Samoa, and Natchez. Non-elite households in these groups, with the exception of the Natchez, occupied small, household-constructed residential mounds like those on Ifaluk. Similar size and energy distinctions can be made for temple mounds (Samoa versus Natchez and Marquesa), community mounds (Ifaluk and Samoa versus Marquesa and Yap), and burial mounds (Choctaw versus Mapuche and Natchez).

As defined in Chapter 1, the seven analyzed groups are classified in terms of increasing complexity as measured by social differentiation; hierarchical organization; and the unequal distribution of goods, resources, and power (Adams 1966; Flannery 1972; Nelson 1995; Redman 1992). Ifaluk and the Choctaw were the least socially differentiated, with few variations in power and resource distribution, and therefore they were the least socially complex. These groups are followed by a mid-

Table 3.1. Selected Attributes of Groups Using Platform Mounds

Group	Population size[1]	Primary subsistence methods[2]	Descent system	Residence rules	Marriage system	Clans present	Leadership system[3]	Social stratification, ranking
Ifaluk	200 - 250	Agriculture, gathering, fishing	Matrilineal	Matrilocal	Monogamous	Yes	Advisory chief (part-time)	Ranked
Yap	28,000 - 34,000	Agriculture, gathering, fishing	Patrilineal	Patrilocal	Monogamous	Yes	Authoritative chief	Stratified
Samoa	35,000 - 60,000	Agriculture, gathering, fishing	Cognatic	None	Monogamous, polygynous	No	Advisory/authoritative chief	Ranked
Marquesa	90,750	Gathering, agriculture, fishing	Patrilineal, cognatic?	Patrilocal, none	Polyandrous?	No	Authoritative chief	Stratified
Mapuche	200,000 - 500,000	Agriculture, gathering, hunting, fishing	Patrilineal	Patrilocal	Monogamous	No	Advisory chief	Ranked
Choctaw	15,000 - 20,000	Agriculture, gathering, hunting	Matrilineal	Matrilocal	Polygynous	No?	Advisory chief	Ranked
Natchez	4,000 - 5,600	Agriculture, gathering, fishing, hunting	Matrilineal	Matrilocal, patrilocal	Monogamous, polygynous	No	Authoritative chief	Stratified

Group	Inherited rank, class (type)	Wealth disparity	Tribute collection	Redistribution, feasting	Specialized priests	Chiefly descent from deity	Residential mounds	Temple mounds	Burial mounds	Other	Correlation of mound size with status
Ifaluk	Yes (matrilineal primogeniture)	Minimal	No	Yes	Part-time	No	Yes	No	No	Men's house	?
Yap	Yes (patrilineal primogeniture)	Great	Yes	Yes	Full-time	No	Yes	Yes	Yes	Men's house	?
Samoa	Yes (patrilineal, cognatic)	Moderate	Yes	Yes	Part-time?	No?	Yes	Yes	No?	Community house, star mounds	Yes
Marquesa	Yes (patrilineal primogeniture)	Great	Yes	Yes	Full-time	No[4]	Yes	Yes	Yes?	Tohua	Yes
Mapuche	Yes (patrilineal primogeniture)	Moderate	Yes?	Yes	Full-time	No	No	No	Yes	Nache-cuel	No
Choctaw	?	Minimal?	?	Yes	Full-time?	No	No	No	Yes		?
Natchez	Yes (matrilineal primogeniture)	Moderate?	Yes	Yes	Full-time	Yes	Yes	Yes	?		?

[1] See Chapter 2 for basis of estimate. Range is purposely broad to include all potential population estimates.
[2] Ranked in a subjective estimation of importance.
[3] It is realized that even "authoritative" chiefs had advisory groups.
[4] Although chiefs are not descended from the gods, inspirational priests had God-given powers when possessed.

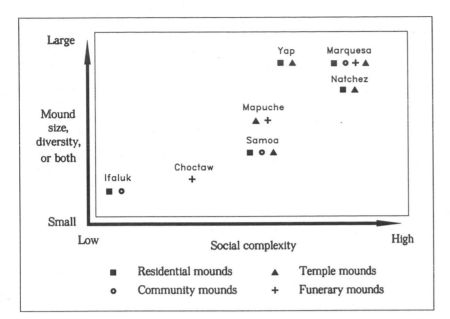

Figure 3.1. Schematic relationship between social complexity and platform mound size and diversity for the seven analyzed groups.

range level containing Samoa and Mapuche. Yap, Marquesa, and Natchez were the most socially complex groups, with well-defined social hierarchies, extreme differences in the distribution of power and resources, and authoritative rulers.

Social complexity is an important attribute because these comparative data indicate that the greater the diversity in mound type and function, the greater the social complexity of the group, and there is a similar relationship between increasing mound size and increasing social complexity. These relationships are shown schematically in Figure 3.1. If the groups are ranked in terms of social complexity and of mound size and diversity (Table 3.2), a Spearman's Correlation Coefficient produces a value of 0.92, indicating a nearly perfect correlation. The pattern shown in Figure 3.1 is strong and is supported by information from other mound-using groups not specifically discussed in Chapter 2.

Mounds could be, and generally were, multifunctional. Mounds that served as chiefly residences or temples also functioned as communal meeting areas, as among the Natchez and Marquesans (Handy 1923; Swanton 1946). In Samoa, the large community mounds also served as temples and were used on occasion for sacred rites and ceremonies (Holmes 1987). Samoan star mounds, although thought to be primarily for the chiefly sport of pigeon-snaring, may have also been defensive features or ritual sites (Herdrich and Clark 1993). The large "old-men's" community house in Yap was used not only for both formal and informal community gather-

Table 3.2. Rank-order Assigned to Variables Used in Spearman's Correlation Coefficient

Group	Social complexity	Mound size, diversity
Ifaluk	1.0	1.0
Choctaw	2.0	2.0
Samoa	3.5	3.5
Mapuche	3.5	3.5
Yap	5.0	6.5
Natchez	7.0	5.0
Marquesa	7.0	6.5

NOTE: Spearman's Rank-Order Correlation Coefficient = 0.92

ings, but as sleeping quarters and as a place for resource redistribution (Lingenfelter 1975). Even mounds that were architecturally similar had very different uses. In Samoa, where temple mounds and small residential mounds were structurally identical, Mead (1968: 266) mistakenly concluded that Samoan temples did not exist (Holmes 1987). Similarly, at Yap the sacred *teliw* mounds were often identical to regular domestic mounds (Intoh and Leach 1985; Jennings and Holmer 1980).

The lack of a direct correlation between mound function and form and the fact that many mounds were multifunctional signify that it is inadvisable to assign a specific primary function to a mound based on architectural attributes, contrary to common archaeological practice in the American Southwest (see Chapter 1). For example, mounds that are structurally similar can be either residential or nonresidential, and sometimes both, depending on the stage of the mound in its life history. Mounds that are structurally different can have similar functions. Determining mound function in general is difficult even when relevant ethnographic data are present, as indicated by Mead's dilemma or by archaeological studies in the Pacific (Jennings and Holmer 1980) and southeastern United States (Blitz 1993). Assigning mound function is even more difficult from an archaeological perspective, where often the superstructure on top of the mound is not preserved. If just the underlying mound was present, the functions of many of the historically documented mounds would have been ambiguous, particularly if multiple size classes were not apparent. Distinctions between the Natchez temple mound and the residential mound of the Great Sun, and of Samoan temple and residential mounds, although functionally very different, would have been difficult to discern because the underlying mounds were structurally alike.

Size, as measured through surface area and volume, is perhaps the primary characteristic that distinguishes mound types. Size, of course, is also correlated with energy expended in mound construction (Abrams 1994). Ifaluk, Samoan, and Yap community mounds were essentially identical to residential house mounds except for their greater size (Burrows and Spiro 1953; Holmes 1987; Lingenfelter 1975). Size was also the distinguishing characteristic between chiefly residential mounds and residential mounds of the commoner classes in Marquesa and Samoa, where volume of the mound (and in Samoa, mound height) was directly correlated with status (Table 3.1; Holmes 1987; Linton 1939). However, this relationship needs to be tempered by the fact that mound size among the Mapuche was not related to status, but to the size of the kin group and the length of the reign of the deceased's successor (Dillehay 1990). It is unfortunate, for archaeological purposes, that the ethnographic and ethnohistoric accounts were not detailed enough to explore the relationship between mound size and the organization and composition of the construction labor group.

A strong pattern in the ethnographic and ethnohistoric sources was that almost all mounds took on a new function after they were no longer actively used for their initial purpose. Abandoned mounds often became "sacred architectural memorabilia" and part of the ancestral property of the group (Dillehay 1990: 233). This practice appeared among all analyzed groups and in all mound categories with the variable exception of the small, household-constructed residential mounds, which may have had new structures built on them and have been more-or-less continuously in use (see Handy 1923: 150). Abandoned mounds were often revisited, were associated with taboos, and were the scenes of ritual offerings and ceremonies. Rarely was a mound reoccupied, however, and sometimes, as among the Natchez, the associated superstructure was purposely destroyed (Anderson 1994). At any moment in time, then, there was a strong tendency for groups to have mounds that were in use and mounds that were abandoned (but still an active part of the social and religious system).

Therefore, the sequential use of mounds was a common characteristic. This pattern was strongest in the more socially complex groups, such as the Mapuche, Yap, Marquesans, and Natchez. Anderson (1994) used ethnohistoric accounts from the Coosa and Cofitachequi to discuss similar patterns among other Southeastern mound-building groups. All these groups constructed new mounds at certain critical points in the individual or group life-cycle, including attainment of puberty or marriage of the eldest son, death of the chief or estate head, or succession of a new chief. Significant remodeling of mounds may have indicated this same process (Blitz 1993), such as the adding of a new platform terrace on the marriage of a Samoan *matai* (Buck 1930).

Unfortunately, little information was available on the processes of mound construction, especially for groups in the Southeast. Data needed to quantify level of effort and energy expenditure for comparative purposes and observations on the social make-up and organization of the mound-building construction group were sparse; the limited view was that mound construction was at both the household and community (suprahousehold, lineage, clan, or tribe) level. Generally, household groups built the mounds and structures used for regular domestic residences, whereas community-wide groups built all other features, including chiefly residences, community houses, temples, and mortuary mounds.

Labor for building the large mound features was under the control of a chief or his representative. In some groups, like the Samoans or Marquesans, a specialized class of master craftsmen directed construction (Buck 1930; Linton 1939). Almost all building, from that of the simplest domestic residence, taking perhaps a few weeks, to the construction of a community house, which might have taken months or years, was accompanied by ritual activities, taboo proscriptions, and feasting. These events were particularly evident in the more socially complex groups, but were present to some degree among those of lower complexity. The larger the structure to be built, the more elaborate the ceremonies. For a simple residential structure, rituals and feasts included just the immediate household or several households who actively helped in the construction (Handy 1923: 150). For more elaborate structures, feasts and ceremonies lasted for several days or weeks and involved the entire lineage, clan, or tribe, all of whom were expected to assist in construction (Buck 1930: 90; Handy 1923: 205).

ENVIRONMENT AND ECONOMY

The environment did not appear to be a significant factor in platform mound construction; mound-building groups inhabited a wide and diverse range of environmental settings. If the environmental data presented for each group in Chapter 2 are combined with information on environment from other ethnographic and archaeological mound-building groups, variation is extreme. The only common characteristic, as noted by numerous archaeologists and ethnographers, is that the environment has to be bountiful enough to provide a surplus of subsistence resources to sustain the construction group during the building of the mound. Even this constraint is variable, however, and not necessarily a diagnostic attribute; in the Marquesa Islands subsistence stress was a real possibility, sometimes in heavy drought years eliminating through starvation up to a third of the population (Linton 1939).

Both Yap and the Marquesa Islands were in marginal environments and suffered periodic subsistence stress (Ferdon 1993; Labby 1976; Lingenfelter 1975; Linton 1939). They were also the two most socially complex Pacific region groups examined in this analysis. Perhaps subsistence stress, or more precisely, the development of social and technological methods to adapt to periodic food shortages, is associated with relatively high social complexity and platform mound construction. However true this may have been for these two specific groups, the relationship appears to be an artifact of the sample chosen for analysis; other Pacific region groups, such as the Tongans and Hawaiian Islanders, achieved similar or greater complexity in more favorable environments (Ferdon 1987; Kirch and Sahlins 1992).

The lack of a relationship between subsistence stress and the attainment of social complexity was even more evident when examining groups in the southeastern United States. Here the ethnohistoric information revealed that increasing complexity and the presence of platform mounds were strongly related to the availability of food surplus (Anderson 1994), brought on, in part, by favorable environmental conditions. Accounts by Cabeza de Vaca on the 1528 Narváez expedition (Hodge 1990) and the Gentleman of Elvas on the 1539 de Soto expedition (Lewis 1990) frequently noted that groups living in less favorable environments exhibited lower social complexity (as measured in the accounts through chiefly wealth and power, hierarchical organization, and social differentiation) than groups living in favorable environments with a surplus of resources. Groups in favorable environments were much more likely to be organized into ranked or stratified societies and to have large villages, sometimes palisaded, with storage facilities and platform mounds.

The amount of surplus food storage of some Southeastern platform mound groups was extremely high. The entire de Soto entrada, consisting of more than 600 men, was able to spend the winters of 1539 and 1540 at the mound villages of Apalachee and Coosa, drawing on the reserves of these chiefdoms (Anderson 1994: 77). De Soto spent five months at Apalachee alone. As another example, there was enough surplus food in the Pacaha (Capaha) chiefdom to feed de Soto and his men for more than 40 days in the summer of 1541 (Lewis 1990: 209–213). Apparently this quantity of surplus was not unusual for Southeastern mound-building groups.

Aside from the presence of a surplus supply of food, there was much variation in the economic and subsistence systems of mound-building groups. Irrigation agriculture was practiced by some, such as groups on Yap and Hawaii, but not by others (Kirch and Sahlins 1992; Lingenfelter 1975). The Samoans and Ifaluk Islanders lived in such bountiful environments that subsistence was never a problem, and sufficient foodstuffs were gathered by periodic visits to the cultivated taro fields and fruit trees. Conversely, agriculture was barely practiced by the Marquesa Islanders, who relied primarily on tree crops, and subsistence stress was common. Groups in the southeastern United States, as well as the Mapuche of South America, practiced standard corn agriculture supplemented by hunting and fishing; both the Choctaw and Natchez produced crop surpluses, which the Choctaw traded to neighboring Creek and Chickasaw groups (Swanton 1946).

The control of subsistence resources is related to increasing social complexity (see also Hayden 1995). In those groups with the highest complexity, resources were controlled by the chief or lineage head. In fact, the relationship was so strong that it can be stated that the greater the diversity and size of platform mounds, the greater the control of resources by the elite or higher classes. Among the Marquesans, Yap, and Natchez, the chiefs collected tribute from the lower classes (Lingenfelter 1975; Linton 1939; Swanton 1946). Several Yap chiefs also collected tribute from other islands, some as far as 650 km (more than 400 miles) distant (Burrows and Spiro 1953). Among the Natchez, the Great Sun had his own personal storage granary supplied by tribute collection. "The subjects of the Great Sun, the people of all the Natchez villages, were conspicuous in giving the Great Sun large presents of food. . . . The head warriors, in fact, cultivated a sacred field of corn, tended entirely by their own labor, and the corn from this field was stored along with other food in the Great Sun's storehouse" (Hudson 1976: 209).

Marquesa and Yap also had well-developed systems of land tenure, with land ownership vested in the higher classes. Members of lower class groups who did not own land were essentially powerless and had no voice in political or social affairs (Labby 1976: 15–16). There is not enough information to determine the nature of land ownership for the Natchez. Some form of land ownership by the chiefs and higher classes was present in all groups examined, but in groups with less authoritative chiefs and lower complexity, such as the Ifaluk and Samoans, land ownership, while conferring certain privileges, was primarily based on the descent group and considered to be held in trust for the common good. Although some notion of the "common good" was present in the more socially complex groups, private ownership for personal benefit was also common, with clear distinctions between land-holding and landless groups. Platform mounds among the Mapuche, and probably the Marquesans, Yap, and Natchez, were used to denote territorial land claims at both the individual and group level. Many of these mounds were large, ostentatious, and designed for public viewing, intimating at least in part a territorial function. Dillehay (1990: 224–225) wrote that "marking territories with lineage architecture" was one of the more important functions of platform mound architecture. A territorial function may have been particularly important for highly sedentary groups who had invested significant energy in landscape modifications such as clearing agricultural fields or constructing irrigation canals or for groups who lived in areas of high population density where land ownership was in dispute.

All mound-using groups examined in this analysis practiced some form of redistribution, involving both subsistence goods and other classes of material culture. Furthermore, all of these groups used feasting as one means of redistributing resources. Although feasting and redistribution cannot be considered to be diagnostic attributes of mound-using groups because they are common in many middle-range societies (see Feinman and Neitzel 1984), they are important characteristics. Redistribution was often used as political strategy by chiefs and religious leaders, thereby establishing debt obligations and patron-client relationships (Lingenfelter 1975: 153). Generosity in giving, as compared to hoarding and personal accumulation of wealth, was a trait held in high esteem by all groups examined (Burrows and Spiro 1953; Linton 1939; Swanton 1946). Among the Natchez, "the Great Sun did not keep all of this [tribute-collected] food for himself, but redistributed it to his people. Above all, the Great Sun was supposed to be generous" (Hudson 1976: 209).

Significantly, platform mounds sometimes played an important role in resource redistribution. One of the specific functions of the large Yap community mound (*pebaey*) was to redistribute food, and a stone table was specially built on top of the mound for this purpose (Lingenfelter 1975: 81). Redistribution may also have occurred at the Marquesan *tohua*, which was the scene of communal feasting (Ferdon 1993).

POPULATION SIZE

The relationship between population size and mound-building groups is unclear. As shown in Table 3.1, population size of the groups studied was highly variable, ranging from a low of 200 to 250 for the Ifaluk Islanders to a high of 500,000 for the Mapuche. Population density would have been a more informative measure, but such figures were not available. There are significant problems with the population data. The population estimates cited in Chapter 2 came from a variety of sources and were made at various times. Population figures from the time prior to European contact would have been the most useful for analysis, but obtaining them was not always possible, and some estimates were for the precontact period whereas others were for the modern period. Unfortunately, estimates for the precontact period often were not reliable, although they were the best available. Additionally, some of the estimates were not for the population of the mound-building group itself, but rather of the entire tribe or, in the case of the Marquesans, of a number of tribes. Because of these problems, population data are not comparable across the seven groups.

The wide variation in the population size of the groups studied intimates that the presence of platform mounds may not have been directly related to population size, although probably it was necessary to reach some sort of threshold number before mounds could be built. Once this threshold was reached, however, population size may not have been a significant factor. The group with the lowest population, Ifaluk, was also the least socially complex, with the fewest types of mounds (Fig. 3.1), and it may have represented the lower end of the mound-building population distribution.

SOCIAL AND POLITICAL ORGANIZATION

Platform mound-using groups encompassed a variety of social and political systems (Table 3.1). Groups that built mounds traced descent through the matrilineal line (Ifaluk, Choctaw, and Natchez), through the patrilineal line (Yap, Mapuche, and lower class Marquesans), and cognatically through both the mother and father (Samoa and possibly higher class Marquesans). Residence rules were similarly variable and related to the descent system: both matrilocal (Ifaluk and Choctaw) and patrilocal (Yap and Mapuche) groups were present, along with groups that had either no defined residence rules (Samoa) or residence rules that differed depending on rank (Marquesa and Natchez). The form of marriage was often rank dependent and was either monogamous (Ifaluk, Yap, Mapuche, and lower class Samoans, Marquesans, and Natchez), polygynous (Choctaw and higher class Samoans and Natchez), or, among the higher class Marquesans, possibly polyandrous. The political system ranged from nearly egalitarian with little chiefly power or privilege (Ifaluk, and possibly Choctaw) to nearly autocratic (Marquesa, Yap, and Natchez).

Even with these variations, there are several important characteristics common to all or most mound-using groups. One of the most significant attributes, specifically because it bears heavily on the issue of social complexity in Southwestern prehistory, is that all mound-using groups that I examined in the HRAF files were either ranked or stratified with a designated chief or leader. Furthermore, both the position of chief and degree of ranking were inherited, although the means of inheritance was group specific (Table 3.1). The degree of chiefly authority varied by group, and all chiefs had some form of advisory council whose power also varied.

Both ranking and stratification are hierarchical forms of social organization present among socially complex groups that have ascribed leadership roles, status distinctions, and unequal access to resources and power.

Ranking can occur at both the individual level, as between individuals within a group, and the group level, as between descent groups. Rank can be measured along a continuum: higher ranked groups have greater social differentiation and centralization of power and resources than lower ranked groups. The distinction between ranking and stratification used in this analysis is based simply on the presence or absence of coercive force available or used by one class in a society to exert their will upon another. In stratified societies the dominant classes had this force, but in ranked societies they did not (Brandt 1994: 14; Schlegel 1992: 381).

One of the strongest relationships in mound-building groups was between the degree of chiefly (or religious) authority and the diversity of mound types and functions; that is, the greater the authority, the greater the degree of mound diversity and the greater the size of the mounds. The association was especially apparent among the Yap, Marquesans, and Natchez (Fig. 3.1), the three most socially complex groups in the analysis and the only stratified groups in which the chiefs unambiguously exercised the right of life or death over their subjects (Lingenfelter 1975; Linton 1939; Swanton 1946).

Similarly, among the Mapuche there was an elaboration of mound function with the emergence of a single "dynastic patrilineage" under the control of a strong chiefly class (Dillehay 1990: 238). This elaboration developed around the turn of the century and probably was at least partly related to the consolidation of lineage land under the authority of the chiefs by order of the Chilean government. At that time, the function of platform mounds changed from being primarily chiefly tombs that were only important to single lineages to being platforms for showcasing lineages and conducting rites associated with multilineage *nguillatun* ceremonies (Dillehay 1992). Interestingly, Faron (1986: 58) reported that Mapuche chiefs gained the power of life or death over their subjects as a result of the consolidation of lineage land. Although not noted by Dillehay (1990, 1992), this new authority may have also been related to the elaboration and change in platform mound function that occurred at essentially the same time.

Dillehay (1990: 237–238, 1992) further posited that chiefly authority and the change in mound function were directly related to the role of the chiefs in scheduling public events and ceremonies. Ethnographic and ethnohistoric sources indicated that participation in these events was time-consuming: Dillehay (1990: 237) estimated that 15 percent of the Mapuche agricultural season was spent attending public affairs, and Blitz (1993:

22) noted that the Natchez undertook 13 feasts a year, some lasting as long as 10 days (Swanton 1911). Although the evidence is not entirely conclusive, it does appear that scheduling was primarily a chiefly role. At Natchez, the Great Sun set the date for the Green Corn ceremony (Swanton 1911: 113–114); in the Marquesas, the chief initiated at least some, if not all, of the ceremonies held at the *tohua* (Linton 1939: 152). Therefore, scheduling of ceremonial activities may also have been related to platform mound use, although the manner in which it was effected is unclear.

All mound-using groups had highly structured descent systems, which operated at the level of the lineage, clan, or tribe, with descent often traced to an apical ancestor. Furthermore, platform mounds were most often directly associated with the entire descent group. This association was especially strong for groups with lower degrees of ranking and chiefly authority, such as the Choctaw or Ifaluk, because the chief derived much of his "advisory" power from continuing lineage support, but it also occurred in those groups with the greatest degree of "autocratic" chiefly authority. For example, platform mounds were still considered to be associated with the lineage, if not an actual part of lineage property, regardless of whether the mound was inhabited by the chief (Natchez), considered to be chiefly property (Marquesa), or served as a chiefly tomb (Mapuche).

The sources reviewed indicated that all members of a descent group shared in the attributes and enjoyed the prestige of their chief, including the built as well as the social environment. In this respect, interpreting prehistoric platform mounds as being solely the domains of elite chiefs or lineageless "aggrandizers" without taking into account the relationship of the associated descent group is not ethnographically supportable. In middle-range societies, platform mounds tended to be primarily corporate features, even though leaders sometimes derived individual benefits from them.

Lastly, many of the chiefly or elite classes examined in this study showed little in the way of material culture besides architecture that could be distinguishable archaeologically as indicative of social rank. Although this observation is perhaps not directly related to platform mound use, it is relevant to the archaeological interpretation of prehistoric groups who built platform mounds and it supports evidence from a much larger sample of middle-range ethnographic groups analyzed by Feinman and Neitzel (1984). Chiefs in Ifaluk and probably Choctaw were virtually indistinguishable from the common people (Burrows and Spiro 1953; Swanton 1946). The

rank of Samoan chiefs was denoted by their carrying perishable wooden artifacts, such as a ceremonial fly-swatter or speaker's staff, and by deferential behavior to the chiefs by those of lower rank (Holmes 1987). Chiefs among the socially stratified Marquesans and Natchez were distinguished only by dress (such as the elaborate feather headdress worn by the Great Sun), by tatoo patterns, and by the deferential behavior accorded to them (Ferdon 1993; Hudson 1976). Although Mapuche chiefs were buried with greater quantities of grave goods and reportedly had well-made artifacts (Dillehay 1992), it is unlikely their higher status would be archaeologically visible in domestic contexts.

The lack of obvious distinguishing indicators of status may, in part, account for the difficulties experienced by Southwestern archaeologists in inferring the presence of prehistoric ranked or stratified societies. Although chiefs generally had greater quantities of goods, or at times, better made goods, much of this material was redistributed at feasts and other ceremonies, and accumulation of wealth was not considered to be a positive attribute in any of the mound-building, middle-range groups examined (see also Feinman and Neitzel 1984). This pattern clearly changed when certain thresholds of scale and hierarchy were crossed, as demonstrated by the often ostentatious displays of individual wealth at highly complex mound-building societies throughout the world (see Nelson 1995).

RELIGIOUS PRACTICES

Like other characteristics, religious practices among mound-building groups were diverse. Religious activities were more similar within a region (such as the Southeast or Polynesia) than between regions, but few attributes crosscut all groups. The presence of full-time religious specialists versus part-time specialists did not seem to be an important factor (Table 3.1), although full-time specialists were more commonly associated with groups of higher social complexity who displayed the greatest diversity in mound form and the largest mound sizes. The presence of full-time religious specialists was also related to the degree of authority exerted by the religious practitioner, which, like the degree of chiefly authority, was related to increasing social complexity. In most groups, however, religious authority was so interwoven with chiefly authority (often the chief encompassed both religious and secular roles, such as the Great Sun of the Natchez or the Samoan *matai*) that it was difficult to separate the two spheres.

In the Marquesa Islands, where religious and secular authority were markedly separate, the high degree of religious authority was a significant factor in mound construction and use. Priests sanctified all mound construction, including that of the small residential mounds, and directed the construction of the temple mounds. Along with the chiefs, priests were the only Marquesans who used the sacrificial temple mounds hidden in the island interiors. Marquesan inspirational priests, like the Great Sun of the Natchez, had god-given powers and exerted tremendous authority. The Natchez and Marquesans were the two most socially complex groups of the sample and had some of the largest mounds, necessitating an impressive expenditure of energy in construction. The interconnections among having an intimate relationship with the gods, either through direct descent (Natchez) or spirit possession (Marquesa), increasing social complexity, and diversity in platform mound form and size are probably not coincidental. Authority figures in other socially complex mound-building groups, such as the Hawaiians and Tongans, also had god-given powers or were directly descended from the deities (Ferdon 1987; Kirch 1990).

Another common attribute of mound-using groups was the fact that construction of almost all mounds, from small domestic mounds to large community mounds and temples, required some sort of religious sanctification. This sanctification generally involved feasting, the extent of which was related to the size of the construction group and the nature of the mound being built.

The final common attribute, less clear, though present in the majority of groups in this study, was the tendency for mound-using groups to practice ancestor worship or at least have an interest in descent group ancestors. Many of the mounds were considered to be the property of the descent group and, once abandoned, continued to be inhabited by mythical lineage ancestors. This pattern included small residential mounds as well as larger temple and community mounds. A concern with descent group ancestors was most pronounced in groups with high social complexity, such as the Yap, Marquesans, Natchez, and Mapuche, who worshipped ancestors directly as deified beings (Faron 1986; Lingenfelter 1975; Linton 1939; Swanton 1946). The Marquesans, Natchez, and Choctaw constructed specialized sacred structures for the bones of their ancestors. The reason for this concern with ancestral remains is unknown, and the relationship may be spurious, but it was a common attribute of most of the analyzed groups and deserves further research.

HISTORIC PLATFORM MOUNDS

One of the more significant findings of this comparative study, although not unexpected, is that platform mounds cannot easily be partitioned into functionally homogeneous categories, despite repeated attempts by archaeologists through the years to do so. Seemingly, then, many of the archaeological analyses of Southwestern prehistoric platform mounds discussed in Chapter 1 are overly simplistic, particularly in their emphasis on assigning a specific function to a platform mound or assuming that all platform mounds in a region functioned in a similar manner. Unfortunately, trying to discern platform mound function from prehistoric remains in the absence of direct ethnographic analogy may be an exercise in futility. The small historic sample examined disclosed that platform mounds had a wide range of functions, that most platform mounds were multifunctional, and that architecturally similar mounds had very different uses. This variability existed both within and between regions. These observations also have a bearing on the debate in Southwestern archaeology over whether platform mounds were inhabited by secular elite leaders, or by religious leaders, or were not inhabited but served as specialized ceremonial centers. Because the study showed that all of these functions are not only possible but highly interrelated and may have occurred at different times in the life of a single mound, it is unlikely that specific mound use can be determined solely from archaeological remains.

Even with these cautions, several common attributes of middle-range groups are identified that can aid in understanding both the use made of the prehistoric mounds and, perhaps more importantly, the groups that used them. Although the attributes specifically apply only to the seven groups analyzed herein, additional information suggests that they generally pertain to most middle-range mound-using groups.

1. Platform mounds were multifunctional and had a wide range of documented uses; at any one time, mounds could encompass one or a number of different functions. The four most common functions were as residential mounds, temple mounds, burial mounds, and community mounds. All mound construction required some type of ceremonial sanctification.

2. Mound-using groups were ranked or stratified with a designated chief or leader; class and rank were inherited. Therefore, groups that constructed platform mounds were socially complex with institutionalized,

hierarchical social organizations. Inferentially, most platform mounds, with the exception of small residential mounds, were associated with some control over the application and organization of community labor and resource distribution.

3. The greater the diversity in mound type and function, and the larger the size of the mound, the greater the social complexity and the authority of the chiefs or religious leaders. Translated into labor-energy measures, this means that the greater the energy invested in mound construction, the greater the social complexity. The greatest elaborations in mound size and function appeared in groups whose chiefs or religious leaders had the unambiguous power of life or death over their subjects.

4. Platform mounds were associated with a specific descent group or with people who considered themselves to be of common ancestry (household, lineage, clan, or tribe) and were constructed by members of that group. The mounds were often used to promote and glorify the corporate group and probably were associated with some form of ancestor worship. There was a focus on the group even if the mound was inhabited by an individual chief or religious leader. The relationship be-tween the size of the social group and mound build-ing is unclear, although it is likely that a minimum population must be reached before mounds are con-structed.

5. As long as the territory continued to be occupied by the descent group, platform mounds took on a new function once they were abandoned, often becoming the mythical home of descent group ancestors. This reuse applied to all mound types, with the variable exception of small residential mounds. Therefore, sequential use of mounds was a common characteristic.

6. The greater the diversity and size of a group's platform mounds, the greater the control of resources by chiefs or individuals of high rank. Environment was not a significant factor except that it had to have been favorable enough to provide a food surplus to sustain the mound construction group. Redistribution and feast-ing were common attributes of mound-using groups.

7. A highly formalized system of land tenure was prev-alent in the more socially complex platform mound-using groups and mounds often served as territorial markers for land claims.

CHAPTER FOUR

Prehistoric Settlement in the Eastern Tonto Basin, Arizona

The Tonto Basin occupies a significant place in the archaeological history of the American Southwest. Containing large and spectacular prehistoric ruins within a dramatic environmental setting, the region has been an area of archaeological speculation for more than a hundred years (Bandelier 1892; Bourke 1891). Early Southwestern archaeologists, such as Erich Schmidt, Harold and Winifred Gladwin, and Emil Haury, conducted research in the Tonto Basin, and some of the most far-reaching theories of Southwestern prehistoric development arose from or were influenced by those investigations. Schmidt recognized the stratigraphic and temporal implications of red-on-buff pottery underlying black-on-white wares, and he speculated on the significance of the platform mounds (Hohmann and Kelley 1988; Schmidt 1928). Haury (1932) defined aspects of the red-on-buff ceramic culture, later named the Hohokam, and the mechanisms of Hohokam colonization based on his work at the site of Roosevelt 9:6. The Gladwins (Gladwin and Gladwin 1935) proposed that the people making red-on-buff pottery were replaced in the Tonto Basin by migrating people making black-on-white vessels, named the Salado, who then went on to influence and dominate much of the southern and central portions of the Southwest. Based on this work, the notion of Salado as an intrusive, pueblo-building people who replaced the Hohokam (and other Southwestern groups) became a central theme in Southwestern prehistory.

The Tonto Basin is perhaps most famous as the "heartland" of the Salado. Despite the years of investigation, the nature of Salado is still not well understood, and debate continues as to whether it represents a migratory group, an indigenous Tonto Basin culture, a regional archaeological horizon, or a religious cult. Although this study of platform mound use has implications for the Salado question, examining the nature of Salado is not the subject of this research. There is no doubt, however, that Salado, in whatever manifestation, strongly influenced much of the central and southern portions of the Southwest for two centuries beginning around A.D. 1250.

Much of the controversy surrounding the Tonto Basin stems from its location in a transitional environmental and cultural zone between the desert-dwelling Hohokam to the south and puebloan groups of the plateau and mountain areas to the north and east (Fig. 4.1). The archaeology of the basin is characterized by varying architectural remains and pottery assemblages that contain a multiplicity of ceramic wares and types. With this diversity, it is not surprising the prehistory of the Tonto Basin has been interpreted in different ways: to some the basin was an uninhabited (or empty) niche colonized by groups from the Hohokam area or from pueblo regions to the north and east of the Tonto Basin (or both), to others it was a cultural sponge that absorbed societies and traditions from neighboring areas, and to still others it was the heartland of Salado populations who used the Tonto Basin as a base from which to spread throughout much of the southern Southwest.

Indeed, the Tonto Basin has been included by various archaeologists at one time or another as part of nearly every prehistoric culture area that surrounds it. Groups identified in the Tonto Basin include the Southern Sinagua (Ciolek-Torrello 1987; Hammack 1969; Huckell 1978; Pilles 1976), the Hohokam (Doyel 1976, 1978; Gladwin and Gladwin 1935; Haas 1971; Haury 1932; Huckell 1977; Jeter 1978; Rice 1985; Wood 1985, 1989; Wood and McAllister 1982, 1984), the Mogollon (Ciolek-Torrello and Whittlesey 1994; Reid 1989; Whittlesey and Reid 1982), and the Anasazi (Gladwin 1957; Gladwin and Gladwin 1935; Morris 1970).

Through the years, much time and energy have been spent debating the cultural affiliation of Tonto Basin inhabitants, generally at the expense of understanding the prehistoric settlement. In many ways, this emphasis reflects an unstated belief that if Tonto Basin inhabitants could be appropriately placed within a defined Southwest culture area, we might then have a clear understanding of Tonto Basin prehistory. Instead, recent research shows that the Tonto Basin population can most productively be understood as an indigenous society, one that interacted and mixed with neighboring groups but maintained a separate and distinct cultural identity for most of its developmental sequence (Elson 1992a, 1996b; Elson, Gregory, and Stark 1995; Wood 1992).

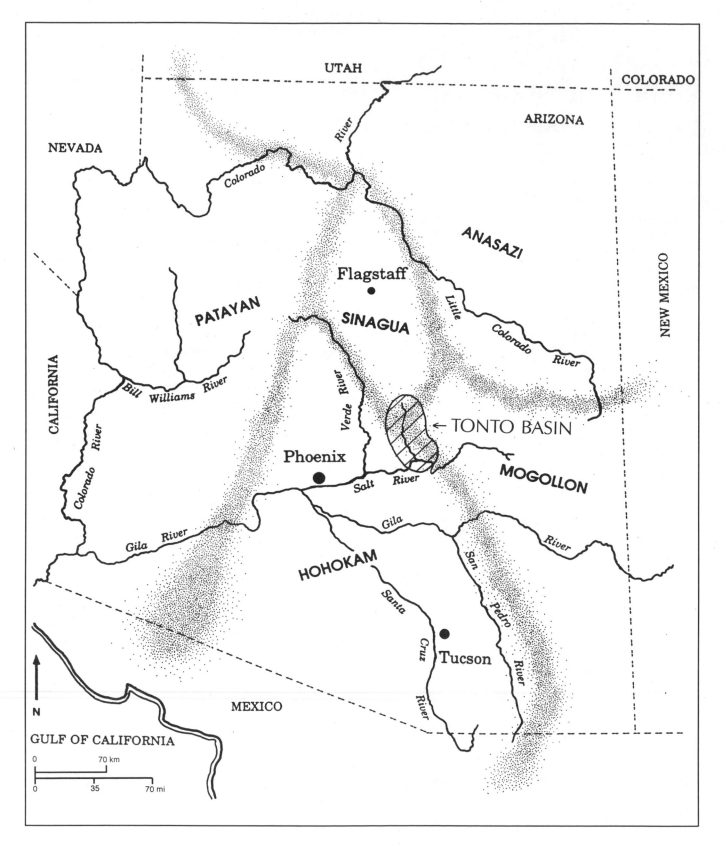

Figure 4.1. The Tonto Basin in relation to surrounding prehistoric culture areas as traditionally defined in the American Southwest.

TONTO BASIN ENVIRONMENT

The Tonto Basin is situated in the mountainous "Transition Zone" of central Arizona (Chronic 1983), which separates the Colorado Plateau to the north from the basin-and-range province of the southern deserts. The basin is characterized as a "typical down-faulted, sediment-filled, basin-and-range trough lying between uplifted mountains" (Royse and others 1971: 8), measuring about 60 km (37 miles) long by 10 km to 15 km (6 to 9 miles) wide (Waters 1996: 2.1). It is bounded by the Mazatzal mountain range to the west, the Sierra Ancha to the east, the Mogollon Rim to the north, and the Pinal, Superstition, and Salt River mountains to the south. Elevation ranges from approximately 580 m (1,900 feet) along the Salt River in the southern portion to more than 2,410 m (7,900 feet) at the top of Mazatzal Peak.

The basin is divided into an upper portion (the Upper Tonto Basin) and a lower portion (the Lower Tonto Basin), separated at the approximate location of a schist deposit that constricts Tonto Creek near the town of Jakes Corner (Elson and Sullivan 1981). The focus of this research and the following discussion is the Lower Tonto Basin, which is further divided into a Salt River arm and a Tonto Creek arm (Fig. 4.2). The Eastern Tonto Basin is a small, 30-square-kilometer area in the southeast portion of the Lower Tonto Basin, situated where the Salt River enters the basin from the deeply downcut Salt River Canyon. The Upper Basin is more rugged, higher, and contains less arable land; it also has a different settlement prehistory than the Lower Basin (Ciolek-Torrello 1987; Elson and Craig 1992; Elson and others 1992; Wood 1992).

Two major drainages flow through the Lower Tonto Basin, providing an ample, if not abundant, supply of water. The Salt River originates in the White Mountains of east-central Arizona and flows east to west through the southern part of the basin; Tonto Creek is a smaller drainage that flows northwest to southeast into the Salt River from the uplands of the Mogollon Rim. The lower portions of both drainages are currently impounded by Roosevelt Lake (Fig. 4.2), which covers approximately 6,885 ha (17,000 acres) and undoubtedly numerous prehistoric sites. Roosevelt Dam and the lake were created in 1911; what lies beneath the lake is known only from early explorers (Bandelier 1892; Bourke 1891) and from brief glimpses of the lake bottom during low-water periods. These reports indicate that some of the largest and perhaps earliest sites are in the inundated area, hampering archaeological interpretation. Fortu-

nately, archaeologists believe they know the locations of all platform mounds, although several, like the large Armer Ranch Ruin, Bourke's Teocalli, and Rock Island, are permanently inundated; only a few early accounts of these sites exist (Lindauer 1995; Wood 1989, 1995).

The Salt River has a drainage catchment of more than 11,150 square kilometers (4,300 square miles) and is one of the major perennial streams of Arizona. As the river enters the Tonto Basin, it leaves the narrow canyons of the Upper Salt and empties into a broad alluvial floodplain. The floodplain, which covers more than 8,100 ha (20,000 acres), contains prime agricultural bottomlands composed of alluvial soils that would have been continually replenished through floodwater deposition (Van West and Altschul 1994; Waters 1996). Tonto Creek has a much smaller floodplain and flow, and it drains approximately 1,750 square kilometers (675 square miles). Paleoenvironmental studies show that, like the Salt River, Tonto Creek may have flowed year-round during the prehistoric occupation (Ciolek-Torrello 1987: 15), although the quantity of water varied by year and by season. Waters (1996: 2.23) estimates that both Tonto Creek and the Salt River contained sufficient water for summer irrigation about 85 percent of the time.

The Salt River and Tonto Creek floodplains in the Lower Tonto Basin are broad and support a Sonoran Desert Scrub vegetation (Brown 1982; Gasser 1987; Lowe 1964). Typical plant species include mesquite, palo verde, acacia, crucifixion thorn, and cholla, prickly pear, and saguaro cacti. The areas adjacent to the streams also support a riparian life-zone, with ash, willow, and cottonwood constituting the dominant species. Economically important fauna include mule deer, jackrabbit, and cottontail rabbit (James 1995; Szuter 1992). Environmentally, the Lower Tonto Basin is similar to the riverine dominated landscape of the Hohokam core area in the Salt and Gila river basins, although the extent of the arable floodplain is significantly less.

The Lower Tonto Basin has a semiarid climate, similar in many respects to the southern deserts but somewhat cooler with slightly more precipitation. Temperature and rainfall are variable within the basin, both being highly dependent on elevation and to a lesser degree on landform and degree of exposure. Although freezing temperatures are common in all areas during the winter months, as are temperatures of over 38° C (100° F) during the summer, most of the basin has a frost-free growing season of at least 180 days (Welch 1994). This period is more than sufficient for agricul-

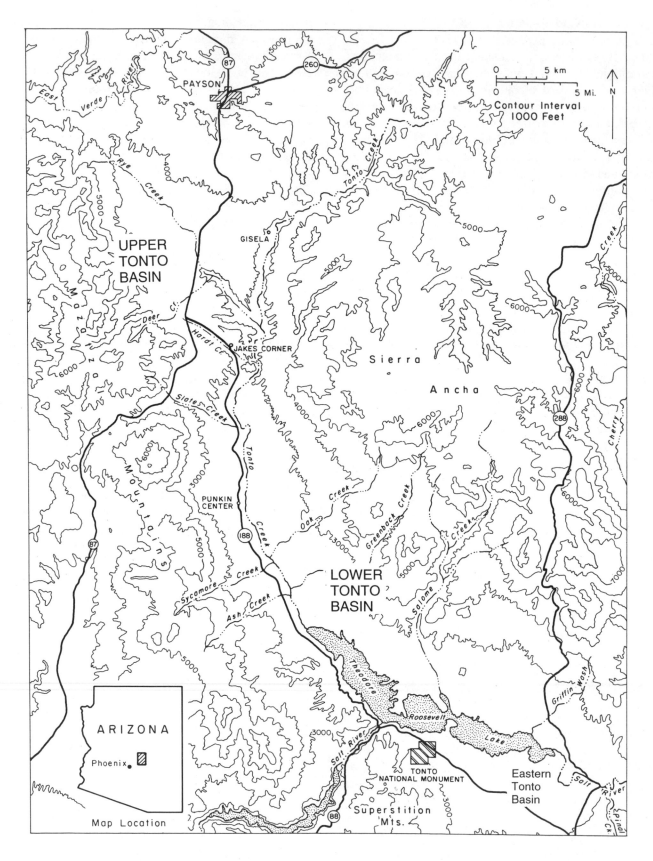

Figure 4.2. The Upper and Lower Tonto Basin, showing the location of the Eastern Tonto Basin.

tural crops to mature. Rainfall, which ranges between 25 cm and 51 cm (10 and 20 inches) a year on the basin floor and lower bajada, is biseasonal: slightly more than half falls during the months of July and August, and most of the remainder falls during December and January. April, May, and June are the driest months, often receiving no rain (Sellers and Hill 1974). It is the amount of precipitation, not temperature, that is the prime factor in successful agriculture.

Elevational differences are a key consideration in understanding the nature of the Tonto Basin environment, because climate, rainfall, and vegetation are all elevation dependent. Environmental variation is evident as one moves east or west out of Tonto Creek, and north from Roosevelt Lake, into areas of higher elevation (Fig. 4.2). Considerable heterogeneity is present within and between these areas, affording a widespread and varied resource base. Resource differences between upland and lowland areas and the subsequent need for both social and resource integration have been stressed in a number of models for the function of Tonto Basin platform mounds (Germick and Crary 1989: 23–24; Rice 1990a: 12–16; Wood and Hohmann 1985: 7). However, the narrow width of the basin (10 km to 15 km; 6.2 to 9.3 miles) means that all but the topmost elevation resources could be procured in a single day's journey (up and back) by inhabitants living along the river: "all principal environmental zones in the basin could have been (and in some cases were) exploited on a regular basis by permanent riverine settlements" (Elson, Gregory, and Stark 1995: 463). The closer proximity, and hence accessibility, of higher elevation resources is an important distinction between the Tonto and Phoenix basins.

Significantly, the location where the Salt River enters the Eastern Tonto Basin is the "first place where the water from the large area drained by this river would have been available in a situation suitable for canal-aided irrigation" (Gregory 1980: 2). Numerous archaeological sites are situated along the banks of the Salt River, both inside and outside the Tonto Basin, indicating the river's importance in prehistoric settlement. Through an examination of soils and landform, Waters (1996: 2.29) estimates that a minimum of 930 ha (2,300 acres) would have been directly accessible to irrigation agriculture in the Lower Tonto Basin. Prehistoric irrigation canals have been recorded along both the Salt River and Tonto Creek arms, although they have yet to be thoroughly investigated (Wood 1995). The earliest documented canal dates sometime between A.D. 850 and 1050 during the pre-Classic Santa Cruz or Sacaton

phase, although canals probably were built earlier (Gregory 1995; Waters 1996: 2.19). As noted by Wood (1995: 34), "Given the environmental constraints on agriculture . . . it can be assumed that any long term successful adaptation to the area would have required the use of irrigation agriculture to sustain stable populations and allow for growth" (see also Van West and Ciolek-Torrello 1995).

PLATFORM MOUND USE IN THE TONTO BASIN

The primary debates concerning the nature of Tonto Basin occupation have centered around whether the region had an indigenous population or whether it was settled by Hohokam, Mogollon, or Anasazi groups, or some combination of them (Elson and others 1992; Lekson and others 1992; Whittlesey and Reid 1982; Wood and McAllister 1982). Continued preoccupation with this focus in Tonto Basin research, particularly in attempts to force Tonto Basin groups into existing cultural categories, imposes limits on understanding the prehistoric settlement. In particular, this emphasis has been stressed in interpretations of the occupation of the basin during the Colonial (A.D. 750–950) and Classic (A.D. 1150–1450) periods, both long suspected to be times of immigration (Gladwin and Gladwin 1935; Haury 1932).

Platform mounds in the Tonto Basin have been most frequently used to argue for a resident population with a Hohokam origin or affiliation because similar features occur in the Phoenix Basin Hohokam core area (Rice 1990b: 36; Wood 1989: 4, 1992: 338; Wood and Hohmann 1985: 6). Some researchers, however, have argued that Tonto Basin platform mounds were simply collapsed two-story pueblos and therefore derived from Mogollon (or Western Pueblo) people. These arguments were prevalent in the 1970s and 1980s prior to any large-scale excavation of a Tonto Basin platform mound, and, although not published, were widely circulated in the Arizona archaeological community. This theory has been somewhat discounted by recent excavations, although claims remain for Mogollon influence, if not an actual Mogollon presence, in the Tonto Basin (Ciolek-Torrello and Whittlesey 1994; Reid 1989; Whittlesey and Ciolek-Torrello 1992; Whittlesey and Reid 1982).

The debate between those who believe that the Tonto Basin is "Hohokam affiliated" and those who believe it is "Mogollon affiliated" has led to the formulation of two different models for the origin and use of Roosevelt phase (A.D. 1250–1350) Tonto Basin platform mounds. Implicit in this debate is the nature of the social complexity of Tonto Basin inhabitants. This argument over complexity is not confined to the Tonto Basin but is present in varying forms throughout the greater Southwest (Cordell and others 1987; Lightfoot and Upham 1989; McGuire and Saitta 1996; Plog 1995; Reid and others 1989; Upham 1982). Later Gila phase (A.D. 1350–1450) platform mounds, which are fewer in number and occur at large aggregated sites, clearly functioned in a different manner and are included only peripherally in the following discussion. Gila phase mounds include both "true" platform mounds, which are similar to Roosevelt phase mounds in their use of cells and retaining walls in construction (Chapter 1), and mounds that were constructed by filling in previously occupied residential and storage rooms to create an elevated platform (Wood 1995: 11). The best excavated example of the latter type of mound in the Tonto Basin is Schoolhouse Point (Lindauer 1996a), although several others exist (Oliver 1994; Wood 1995).

A typical example of a Roosevelt phase Tonto Basin platform mound is the mound at the Meddler Point site in the Eastern Tonto Basin (Fig. 4.3). In general, Roosevelt phase mounds consisted of a raised platform, constructed from underlying structural cells, that was used to support a few mound-top rooms. The mound itself was directly associated with a small number of ground floor rooms and extramural features within an enclosing compound wall. There is considerable debate over whether the rooms on top of the mound and in the mound compound were residential habitations or were used solely for nonresidential ceremonial or communal purposes. The mound compound is generally part of a larger settlement containing a number of dispersed residential compounds, along with trash mounds, cemetery areas, roasting pits, and other features. At Meddler Point, the platform mound compound is associated with 12 additional compounds. Each of the separate compounds probably contained one to three households or family groups (Craig and Clark 1994). The accurately scaled reconstruction of the Meddler Point platform mound and compound shown in Figure 4.4 shows what these features may have looked like prehistorically.

For researchers who support a Hohokam affiliation, Tonto Basin platform mounds are either attributed to peer-polity emulation processes as defined by Renfrew and Cherry (1986) or to the immigration of elite members of Phoenix Basin groups who subsequently built the Tonto Basin mounds (Hohmann and Kelley 1988; Rice 1990a, 1990b; Wood 1989; Wood and Hohmann

1985). In the past, models of Phoenix Basin platform mound use and function were, for the most part, simply transferred to the Tonto Basin (Wood 1992: 338), often with little consideration for the differences between the two areas (Wood and McAllister 1980, 1982). For example, Wood and McAllister (1982: 88) asserted that Tonto Basin platform mounds were "identical to those used by other Classic period Hohokam groups in the Salt-Gila Basin and elsewhere. . . . The fact that Salado platform mounds are found only in Tonto Basin and not farther north or east argues that they arrived there from the Hohokam core area where they have a much greater time depth."

Despite the current recognition of environmental and cultural differences between the Hohokam core area and the Tonto Basin, the overall Phoenix Basin orientation of these models remains: platform mounds are generally viewed as the upper tier of a hierarchical settlement system that functioned in the administration of irrigation systems, land tenure, and trade networks (Hohmann and Kelley 1988; Wood 1989, 1992, 1995; Wood and Hohmann 1985). Mound communities were controlled by an institutionalized elite class who lived on top of the platform mound and received a larger share of the available wealth. Wood (1995: 43; Wood and Hohmann 1985: 10) further suggested that the elites (or elite lineages) who occupied the mounds initially rose and then stayed in power through "entrepreneurial" behavior. In Tonto Basin models, this power was achieved by taking advantage of the increased economic opportunities associated with the mounds, particularly in the control of trade.

A second set of Hohokam-oriented scholars has used platform mounds in areas outside the Phoenix Basin as models for Tonto Basin settlement. Rice (1990a: 12–17) posited two different models for platform mound settlements: the "Escalante model" of the Phoenix Basin core area (Doyel 1974), and the "Marana model" of the outlying northern Tucson Basin–Picacho Peak area (Bayman 1994; S. Fish and others 1992).

In Rice's version of the Escalante model, platform mounds were located in the valley bottoms and inhabited by managerial elites who controlled large tracts of irrigable land. The less important upland regions were exploited through a variety of temporary camps, but all permanent habitation occurred within the riverine-focused mound and associated compounds. This settlement pattern resulted in a nucleated mound community centered on a canal system.

In the Marana model, the mounds were still occupied by elites but the focus was less on irrigation than on the

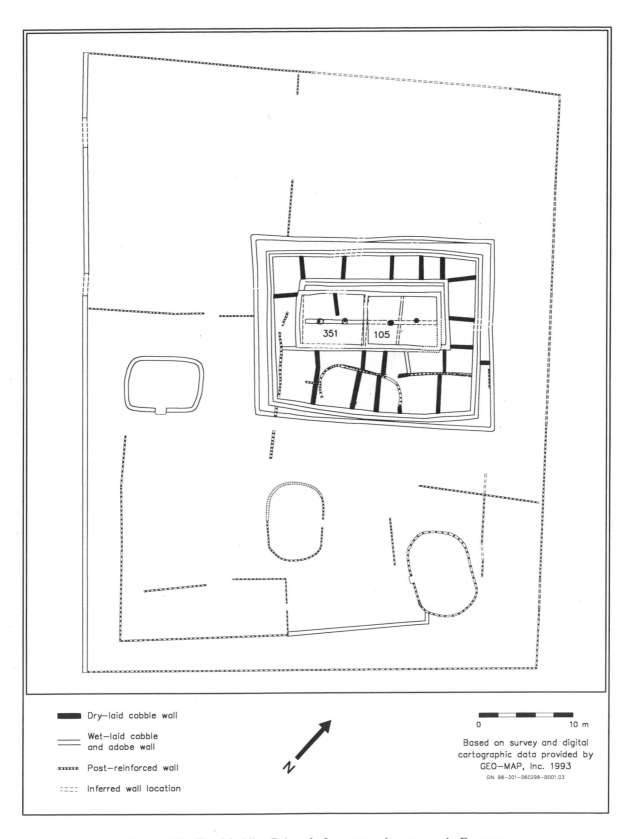

Figure 4.3. The Meddler Point platform mound compound. Features 351 and 105 are the two rooms on top of the platform mound supported by underlying filled cells (after Craig and Clark 1994, Fig. 7.39).

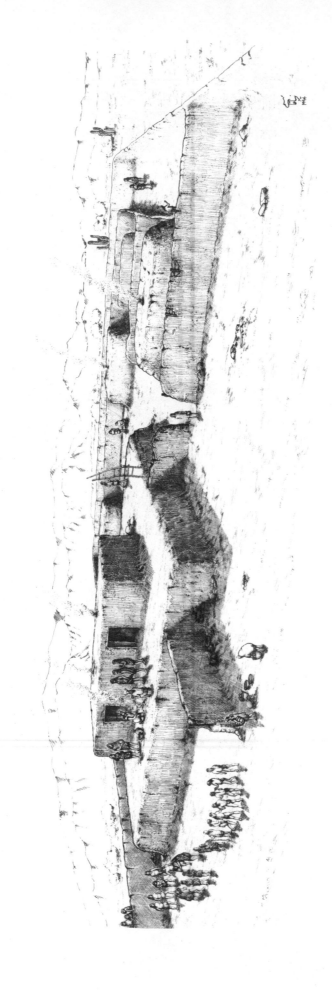

Figure 4.4. Artist's reconstruction of the platform mound compound (Compound 1) at the Meddler Point site, facing east. Reconstruction by Ziba Ghassemi (from Stark and Elson 1995, Fig. 1.10).

integration of permanent settlements in both the uplands and lowlands that were exploiting a series of different resource zones, a pattern that resulted in a dispersed community settlement. In this model, platform mounds functioned largely to ensure distribution of resources, through feasting and other redistributive mechanisms, with more going to the elites in the mound compound than to others. Rice (1990a) posited that Tonto Basin platform mounds were similar to those in the Marana model and functioned to integrate groups in the uplands with those settled in the riverine lowlands, a position previously suggested by Wood and Hohmann (1985: 7) and supported in part by several other Tonto Basin researchers (Germick and Crary 1992: 299; Lindauer 1992: 2–3, 1995: 425).

Mogollon-derived models of platform mound function differ from the Hohokam-derived models primarily in the degree of social complexity attributed to the mound builders and in their characterization that platform mounds in the Tonto Basin were not used as elite residences. In the Mogollon models, high status elite leaders did not exist in the Tonto Basin or, for the most part, elsewhere in the Southwest: leadership positions were based on achievement and organized through religious or kinship associations. Tonto Basin platform mounds, then, functioned solely as nonresidential ceremonial structures among primarily egalitarian groups. Platform mounds served to "meld various clan segments or small residential units into small villages . . . [and] as ritual contexts for the administrative and integrative functions of clans and sodalities, rather than as residences of the elite" (Ciolek-Torrello and others 1994: 470).

The Mogollon models essentially dispute the Hohokam model premise that platform mounds indicate a hierarchical social organization (Ciolek-Torrello and Whittlesey 1994). In these scenarios, which are based primarily on pueblo ethnography, the archaeological record of the Tonto Basin and other areas in the Southwest is considered to be "complicated" but not necessarily "complex" (Reid and Whittlesey 1990; Whittlesey and Ciolek-Torrello 1992: 314). Although these researchers acknowledged that platform mounds were "unique public structures . . . not reflected in the ethnographic record" (Whittlesey and Ciolek-Torrello 1992: 323) and that platform mounds required "a considerable and long-term labor investment for construction and maintenance" (Ciolek-Torrello and others 1994: 468), the Mogollon model drew on the Hopi ethnographic record to propose that groups who built and used the mounds were primarily organized through kin-based social units, with clans and possibly sodalities providing group leadership. Even with this fundamental disagreement on complexity, many of the basic functions of the platform mounds listed by the Mogollon proponents, such as the redistribution of resources, land tenure, community integration, and labor organization, particularly for constructing and maintaining irrigation systems (Ciolek-Torrello and others 1994: 470), are similar to the functions listed by proponents of the Hohokam model.

In the Mogollon model, ritual organization, rather than control by elite leaders, played the primary role in group and community integration: "As in the case of ethnohistoric village farming communities of the Southwest, redistribution among Roosevelt phase settlements was probably carried out in a ritual context for the benefit of the larger community rather than for individuals" (Ciolek-Torrello and others 1994: 471). Even though the Hopi ethnographic record details inherited leadership roles and status distinctions (Brandt 1994; Levy 1992; Parsons 1939; Schlegel 1992), Whittlesey and Ciolek-Torrello (1992: 323) argue that these distinctions are largely the result of historic Anglo-European contact and influence: "Prehistoric cultures in the Southwest, were, perhaps, less complex than the historic pueblos."

In summary, the Mogollon-derived model and the Hohokam derived-model differ primarily in the nature of the social complexity attributed to Tonto Basin mound-building groups. Both models, however, posit that Tonto Basin platform mounds were used for similar purposes: they functioned to integrate smaller segments of the population and played a primary role in resource distribution, land control, and the organization of labor. The organization of labor was of critical importance in the construction and maintenance of canal irrigation systems, without which the prehistoric occupation of the Tonto Basin would have been marginal at best. Although there is some recognition in both models that the ritual and political realms are often interconnected and difficult to separate and that truly egalitarian groups probably did not exist in the late ceramic period Southwest, the models clearly differ in their primary emphasis and theoretical orientation. In the Hohokam (or high complexity) model, social control and community integration were accomplished by institutionalized elite leadership, possibly through the use of ritual mechanisms, with the elites reaping a greater share of available resources. In the Mogollon (or low complexity) model, there is relatively equal distribution of resources, and social control and integration were accomplished primarily through ritual means without inherited elite leadership; leadership was based on achievement and centered on religious or kin-based social organizations.

TONTO BASIN SETTLEMENT SYSTEMS

Archaeologists have divided the Tonto Basin into a series of "irrigation districts" or "local systems" based on land form, hydrological factors, and prehistoric settlement patterns (Craig and others 1992; Elson, Gregory, and Stark 1995; Gregory 1995; Wood 1989, 1995; Wood and others 1992). In overall concept, these terms are similar and define a spatially bounded area in which the components (prehistoric settlements) were strongly integrated through some sort of overarching organizational framework. As used in Tonto Basin research, irrigation districts and local systems are also interchangeable with the term "community," particularly as defined for the Marana platform mound settlement in the northern Tucson Basin (S. Fish and others 1992).

Wood (1995: 35) has postulated eight (or possibly nine) irrigation districts in the Lower Tonto Basin and three in the Upper Basin. His division is based primarily on platform mound distribution and hydrology and specifically on likely places for irrigation canals. Because the actual locations of prehistoric canals are unknown, these divisions are largely theoretical. By definition, irrigation districts consisted of habitation sites, agricultural fields, and specialized sites such as field houses along the same canal or canal system (Doyel 1980; Gregory and Nials 1985: 383–386; Masse 1991: 202–203). The districts are assumed to have been socially integrated because construction and maintenance of a canal system was a cooperative, generally community-level venture where some form of leadership was necessary (Craig and others 1992; Howard 1993). In Wood's reconstruction, each district was roughly similar in size and associated with a single platform mound per phase, although some of the districts were abandoned by the start of the Gila phase (about A.D. 1350). He suggested that the elite groups living on the platform mounds controlled their respective irrigation districts through the establishment of a hierarchical settlement organization. Wood (1995: 33) contrasted Tonto Basin irrigation districts with those defined in the Phoenix Basin core area by indicating that each "[irrigation] district, regardless of size, may have been the focus of mound placement rather than a specific canal system."

To identify what he called local systems, Gregory (1995) used a method similar to Wood's but stressed the influence of social factors and shared history.

Local systems represent social units whose constituent settlements, subsistence regimes, and organizational forms were all closely integrated. . . . Local systems have a very important historical dimension and are shaped by internal, as well as external dynamics. The scale and boundaries of the local system are affected by various environmental factors, like topography, access to arable land, and access to water. Boundaries are also shaped by social factors, such as the presence of a neighboring local system (Elson, Gregory, and Stark 1995: 442).

Like irrigation districts, local systems were based on a combination of topographic, hydrological, and cultural variables, but in contrast to Wood, there was no assumption that each system contained only a single platform mound per phase. Local systems were composed of various kinds of habitations, some having different functions, as well as agricultural fields, resource procurement areas, and other specialized loci. Following Gregory (1995: 130–131), in this discussion field house, farmstead, hamlet, and village are used as relative terms referring to the size of the settlement based on the probable number of inhabitants. Villages and hamlets are considered to be permanently occupied agricultural settlements differing primarily in size: villages contained more than 100 individuals; hamlets contained between 50 and 100 individuals. Farmsteads were smaller than hamlets and were either seasonally or permanently occupied. Field houses consisted of one or two structures that were inhabited by a few individuals on a seasonal basis specifically for some type of resource procurement. Based on settlement data, particularly breaks between clusters of prehistoric sites as well as "natural barriers to irrigation systems [such as major washes and geologically stable terraces] and the position of suitable [canal] intake locations," seven local systems were defined for the Lower Tonto Basin and two for the Upper Basin (Elson, Gregory, and Stark 1995: 466–469, Fig. 14.3).

Differences between Wood's (1995) irrigation districts and Gregory's (1995) local systems are minor; both researchers define bounded units in essentially the same locations and there is undoubtedly prehistoric validity to these definitions. However, there are problems in the use of both of these terms, as well as in the use of the term 'community,' to describe these relatively large spatial areas because of the assumption that all settlements within them were socially and politically integrated and functioned for the most part as a single unit. In the Tonto Basin, this assumption is difficult to support with archaeological evidence because of the lack of excavation information and because the actual locations of the irrigation canals are largely theoretical. For example, in previous work I identified the Eastern Tonto Basin, containing five platform mounds and numerous smaller residential settlements in a 30-square-kilometer area, as an integrated local system or prehistoric community (Elson, Gregory, and Stark 1995). However, in the following chapter, I argue that the Eastern Tonto Basin was actually occupied by two competing descent groups who, although sharing a similar background, were not socially or politically allied. Each of the descent groups was internally integrated, but there was no coherent leadership or organizational framework that joined the two groups. Yet, due to their spatial proximity, the two groups heavily interacted and shared a similar settlement history; perhaps most importantly, the behavior and actions of one group strongly affected the behavior and actions of the other. The difference between 'integration' and 'interaction' here is that integration implies the presence of an overarching social or political organizational system whereas interaction does not.

This interpretation could not have been achieved without the wealth of information derived from excavations in the Eastern Tonto Basin and from the analysis of historic mound-building societies. I suspect that other defined spatial units, whether called irrigation districts or local systems, actually contained a number of different, nonintegrated groups. If these groups were not integrated, a problem arises in what terminology to use to describe these units. By definition, the use of the terms community and irrigation district indicate internal integration; they are also commonly used in the archaeological literature and redefining their meanings here would cause confusion. Gregory's definition of local system also included the concept of integration. Until we are better able to archaeologically demonstrate the areal extent of the integration, I am defining individual settlement systems without making integration one of the defining characteristics. By doing so, we are free to describe which portions of any given settlement system may have been integrated and which not, thereby more accurately portraying the archaeological evidence. A "settlement system," then, was composed of interacting parts, but this does not mean that the whole system was

internally cohesive or shared an overarching social and leadership structure. Figure 4.5 shows the settlement systems identified in the Tonto Basin (defined by Gregory as local systems), along with associated platform mound sites.

In this sense, the region is the Tonto Basin; it contains two primary subregions, the Upper Tonto Basin and the Lower Tonto Basin. The smaller spatial divisions of the Lower Tonto Basin include, for example, the Eastern Tonto Basin settlement system, the Armer Ranch settlement system, and the Oak Creek settlement system. Each of these was in turn composed of internally integrated communities made up of one or several descent groups. In the following chapter, I propose that in the Eastern Tonto Basin the descent group and the community were the same. Whether communities in the other defined Tonto Basin settlement systems contained a number of different descent groups and whether the communities themselves were further integrated (that is, joined together under a common social structure and leadership) await future archaeological resolution.

All of these divisions, from the region down to the community and descent group, shared common attributes that set them apart from other areas with like units. Groups that were usually not integrated may have joined together at various levels of inclusiveness (settlement system, subregion, region) during periods of stress, such as with the threat of conflict or during food shortages. These sorts of temporary alliances, however, broke down during normal periods when, at least in the Eastern Tonto Basin, I believe that a high degree of integration occurred only at the descent group level.

THE EASTERN TONTO BASIN SETTLEMENT SYSTEM

The Eastern Tonto Basin encompasses a 6–km (3.7-mile) stretch along both sides of the Salt River, extending from Meddler Point, which is the first major site location after the river enters the Tonto Basin, to the Griffin Wash–Schoolhouse Point area (Fig. 4.6). All available evidence indicates that the prehistoric occupation here was primarily riverine in its focus (Elson, Gregory, and Stark 1995; Gregory 1995), although some nonriverine settlements may have been included. The Eastern Tonto Basin covered about 30 square kilometers (11.6 square miles) and was continuously occupied from the Colonial period Gila Butte phase (A.D. 750–850) through the Gila phase (A.D. 1350–1450) of the Classic period (see Fig. 1.3). A small population dating to the Early Ceramic period (A.D. 100–600) also

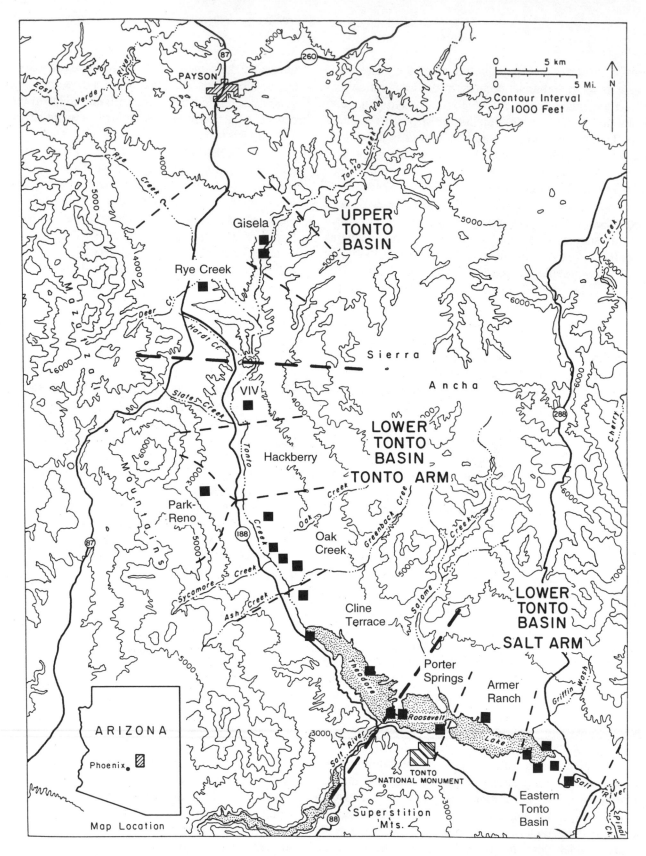

Figure 4.5. Hypothesized Classic period local settlement systems in the Tonto Basin. Thick dashed lines mark the three major physiographic divisions of the basin and thin dashed lines indicate local system boundaries. Solid squares indicate the approximate location of sites with platform mounds (after Elson, Gregory, and Stark 1995, Fig. 14.3).

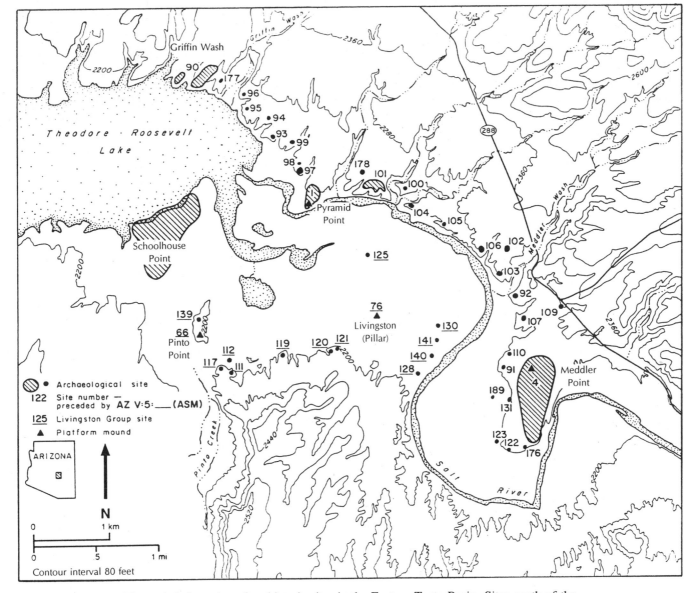

Figure 4.6. Location of prehistoric sites in the Eastern Tonto Basin. Sites north of the Salt River were investigated by Desert Archaeology; underlined sites south of the river were studied by Arizona State University (from Stark and Elson 1995, Fig. 1.4).

occupied this area (Elson and Lindeman 1994), but because of the approximately 150–year hiatus between A.D. 600 and 750, its relationship to the settlement that began during the Gila Butte phase is unknown.

Archaeological field work in the Eastern Tonto Basin was undertaken between 1991 and 1992 by Desert Archaeology and Arizona State University as part of the U.S. Bureau of Reclamation Roosevelt Lake Project. The 44 numbered sites these two teams examined, many with multiple residential loci, comprise the majority of known archaeological sites in the Eastern Tonto Basin. The intensity of investigation varied: some sites were completely excavated, others were partially excavated, and many others were only tested (Elson and Swartz

1994; Elson and others 1994; Jacobs 1994a; Lindauer 1996a, 1997a). The most intensive excavations were conducted at platform mound settlements and at village sites without mounds, although their large size and time constraints required the teams to use sampling procedures on these sites as well.

For brevity and readability, in this brief archaeological overview I do not cite repeatedly the extensive literature on the Roosevelt Project excavations; nearly every sentence would require several lengthy citations. Instead, I have compiled this summary from the thorough work and thoughtful evaluations presented by my colleagues. I note the primary monograph for each major site discussed, and more details may be obtained

[65]

from the authors listed alphabetically in the References, where all literature pertaining to the Roosevelt Project is preceded by an asterisk. Additionally, in the Appendix Roosevelt Project reports are listed by contractor with chapter titles and authors.

The Eastern Tonto Basin was most densely occupied during the Roosevelt phase (A.D. 1250–1350), when it contained four platform mounds (Meddler Point, AZ V:5:4; Pyramid Point, AZ V:5:1; Pinto Point, AZ V:5:66; and Livingston, AZ V:5:76), two large villages without mounds (Schoolhouse Point, AZ U:8:24, and Griffin Wash, AZ V:5:90), and numerous smaller habitation loci, agricultural fields, field houses, temporary campsites, and resource procurement areas. The Roosevelt phase occupation of the Eastern Tonto Basin encompassed the largest clustering of platform mounds of any local settlement system in the Tonto Basin (Fig. 4.5), with a distance between platform mounds of 1.3 km to 2.1 km (0.8 to 1.3 miles). During the following Gila phase (A.D. 1350–1450), several habitation rooms at Schoolhouse Point were modified into a platform mound, but all other platform mounds and the majority of habitations in the Eastern Basin were abandoned.

Along with topographic and hydrological factors, several aspects of the archaeological record suggest that the prehistoric settlements in the Eastern Tonto Basin were associated to some degree and strongly interacted with one another. For one, a roughly 3-km (1.9 mile) break in Roosevelt phase settlements separated the western end of the Eastern Tonto Basin from the larger Armer Ranch settlement system downstream (Fig. 4.5). The distance between the two systems was even greater during the earlier pre-Classic occupation. Considering the relatively high density of Roosevelt phase settlement in both the Eastern Tonto Basin and Armer Ranch systems, this discontinuity is significant and most likely indicative of an areal boundary.

Pottery also provided evidence of the presence of an interacting settlement system. Petrographic analysis of ceramics indicated that the Roosevelt phase inhabitants of Griffin Wash specialized in the production of corrugated vessels that were distributed to the other settlements in the Eastern Basin (Heidke and Stark 1995).

There are also regularities in the continuous expansion of the original occupation from a single hamlet at Meddler Point founded during the Gila Butte phase, to a Roosevelt phase settlement system that contained several hamlets or villages at Meddler Point, Griffin Wash, Pinto Point, and Schoolhouse Point. Gregory (1995: 164–168) noted that this pattern of expansion

followed a model set forth by Chisholm. In his model, Chisholm (1979: 127) argued that new settlements were constructed at distances greater than 3 km to 4 km (1.8 to 2.5 miles) from the original founding settlement because of increasing transportation time between a settlement and its associated fields.

This pattern was present in the Eastern Tonto Basin where Pinto Point, Schoolhouse Point, and Griffin Wash, the first large settlements established away from the founding Meddler Point, were located just beyond the 4–km zone (Fig. 4.6). The implication is that these sites were initiated as satellite settlements by small groups moving away from Meddler Point. The following Gila phase population witnessed both reduction and an occupation aggregation centered on a single large village at Schoolhouse Point. This historical continuity indicates a shared origin for the settlements within the Eastern Tonto Basin, although, as I argue in the following chapter, it does not necessarily mean that these settlements were united under a single social and political framework.

Developmental History of the Eastern Tonto Basin

The earliest documented occupation in the Eastern Tonto Basin is in the Early Ceramic period (A.D. 100–600) component of the Eagle Ridge site (AZ V:5:104, Figs. 1.3, 4.6). Eagle Ridge was inhabited by an indigenous, ceramic-using population that established a permanent agricultural settlement on a ridge finger overlooking the Salt River. The settlement contained 30 to 50 pit houses and one much larger pit house with a floor trench or "foot-drum." Because no Archaic period remains (except a few projectile points) were recovered from the Eastern Tonto Basin, the Early Ceramic population probably came from local Late Archaic or Early Agricultural period groups living in other areas of the Tonto Basin. Eagle Ridge inhabitants maintained their closest affinities with contemporaneous groups in the Mogollon highlands, such as those that occupied the Bluff site (Haury and Sayles 1947), and were distinct from groups in the Phoenix and Tucson basins.

Phoenix Basin Hohokam groups migrated into the sparsely populated Lower Tonto Basin sometime during the late Snaketown or early Gila Butte phases (about A.D. 700–850) and established a number of permanent and temporary settlements. Meddler Point in the Eastern Tonto Basin and Roosevelt 9:6 (Haury 1932) situated about 7 km (4.4 miles) downstream are the two largest Gila Butte phase settlements recorded. The degree of interaction with the local population, or whether a local population was even present in the Eastern Basin at this time, is unclear because of the 100–to–150–year occupational hiatus in the area. By all appearances, Meddler Point resembled a typical, permanently occupied, Phoenix Basin Hohokam settlement, with a central plaza containing a cremation cemetery surrounded by trash mounds and pit house courtyard groups. This layout, which was maintained throughout the nearly 600–year occupation, denotes an intimate knowledge of Hohokam settlement structure and the proper arrangement of domestic and ritual space. Additional evidence for migration comes from the petrographic analysis of the utilitarian ceramics, which underscores a Phoenix Basin origin for the intrusive groups, specifically areas along the Gila River (Miksa and Heidke 1995).

The Meddler Point settlement slowly expanded and its inhabitants interacted with other Tonto Basin settlers throughout the Santa Cruz (A.D. 850–950) and Sacaton (950–1050) phases. During this time, several small farmsteads sprang up and resource procurement zones were established away from Meddler Point, but Meddler Point itself remained the only sizable center in the expanding settlement system. All evidence indicates that Tonto Basin inhabitants still strongly participated in Hohokam regional society. To date, no ballcourts have been recorded in the Tonto Basin, although some may exist unseen beneath Roosevelt Lake. If ballcourts were part of Tonto Basin settlement, Meddler Point should have had one, because it contained one of the largest pre-Classic occupations in the basin. The intensity of investigation at this site rules out the possibility that one was overlooked. It is more likely that the pre-Classic Tonto Basin did not have a sufficiently large population to support the construction and use of this type of feature (Doelle 1995b). Perhaps Eastern Basin inhabitants used relatively nearby courts in the Globe-Miami area and on the outskirts of the Phoenix Basin, at most, a two-day walk (around 50 km or 30 miles distant).

Relations with the Phoenix Basin were curtailed sometime just prior to or during the Ash Creek phase (A.D. 1050–1150), when the widespread sphere of Hohokam influence retracted and was reorganized. Curtailing of relationships with the Phoenix Basin was not confined to the Tonto Basin and it is evident in other Hohokam-related areas in the southern Southwest, such as in the Tucson Basin (Doelle and Wallace 1986, 1991), the Lower Verde Valley (Ciolek-Torrello 1997), and New River areas (Doyel and Elson 1985). In the Eastern Tonto Basin, the retraction of the Phoenix Basin network, possibly in conjunction with the expansion of

the Chaco network (Lekson 1991), resulted in increased interaction with groups to the north and east that were producing or using Cibola White Ware pottery. During this time, Hohokam Buff Ware was almost completely replaced by Cibola White Ware in Eastern Basin ceramic assemblages. An increase in cotton production in the Eastern Basin at approximately the same time may mean that cotton was exchanged for white ware vessels (Adams 1996).

Following established ceramic trade connections, migrant populations entered the Eastern Tonto Basin sometime during the Roosevelt phase in the mid- to late-thirteenth century (Clark 1995b). The exact place of origin of the migrants remains unknown and somewhat controversial, but the immigrants were most likely from Cibola White Ware and White Mountain Red Ware ceramic-using populations in regions north and east of the Tonto Basin. Evidence for migration is based on multiple lines of information, including architecture, pottery, and botanical remains, and is presented in detail in the Roosevelt Project reports listed in the Appendix and in the References with asterisks. Some of the migrant groups joined a small existing settlement at Griffin Wash and others settled at Saguaro Muerto (site AZ V:5:128) to the southeast. A small site on Schoolhouse Mesa (AZ U:8:454) may also represent a migrant settlement, and migrants may have comprised part of the occupation of Locus B at Meddler Point. Migration into the Tonto Basin was probably in response to "push" factors such as environmental stress and conflict in various portions of the northern Southwest at this time (Cameron 1995; Clark 1997; Dean and others 1985, 1994; Wilcox and Haas 1994).

Chronometric information from both tree-ring samples and cross-dated decorated pottery indicate that the first platform mounds were constructed in the Eastern Tonto Basin during the Roosevelt phase, around A.D. 1280 or slightly earlier. In contrast to the Phoenix Basin, where mounds may have been constructed as early as the twelfth century (Chapter 1), there is no evidence of earlier mound construction in the Eastern Tonto Basin (or the Tonto Basin in general), and all investigated mounds were constructed relatively quickly, possibly from a preconceived plan. For whatever reasons, most likely ones related to continuing environmental and social stress, the Roosevelt phase mound settlements in the Eastern Tonto Basin were abandoned within 50 to 75 years. Documented variability in Tonto Basin stream flow during the early 1300s, particularly a period of increased flooding between A.D. 1295 and 1320, may have impacted canal

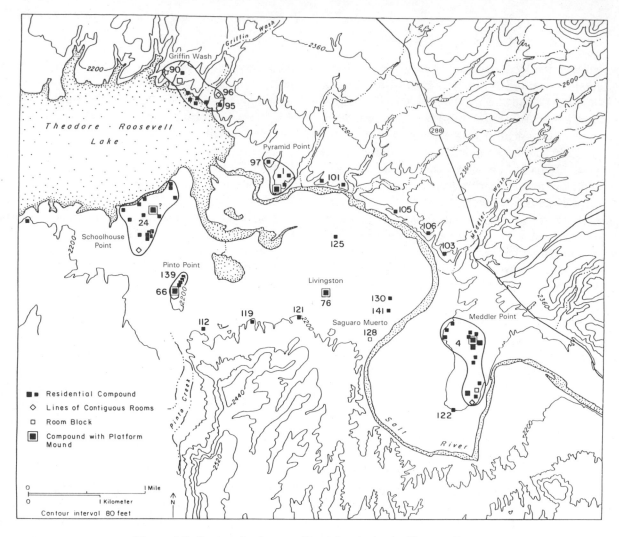

Figure 4.7. Roosevelt phase residential units in the Eastern Tonto Basin, excluding field house sites (from Clark 1995a, Fig. 9.9).

systems and therefore subsistence resources. According to Waters (1996: 2.36):

> The abandonment at the end of the Roosevelt phase is most dramatic along the Salt River at the easternmost end of the basin [the Eastern Tonto Basin]. This . . . is probably no coincidence. Here flooding would probably have been the most severe of any stretch of the Salt River, because at this point the river leaves its confined bedrock gorge to flow out into its broad alluvial basin. Floods immediately downstream of the gorge would have been intense and may explain the abandonment of this area and its near absence of occupation since A.D. 1320.

Conflict between upstream and downstream settlers over water may also have been a factor. Most settlements in the Eastern Tonto Basin were abandoned by A.D. 1325, just prior to the widespread use of Gila Polychrome and

Fourmile Polychrome pottery. At this time, some groups apparently moved to the large settlement at Schoolhouse Point; most of the population, however, left the Eastern Tonto Basin. The remodeling of a portion of Schoolhouse Point into a platform mound occurred at the beginning of the Gila phase and the settlement was occupied into the early fifteenth century when it, too, was abandoned.

The Roosevelt Phase in the Eastern Tonto Basin

The Eastern Tonto Basin contained its greatest population during the A.D. 1250 to 1350 Roosevelt phase. Roosevelt phase settlement included four platform mound sites (Meddler Point, Pyramid Point, Pinto Point, and Livingston), two large villages without mounds (Schoolhouse Point and Griffin Wash), and about 15 other numbered residential sites (Fig. 4.7).

Many of these sites and the platform mound complexes contained multiple residences, and counting all Roosevelt phase field houses, compounds, and room blocks yields a total of 74 residential units. These units ranged from one-room field houses to large room blocks with up to 100 rooms; most units, however, were small masonry compounds with 3 to 10 rooms.

Doelle (1995b, Table 7.2) used several different methods to estimate that the Roosevelt phase population of the residential units excavated by Desert Archaeology was between 180 and 290 persons. This calculation represents slightly more than half of the residential units in the combined Desert Archaeology and Arizona State University project areas, and because both areas contained similar types of features, the total Roosevelt phase population for the Eastern Tonto Basin is roughly estimated at between 360 and 580 inhabitants, or a density of 12 to 19 persons per square kilometer. This density contrasts with earlier and later periods, which have markedly lower populations, and Doelle postulated that both internal growth and immigration of outside groups augmented the Roosevelt phase population.

The contemporaneity of the Eastern Tonto Basin residential units is problematic. Ceramically, all these sites and platform mounds date to the 100–year Roosevelt phase, but achieving temporal resolution at a finer scale is difficult. Dating sites and features here is primarily based on cross-dated decorated pottery, most of which was not manufactured in the Tonto Basin. Ceramic cross-dating is necessary because of the general lack of datable tree-ring material from Tonto Basin contexts and because the standard deviations or confidence intervals associated with radiocarbon and archaeomagnetic determinations are often in the 150–to–250–year range.

Unfortunately, many of the common diagnostic ceramics, particularly the decorated white wares but some of the polychrome pottery as well, are not well dated and either have ranges of 100 years or more or overlap with phases that are earlier or later than the Roosevelt phase. The most common pottery types represented in the Roosevelt phase Tonto Basin are Reserve, Tularosa, and Pinedale black-on-white; St. Johns Polychrome and St. Johns Black-on-red; Pinto Polychrome and Pinto Black-on-red; and McDonald Corrugated. The three ceramic types most diagnostic of the Roosevelt phase, Pinedale Black-on-white (A.D. 1250–1350), Pinto Polychrome (1270–1350), and Pinto Black-on-red (1250–1350), have production spans extending through all or most of the phase, making seriation within the phase itself difficult. Although using percentile or simple

graphic methods for ceramic dating sometimes may assign individual features or strata to intervals as brief as 50 years, resolution at the site level of fewer than 100 years is rare. Still, there are indications, such as lack of accumulated trash deposits or the absence of architectural remodeling, that many of the small residential compounds and even some of the platform mounds were occupied for substantially less than a hundred years. Considering the contemporaneity problem, Doelle's (1995b) population estimates should be viewed as maximum numbers.

The major Roosevelt phase platform mound sites and villages in the Eastern Tonto Basin are briefly described below. The primary site reports are indicated; descriptions of some of the smaller excavated field house, compound, and room block sites are in Elson and Swartz (1994), Jacobs (1994a), and Lindauer (1997a).

Pyramid Point Site (AZ V:5:1 ASM)
(Elson 1994)

The Pyramid Point site contained a small platform mound within a 15–room masonry compound (Figs. 4.8, 4.9, 4.10). The platform mound compound was associated with three small outlying compounds and it was located on one of the most prominent points in the Eastern Tonto Basin, on a ridge overlooking a major bend in the Salt River (Fig. 4.7). The mound itself was positioned at the end of the ridge. The other three platform mound sites in the Eastern Tonto Basin are visible from the top of the Pyramid Point platform mound, as are the Schoolhouse Point and Griffin Wash sites. Occupation was primarily confined to the Roosevelt phase, although there is evidence of a small, earlier Miami phase component. Two small pre-Classic pit house components were recorded, one east of Compound 1 and one north of Compound 4, each estimated to contain six to eight pit houses. Diagnostic ceramics recovered from these areas date the pit houses to the Santa Cruz and Sacaton phases. A few earlier Gila Butte phase ceramics were also represented.

The Pyramid Point platform mound was one of the smallest mounds in the Tonto Basin; it consisted of a single 2–m high cell (Feature 47) with a 2–m high room on its top, and it contained 94 cubic meters of fill. The mound surface was 47 square meters in area, including a small structure (Feature 63) adjoining the mound to the south that was converted into a cell and filled some time after initial mound construction (Fig. 4.10). Unlike other platform mounds in the Eastern Tonto Basin, the location of the mound at the tip of the

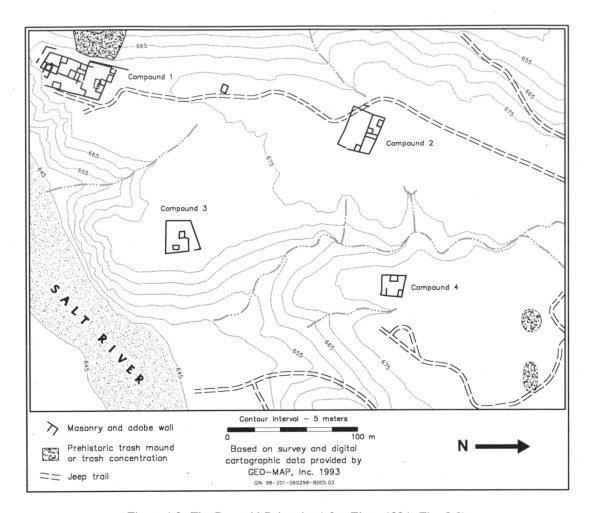

Figure 4.8. The Pyramid Point site (after Elson 1994, Fig. 8.2).

ridge and the layout of the associated compound indicate that the mound was designed for viewing from a distance rather than from the immediate area (Fig. 4.9). This placement suggests that the mound functioned as a tower to facilitate long-distance communication.

Occupation at Pyramid Point, although permanent, was quite small: no more than four households with an estimated maximum of 20 to 30 people. These few people probably were responsible for maintaining the platform mound and compound and for conducting ceremonies associated with the mound. Feature 43, the room adjoining the platform mound to the north (Fig. 4.10), contained an extensive floor assemblage indicative of ritual activity and the manufacture of personal ornaments. The relatively large number of granary platforms included some that had been placed in areas with restricted access, such as the courtyard associated with the platform mound. There are both archaeological and ethnographic examples of granary platforms serving as

bases for large baskets used to store food. The three outlying compounds contained little evidence of habitation, but there was a clear line-of-sight between the mound and the compounds; their function, length of occupation, and relationship to the platform mound remain unknown.

Meddler Point Site (AZ V:5:4 ASM)
(Craig and Clark 1994)

Meddler Point was the largest and longest-occupied settlement in the Eastern Tonto Basin, and one of the most intensively excavated sites in the project (Fig. 4.11). Migrant groups from the Phoenix Basin area initially settled here during the Gila Butte phase, and habitation continued through the Roosevelt phase. Occupation of this area was continuous, although less intensive in some phases than others; demographic reconstructions by Craig and Clark (1994: 166–174) and Wallace

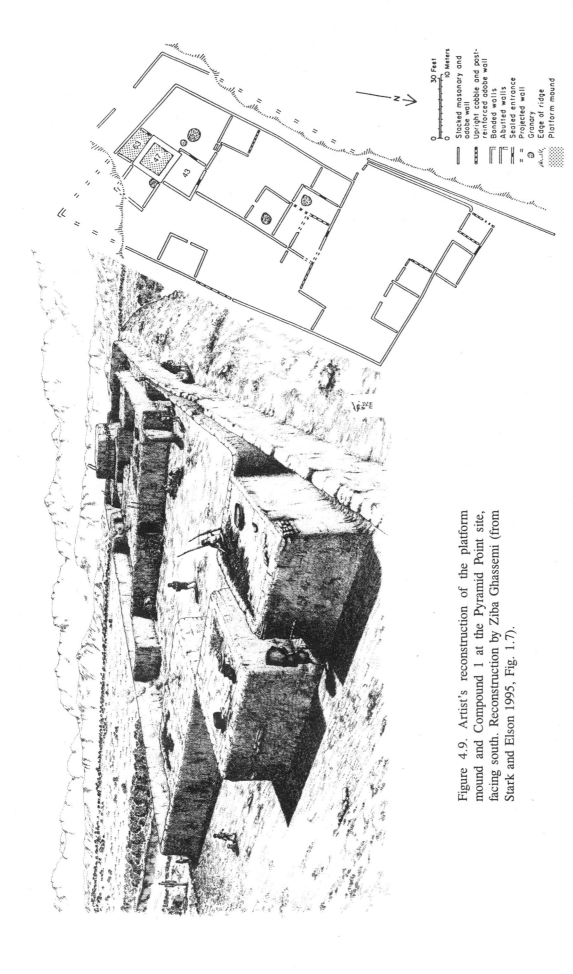

Figure 4.9. Artist's reconstruction of the platform mound and Compound 1 at the Pyramid Point site, facing south. Reconstruction by Ziba Ghassemi (from Stark and Elson 1995, Fig. 1.7).

Figure 4.10. Plan of Compound 1 at the Pyramid Point site. The platform mound is composed of Features 47 and 63 (after Elson 1994, Fig. 8.38).

Stacked masonary and adobe wall
Upright cobble and post-reinforced adobe wall
Bonded walls
Abutted walls
Sealed entrance
Projected wall
Granary
Edge of ridge
Platform mound

30 Feet
10 Meters

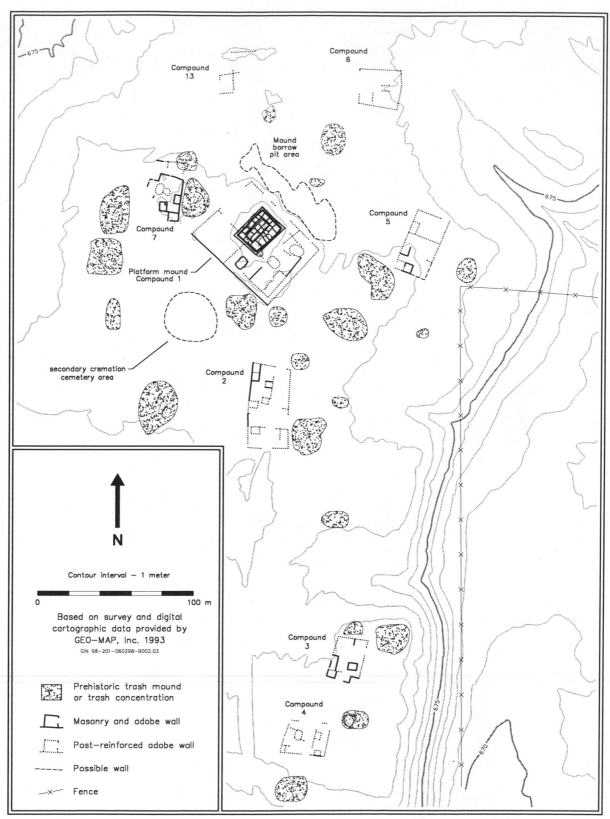

Figure 4.11. Locus A at the Meddler Point site. The platform mound is in Compound 1 (after Craig and Clark 1994, Fig. 7.17). Locus B contains five additional compounds and is approximately 250 meters south of Locus A.

(1995a: 95–104) indicated relatively continuous growth except during the Sedentary period, when there may have been a decrease in the population. The pre-Classic component contained between 75 and 120 pit houses, identified through backhoe trenching. The structured layout of the settlement, including formal trash areas, a central plaza, and a large cremation cemetery containing a full range of Hohokam-related mortuary goods, is evidence for a small hamlet, permanently occupied during most of the pre-Classic.

The settlement was most intensively inhabited during the Roosevelt phase, when it reached village proportions. At that time, a platform mound was constructed, along with 12 outlying residential compounds (Figs. 4.3, 4.4, 4.11). Several nearby compounds (with separate site numbers AZ V:5:91 and AZ V:5:110) also appeared to be associated with the mound (Fig. 4.6). Probably not all the compounds were contemporaneous, but demographic reconstructions indicate a population of approximately 100 to 150 people during the Roosevelt phase.

The platform mound was built around A.D. 1280, based on a tree-ring date of 1277vv from a preexisting wall. Construction probably took less than two years and might have involved the help of people from outside the Meddler settlement. The mound platform, which contained an estimated 966 cubic meters of fill, was 2 m high and designed solely to support two large rooms (Features 105 and 351) within the 483–square-meter area on top of the mound (Fig. 4.3). Excavation revealed that the rooms on top of the mound were not residential, at least that was not their primary function, although both rooms had doorways and internal hearths. Craig and Clark (1994) suggested that these rooms served ceremonial purposes and might have functioned as stagelike areas for public displays (see Fig. 4.4). The compound (Compound 1) surrounding the platform mound was probably not primarily residential either. The area behind the mound contained three pit rooms, which might have been preparation rooms for mound activities; access to this area was restricted through a series of partitioning walls. The nonresidential nature of the platform mound compound is particularly apparent when it is compared to some of the other surrounding compounds (such as Compounds 2 and 7), which contained evidence for food storage and domestic activities. Unlike some of the other mound sites in the Eastern Tonto Basin, such as Pyramid Point and Schoolhouse Point, the Meddler mound compound did not have granary platforms or storage rooms, suggesting that domestic food preparation and consumption were not occur-

ring in the mound area on a regular basis. Also unique to this platform mound was its placement at a 45–degree angle from the other residential compounds, further attesting to its specialized, and probably nonresidential, function.

Griffin Wash Site (AZ V:5:90 ASM)
(Swartz and Randolph 1994)

The Griffin Wash site contained approximately 100 masonry rooms in three room blocks designated Loci A, B, and C (Figs. 4.12, 4.13). A nondescript fourth masonry area, Locus D, had been badly depleted of stone, so its original size is unknown. Locus D also contained a small pre-Classic pit house component represented by three to four pit houses dating to the Santa Cruz and Sacaton phases. Based on remains from the trash mounds, additional pit houses probably existed in the area between Locus A and Locus B.

The three room blocks were roughly contemporaneous and were occupied primarily during the Roosevelt phase. Locus B was abandoned slightly earlier than Loci A and C; Locus C may have continued in use after Locus A. The most intensive excavations were in Locus A and they focused on comparative households in two areas (Fig. 4.14). These excavations, many in burned structures with large floor assemblages, produced some of the most temporally unmixed sets of evidence recovered from Desert Archaeology's project area.

The room unit associated with Feature 9 (Fig. 4.14) was the first constructed at the settlement. It was the most architecturally impressive area, having two rooms (Features 9 and 43) with walls two courses wide. Feature 9 contained two stories and an extensive floor assemblage that indicated the storage of ritual goods. Feature 43 also may have had two stories, but the room was not excavated. The largest room at the settlement, Feature 73, was an oval structure isolated within its own plaza. Although excavation of the structure revealed little about its nature, its size and placement suggested a specialized, settlement-level integrative function. Other isolated oval structures in plazas occur in the Eastern Tonto Basin (Compound 7 at Meddler Point) and elsewhere in the Lower Tonto Basin.

A view of Locus A, with Locus C on the next ridge in the background, is shown in the artist's reconstruction (Fig. 4.13). The Griffin Wash settlement had a more pueblolike appearance than other settlements in the study area and was almost certainly settled by immigrant groups. The immigrants joined an already existing small, local settlement that contained several com-

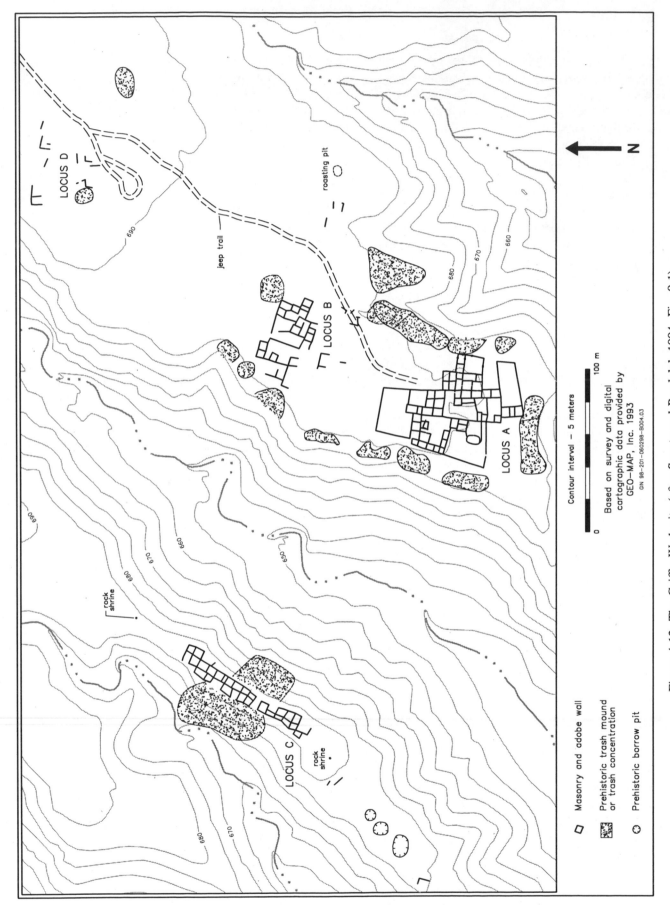

LOCUS D

roasting pit

jeep trail

LOCUS B

LOCUS A

LOCUS C

rock shrine

rock shrine

N

Contour interval — 5 meters

0   100 m

Based on survey and digital
cartographic data provided by
GEO—MAP, Inc. 1993

GIN 98—201—060298—B004.03

⬚ Masonry and adobe wall

▨ Prehistoric trash mound
   or trash concentration

◎ Prehistoric borrow pit

Figure 4.12. The Griffin Wash site (after Swartz and Randolph 1994, Fig. 9.1).

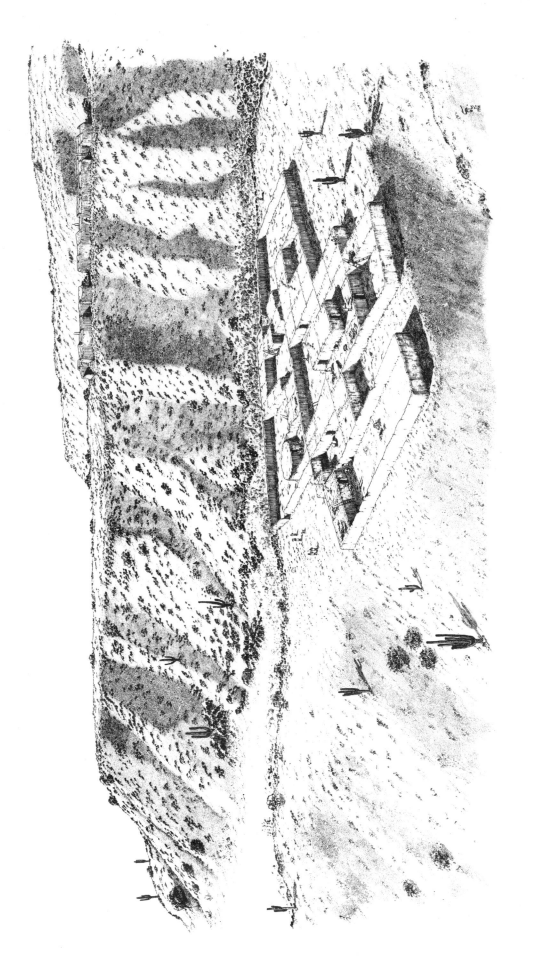

Figure 4.13. Artist's reconstruction of Locus A (with Locus C on the ridge in the background) at the Griffin Wash site. Reconstruction by Ziba Ghassemi (from Stark and Elson 1995, Fig. 1.13).

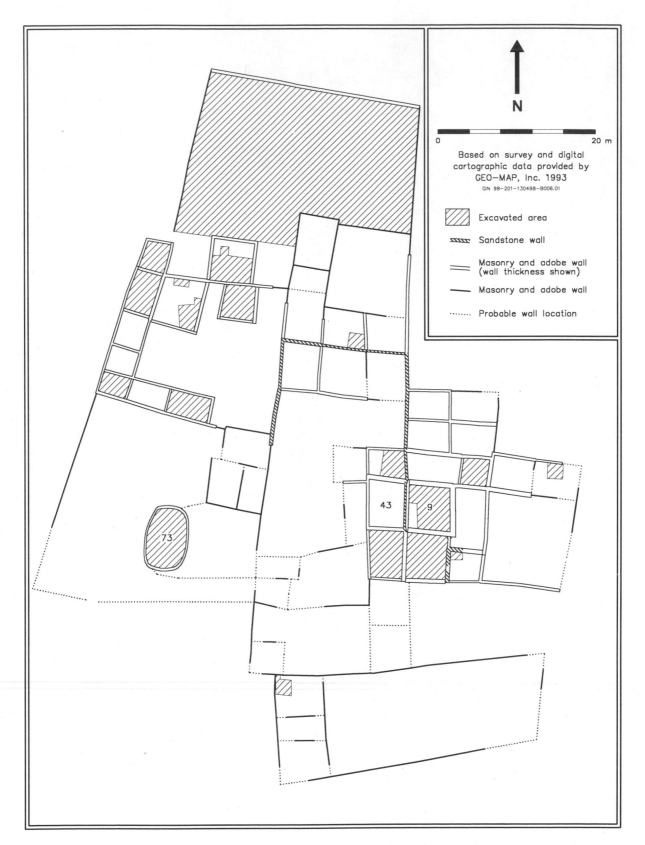

Figure 4.14. Plan of Locus A at the Griffin Wash site, showing
excavated areas (after Swartz and Randolph 1994, Fig. 9.2).

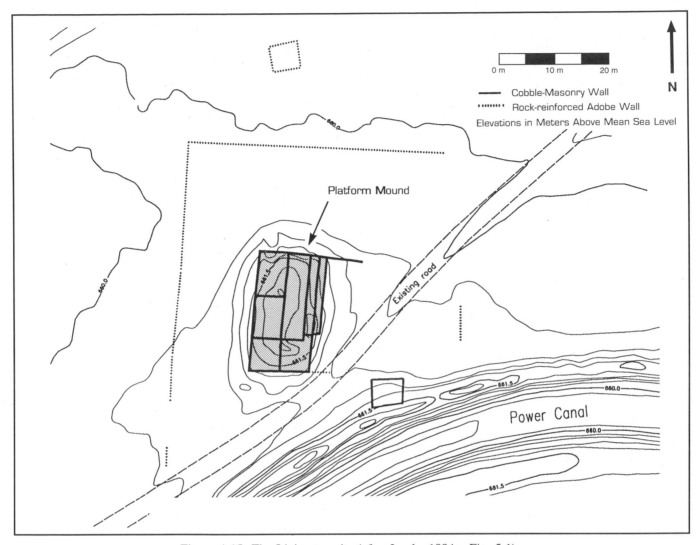

Figure 4.15. The Livingston site (after Jacobs 1994a, Fig. 5.1).

pounds. The nature of the original settlement is unclear because it is currently covered by Roosevelt Lake, but a rough sketch map exists from a period when water in the lake was at a low level. The location of Locus C on a narrow ridge suggests a defensive orientation, but the limited excavation here was unenlightening.

Livingston (Pillar) Site (AZ V:5:76 ASM)
(Jacobs 1994a)

The Livingston platform mound consisted of three ground floor rooms and a small plaza that had been filled to a height of approximately 2 m to make an elevated platform for supporting at least two large rectangular rooms (Fig. 4.15). Evidence for two other smaller mound-top rooms is less certain because of erosion. Neither the ground floor structures nor the structures on top of the mound were used as habitation rooms, although, like Meddler Point, the two mound-top rooms contained doorways and internal hearths. The ground floor rooms were apparently constructed for some sort of specialized use and not as internal cells, because they had doorways and interior plastered walls but no hearths. The mound had a surface area of 302 square meters with an estimated volume of fill of approximately 604 cubic meters.

Jacobs (1994b) thought that the ground floor rooms were built prior to the Roosevelt phase, whereas evidence from the platform mound fill indicated a Roosevelt phase date for the construction of the mound itself. The ceramic assemblages from the floors of the ground floor rooms, however, consisting primarily of Pinedale Black-on-white, Pinto Black-on-red, and McDonald Corrugated, indicated a Roosevelt phase use, and it is

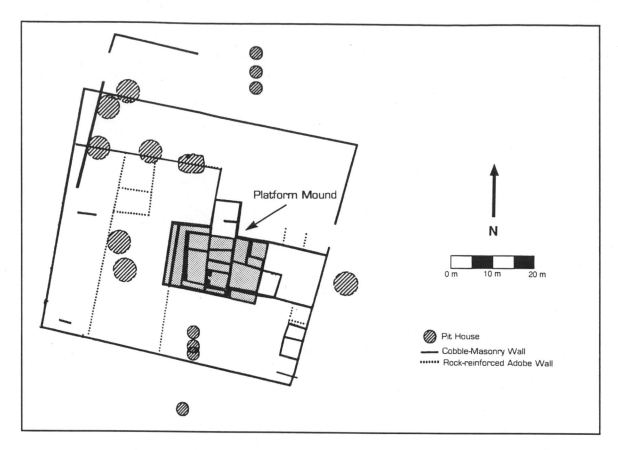

Figure 4.16. The Pinto Point site (after Jacobs 1994a, Fig. 7.3).

likely that the mound complex was constructed quickly. The site, and particularly the compound wall, were severely disturbed by the construction of an early historic period canal associated with Roosevelt Dam. As a result, portions of the compound were missing; even so, it appears that the compound never contained more than a few rooms in addition to the platform mound.

An interesting aspect of the platform mound was the construction of large cobble and adobe pillars in both ground floor and elevated rooms to serve as bases for wooden roof-support posts. Although at one time Rice and Redman (1993: 60) postulated that the Livingston pillars had an astronomical function, researchers now think that they were used solely as roof supports. In the Tonto Basin, this use of large pillars in construction has only been found at Livingston, but similar features existed at the platform mound site of University Indian Ruin in the Tucson Basin (Hayden 1957).

The Livingston mound is unique in two other respects. For one, it was isolated: the nearest Roosevelt phase compound (AZ V:5:121) was approximately 400 m to the southwest; the only other habitations possibly associated with the mound, three other compounds and

a room block (Saguaro Muerto), were at distances between 700 m and 900 m (Fig. 4.7). For another, the site itself contained very little cultural trash; in fact, no associated trash middens were located. Combined with the subsistence remains, which Spielmann (1994: 920) characterized as "depauperate," these aspects denote either a specialized or notably short-term occupation.

Pinto Point Site (AZ V:5:66 ASM)
(Jacobs 1994a)

The Pinto Point platform mound contained at least nine elevated rooms, along with several elevated plazas and miscellaneous spaces within a mound area of 340 square meters (Fig. 4.16). The volume of the mound, which stood approximately 2 m high, is estimated at 680 cubic meters. At least 12 ground floor rooms were inside the associated compound. The mound and compound had been severely disturbed through vandalism and erosion, destroying important information on the number of features and the nature of the site. Unlike Meddler Point and Livingston, both of which were constructed relatively quickly in nearly final form, the

Figure 4.17. Construction sequence of the Pinto Point
platform mound (after Jacobs 1994a, Fig. 8.5).

Pinto Point mound grew in a more accretionary manner. Jacobs (1994c) documented at least one major building episode after the initial Roosevelt phase mound construction, with a second minor addition in the late Roosevelt phase or early Gila phase (Fig. 4.17).

An underlying Sedentary period pit house component and a premound Roosevelt phase residential compound were recorded, but the nature of these occupations is obscure. Some of the earlier compound rooms, along with newly constructed cells, were apparently filled to construct the mound platform. Even though archaeologists were not specifically searching for them, 15 underlying pit houses were discovered (Fig. 4.16), indicating

that the Sedentary period occupation was relatively substantial. Four, and perhaps five, additional residential compounds existed within 300 m of the platform mound compound (Fig. 4.7).

Jacobs and Rice (1994: 924) suggested that the ground floor rooms within the mound compound were used as residences and areas for craft production. Residential use of this area is supported by the subsistence remains and moderate quantities of cultural trash. The rooms on top of the mound, however, even though some contained hearths, did not appear to be residential and, like the Meddler and Livingston mounds, a ceremonial and communal function is assigned to them.

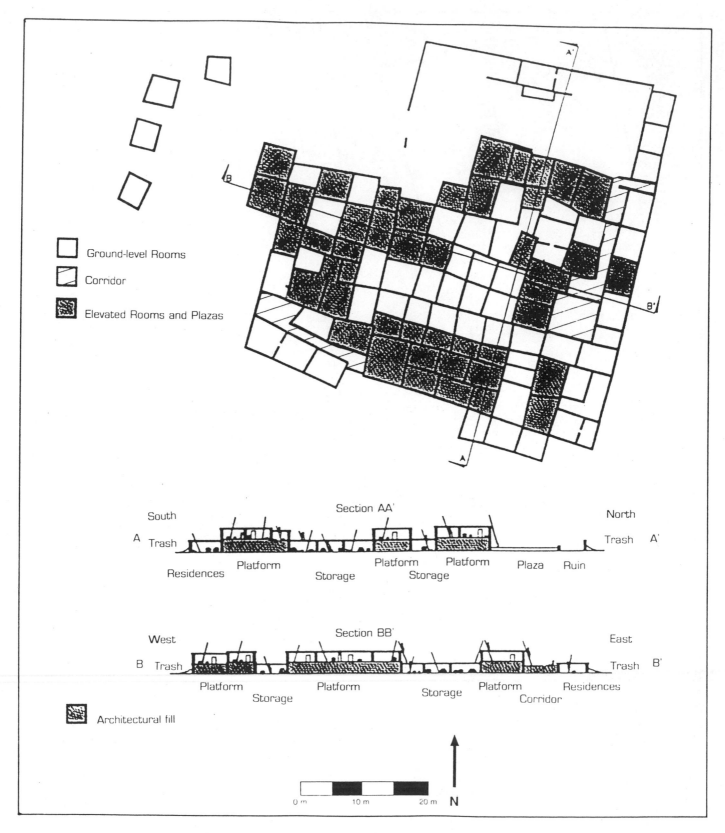

Figure 4.18. The Schoolhouse Point platform mound compound, showing
plan and reconstructed profile views (after Lindauer 1996a, Fig. 5.13).

Schoolhouse Point Site (AZ U:8:24 ASM)
(Lindauer 1996a, 1997a)

Schoolhouse Point, located on Schoolhouse Mesa (Fig. 4.7), was a moderately sized dispersed village during the Roosevelt phase, with at least 15 residential compounds and a room block. Most of the compounds, although relatively small, contained well-defined trash middens, probably signifying permanent occupation. The compound that ultimately was modified to become the Schoolhouse Point platform mound during the following Gila phase may have functioned in the Roosevelt phase as a specialized integrative center: it was unusually large, with substantial trash mounds, a large granary, and a cremation cemetery. The later construction of the platform mound obscured any other early compound features.

At some time during the early Gila phase, around A.D. 1350, the Roosevelt phase compound was dramatically expanded, eventually reaching a total of 92 rooms (Fig. 4.18) with an estimated population of between 125 and 155 people. Some of the rooms were converted into elevated platforms by filling in earlier ground floor rooms; other rooms were newly constructed at ground level around the peripheries of the elevated rooms. The expansion of the Schoolhouse Point settlement corresponds with the abandonment of the Roosevelt phase compounds on Schoolhouse Mesa and with the abandonment of the platform mounds and most of the other compounds throughout the Eastern Tonto Basin.

The Schoolhouse Point mound compound was only sampled, but excavations uncovered 47 granary platforms and a relatively large number of storage rooms. Many of the granary pedestals were hidden from public view in ground level rooms in the center of the mound area and are indicative of large-scale storage. "The many storerooms at the site and the site's proximity to floodplains where surpluses of food could have been grown suggest that Schoolhouse Point Mound may have ultimately served as a regional center for food storage and surplus distribution" (Lindauer 1996b: 841). According to Lindauer, control of food surplus and resource redistribution were maintained and carried out by one or several elite lineages who lived at Schoolhouse Point. Therefore, instead of a primarily nonresidential ceremonial function, as proposed for the earlier Roosevelt phase platform mounds, Lindauer (1996b: 855) viewed the Gila phase Schoolhouse Point mound as residential, socially differentiated, and the locus of elite control: "The position of storerooms—encircled by elevated rooms, some of which were residences—created

a physical structure in which social distinctions could have been reinforced."

Interpretations of Platform Mound Use in the Eastern Tonto Basin

Archaeologists working with the Roosevelt Lake Project excavation data have postulated several models for platform mound use that are specific to Roosevelt phase settlement in the Eastern Tonto Basin. One is a variation of the Hohokam model discussed above, but without the presence of managerial elite leaders, making it similar to the Mogollon or low complexity models. This model is posited by Jacobs and Rice (1994), who, based on information from the Pinto Point and Livingston sites, suggested that at least some Roosevelt phase platform mounds functioned not as elite residences, but as primarily nonresidential ceremonial or community centers. Platform mounds, however, were still "important" places, and they contained high frequencies of certain kinds of artifacts, including "greater densities of rare lithic materials (turquoise and obsidian), more marine shell and imported shell jewelry, and more bowls than the residential compounds" (Jacobs and Rice 1994: 924). Similar to interpretations of the mounds in the Marana model, Jacobs and Rice (1994: 924) further suggested that Eastern Tonto Basin platform mounds may have functioned in the redistribution of resources, generally by way of feasting: "The relative importance of the mound sites compared to the surrounding residential compounds could not have been based on the status of individuals if V:5:76 [the Livingston mound] was not occupied as a residence. Instead, the gathering of people to these locations for the purpose of holding community-wide activities was apparently the main process leading to distinctive and more elaborate artifact assemblages." In keeping with a general Hohokam orientation, they posited that a peer-polity interaction model explained the adoption of mounds, with Tonto Basin mounds emulating "the previously established mound tradition of the Hohokam area to the south and west" (Jacobs and Rice 1994: 923).

In an earlier analysis made prior to full examination of the excavation results, Rice (1992: 21) wrote that each of the five Eastern Basin platform mounds might represent "highly autonomous and self-sufficient" corporate descent groups or lineages. Using the concept of a segmentary lineage, Rice proposed that the separate mound lineages may have banded together into larger and more inclusive descent groups when undertaking labor intensive communal tasks, such as warfare or the construction and maintenance of irrigation systems.

These larger groups were ruled by the "senior" lineages who had the "allegiance of the junior lineages." At the start of the Gila phase, this more inclusive organization became permanent at the aggregated Schoolhouse Point settlement:

> By A.D. 1350 . . . the heads of the various lineages appear to have been drawn together into a single settlement at Schoolhouse, presumably under the authority of the senior lineage. . . . Some of the non-elite members of the society also lived at Schoolhouse, but at least part of the population was housed in other communities (Rice 1992: 21–24).

Although Jacobs and Rice (1997) used a variation of this model to explain the occupation of the Gila phase Cline Terrace platform mound on Tonto Creek, it is not mentioned in their final analysis of the Eastern Tonto Basin settlement system (Jacobs and Rice 1994).

In Desert Archaeology's analysis of the Eastern Tonto Basin, I suggested that Roosevelt phase mounds functioned primarily as nonresidential ceremonial centers (Elson, Gregory, and Stark 1995; Elson and others 1996). In this interpretation, mounds were used to integrate migrant and local groups and to manage irrigation and other subsistence related activities (see also Doelle and others 1995). The impetus for mound construction was believed to be related to both social stress, brought about by immigrant groups, and subsistence stress, brought on by deteriorating environmental conditions. Although some form of leadership was necessary to construct and maintain both the platform mounds and irrigation systems, in general I agreed with Ciolek-Torrello and others (1994) that social organization was of relatively low complexity.

The low-complexity view is also supported by Craig (1995), who, through an analysis of population size and resource productivity at the Meddler Point site, posited that the Meddler mound functioned primarily to regulate irrigation systems through ceremonial means. Craig (1995: 249) reported that initially the Meddler Point irrigation systems were "decentralized," with "only a few households . . . using a single canal system," and therefore sequential rather than simultaneous forms of decision-making were used in social organization (Johnson 1982, 1983). The onset of environmental degradation and subsequent subsistence stress in the late thirteenth century, however, required expansion of the canal systems; platform mound construction, along with a greater degree of centralized decision-making, were responses to increasing scalar stress in the Meddler community. Even with increasing complexity in decision-making, however, Craig (1995: 248–249) saw little evidence for social differentiation:

> the Meddler platform mound served a primarily nonresidential function, and . . . decision-making within the settlement was structured primarily by consensus. . . . Centralization in irrigation management does not appear to have led to social inequality or political coercion at Meddler.

In summary, previous models for Tonto Basin platform mounds have focused mainly on the question of mound function, specifically on whether mounds were occupied by institutionalized elite leaders or whether they were vacant ceremonial structures used by essentially undifferentiated groups. Most models for Classic period settlement stem from these two divergent views, which reflect a long-term and ongoing debate on the nature of the social complexity of Tonto Basin groups and Southwestern groups in general.

Models specific to the Roosevelt phase of the Eastern Tonto Basin fit somewhere between the two extremes: the mounds are viewed as nonresidential and largely ceremonial, but the groups that used them, at least to some degree, showed indications of centralized decision-making and leadership. Almost all models are in accordance that the mounds functioned in the control of irrigation and other subsistence activities, in the redistribution of resources, and in the integration of smaller groups within the larger settlement system. With this review of archaeological platform mounds in hand, in the next chapter I use the information gathered from the ethnographic and ethnohistoric sources about historic mound-using groups to develop a new model for prehistoric platform mound use and the settlement of the Eastern Tonto Basin.

CHAPTER FIVE

Modeling Platform Mound Use in the Eastern Tonto Basin

Applying the attributes of the historic mound-using groups discussed in Chapters 2 and 3 to the archaeological evidence presented in Chapter 4 provides insights into both the nature of the prehistoric groups who used platform mounds and the manner in which the mounds may have been used. Let me note here that it is not the goal of this analysis to determine specifically why platform mounds were built in the Tonto Basin and elsewhere. The impetus for building platform mounds most likely originated from a number of interrelated factors rather than from a single causal event, and in the Tonto Basin these factors probably included environmental change with resulting subsistence and social stress, migration of new groups into the basin, intensification of irrigation and other subsistence activities, and some degree of emulation of Phoenix Basin mounds. Therefore, although the origin of the platform mounds is an important research question, and some thoughts on this topic are offered below, the focus of the analysis is primarily on how the mounds were used and the social dynamics of the mound-using groups.

DEVELOPING A MODEL FOR PREHISTORIC PLATFORM MOUND USE

Characteristics of platform mound use derived from historic period groups are particularly informative in two areas: modeling the social organization of the groups that used the mounds and modeling the general manner in which the mounds were used. Information on the specific functioning of the mounds is less illuminating because of the wide range of documented functions in the ethnographic and ethnohistoric literature.

The Social Organization of Groups with Platform Mounds

The ethnographic and ethnohistoric sources indicated that mound-using groups were either ranked or stratified with some form of inherited leadership: every mound-building group surveyed in this research had these attributes. The degree of social differentiation in these groups can be equated with the size and diversity of the platform mounds; those groups that were the most highly ranked or stratified had the largest mounds (in volume) and the greatest number of functionally different mounds.

These facts strongly support the idea that Roosevelt phase mound-building groups in the Eastern Tonto Basin were ranked with institutionalized leadership positions. Ranking may have included distinctions between individuals within groups and between the groups themselves, such as differentially ranked clans and lineages. Stratification, which by definition (Chapter 3) indicates the use of coercive force on lower class members by those in the higher classes, was probably not present, a judgment in keeping with the moderate size and limited diversity of Eastern Tonto Basin mounds (Fig. 5.1). As defined by Doelle and colleagues (1995: 398–410), Roosevelt phase mounds in the Eastern Basin represented just two types: the Meddler Point, Livingston, and Pinto Point mounds were all classified as the "Meddler-type," whereas the small Pyramid Point mound was the only example of the "tower-mound" type. Similarities among the Meddler-type mounds was apparent in construction technique, general form, and basic layout (see Figs. 4.3, 4.15, 4.16). The three mounds averaged 375 square meters in surface area, 2.0 m in height, and 750 cubic meters in volume. Meddler Point was the largest, with a volume of 966 cubic meters, and Livingston was the smallest, with a volume of 604 cubic meters. Minor variations in these mounds are discussed below.

Mound size and diversity can be equated with energy expended in construction (Abrams 1989, 1994; Craig and Clark 1994; Kolb 1994; Trigger 1990); therefore, the relationship between mound size and social complexity may be restated as the greater the energy expended in mound construction, the greater the social complexity. Unfortunately, the lack of construction-related information from the ethnographic and ethnohistoric sources means that energy expenditure is not

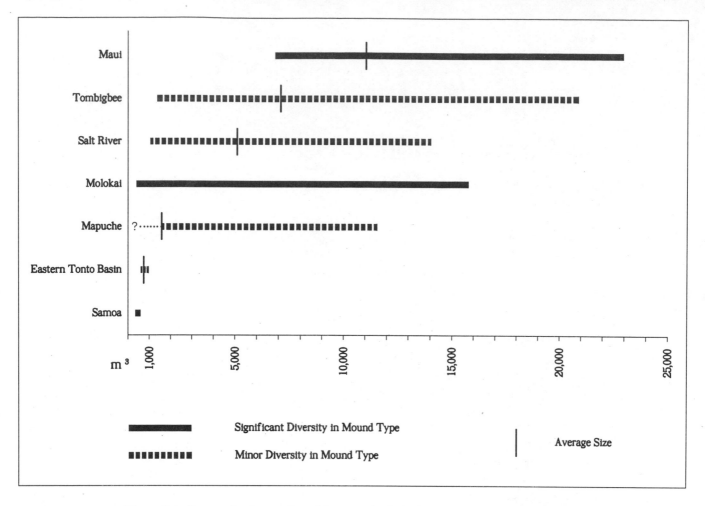

Figure 5.1. Range of volumes (in cubic meters) of platform mounds in selected areas.

quantifiable for the historic mound-building groups. Energy expenditure would be a promising area of research that would give archaeologists a more-or-less objective measure for comparing complexity between historic and prehistoric groups. Meanwhile, I use mound volume as a proxy measure for labor energy (Doelle and others 1995), with the understanding that the measure is not entirely satisfactory because it does not take into account differential costs associated with mound construction (for example, in materials procurement and transportation or building methods; see Abrams 1994, Erasmus 1965).

Platform mounds in the Eastern Tonto Basin appear to be most similar in size to mounds in the analyzed historic sample from Samoa, where the average volume of the *matai's* house platform ranged from 350 to 600 cubic meters (Jennings and Holmer 1980, Table 4), and Mapuche, where the average mound volume was approximately 1,570 cubic meters (Fig. 5.1; Dillehay 1990: 231). Accurate mound volumes from the other analyzed historic period groups were not available. Diversity in mound type occurred in Samoa (residential mounds,

community mounds, temple mounds, and star mounds) and to a limited degree in Mapuche (mortuary mounds and possibly the ancestral mound at the *nache-cuel* site). Both of these were ranked groups, with well-defined, inherited chiefly roles (Chapter 2), positioned in the approximate center of the complexity scale for the analyzed groups (Fig. 3.1.)

In contrast, a set of six prehistoric Southeastern mound centers along the central Tombigbee River in Mississippi and Alabama had an average mound volume of 7,069 cubic meters, ranging between 1,375 and 20,865 cubic meters (Blitz 1993, Table 5). Similar measures have been recorded by Anderson (1994) for prehistoric residential-temple mounds in the Savannah River group in Georgia, by Thomas (1894) for mounds in Louisiana and Mississippi, and by Lindauer and Blitz (1997) in a more general comparison of Southeast and Southwest platform mounds.

The size of some mounds in the Southeast far exceeded any mounds in the Southwest: for example, Mound 1 at Troyville in Louisiana had an estimated volume of more than 65,500 cubic meters, and the great mound at Etowah in Georgia had an estimated volume of 121,725 cubic meters (Thomas 1894: 251, 300). The two largest mounds in the Southwest were the Phoenix Basin mounds of Pueblo Grande and Mesa Grande, each estimated to contain approximately 14,000 cubic meters of fill. As documented in the ethnohistoric and archaeological literature, most Southeastern mound-building groups were highly ranked and possibly stratified (Anderson 1994; Blitz 1993; Scarry 1994).

The size and diversity of Eastern Tonto Basin mounds may also be contrasted with archaeological evidence from the societies of Hawaii, Yap, and Marquesa, all exhibiting a high degree of social complexity (Kolb 1994; Labby 1976; Linton 1939). On Molokai Island, a small Hawaiian island occupied by a line of relatively minor chiefs, the volume of fill used for the temple platforms (*heiau*), which were just one of several mound types, ranged from 400 to 15,750 cubic meters (Kirch 1990: 216). On Maui, home of one of the most powerful Hawaiian chiefly lineages, the volume of fill from five excavated *heiau* ranged from 5,834 to 21,938 cubic meters, with an average of 11,014 cubic meters (Kolb 1994: 221). Although the volumes of individual platform structures on Yap and Marquesa were not directly available, illustrations reveal that they were of similar size or smaller than the mounds in the Eastern Tonto Basin (Gifford and Gifford 1959; Handy 1923; Intoh and Leach 1985; Linton 1923). However, they were part of multiplatform complexes with significant diversity in mound type, and the total expenditure of energy in construction would have been much greater than in the Tonto Basin.

The differences in magnitude between the Eastern Basin mounds and those from the highly stratified Maui chiefdom may be further compared through energy expenditure measures based on the work of Craig and Clark (1994: 188–194) and Kolb (1994). These measures take into account labor needed not only for actual mound construction, but for gathering and transporting building materials, mixing adobe, plastering walls, roofing structures, carving rock, and facing platforms. They are, therefore, a far more realistic and comparable measure than straight volume. Craig and Clark (1994, Fig. 7.58, Tables 7.27 and 7.28) estimated that construction of the Meddler mound complex would have taken 3,806 person-days: the mound itself 2,527 person-days and the surrounding compound wall and compound rooms another 1,279 person-days. In contrast, the five excavated *heiau* on Maui (Kolb 1994, Table 1) included two residential-ceremonial temples (39,368 and 128,155 person-days), two war temples (21,462 and 24,011

person-days), and a single refuge (53,537 person-days). The average labor expenditure for these five Maui complexes was 53,307 person-days or 14 times the labor energy expended on the Meddler mound, a comparison that underscores the significant differences in labor organization and social complexity.

Although the presence of mound architecture in the Eastern Tonto Basin denotes social differentiation, differences between groups or individuals are not overtly visible in the nonarchitectural archaeological record. There are differences in the distribution of some goods, like decorated pottery, shell, and turquoise and obsidian artifacts in mortuary, ceremonial, and residential contexts (Rice 1994; Stark 1995, Tables 10.5–10.7), but most researchers think that these apportionments are minor and result from factors other than status differentiation (Elson, Gregory, and Stark 1995: 476–477; Jacobs and Rice 1994: 924; Stark 1995: 341–342). The lack of indicators of social differentiation extends to some degree to the later Cline Terrace platform mound, the largest Gila phase mound in the Tonto Basin (Jacobs and Rice 1997), and to platform mounds in the Phoenix Basin, where differences in individual status are not always readily apparent in artifact assemblages (Bostwick and Downum 1994; Doyel 1974; Gregory 1988a). As Wilcox (1991: 269) wrote about Hohokam mortuary remains, "if there were significant differences in status, its costumes were perishable textiles and feathers that have yet to be documented. . . . nothing comparable to the wealth of Mississippian burial assemblages . . . is present in the Hohokam area."

Archaeologists use the lack of clear, unambiguous status markers to argue for low social complexity in the Tonto Basin and elsewhere in the greater Southwest (Ciolek-Torrello and others 1994; Elson, Gregory, and Stark 1995; Stark 1995; Whittlesey and others 1995). Burials have been studied at Snaketown (Haury 1976), Casa Grande (Wilcox 1991), Chaco Canyon (Akins 1986), Grasshopper (Whittlesey 1978), and Ridge Ruin (McGregor 1940) that clearly indicate differential mortuary treatment and possibly institutionalized status distinctions, but interpretation of them varies. Some researchers suggested interments were of leaders of religious orders or social sodalities where status was achieved (Reid 1989: 87; Whittlesey 1978), whereas others suggested that the burials were of elite leaders with ascribed status (Akins 1986; Wilcox 1991).

The analysis of historic mound-using groups indicates that clear material signatures of status are not necessarily to be expected in the archaeological record, particularly for middle-range groups at the level of ranking proposed for the Roosevelt phase Eastern Tonto Basin. If architecture is excluded from consideration, many of the material indicators of status found among historic period groups are items that would either not survive in the archaeological record or would be difficult to interpret without direct ethnographic analogy. Status may be designated by the carrying of wooden artifacts (Samoa), the wearing of elaborate feather headdresses and other clothing (Marquesa, Yap, and Natchez), tattoo patterns (Marquesa and Natchez), and deferential behavior to chiefs and nobles by those in lower positions (Samoa, Yap, Marquesa, and Natchez). In fact, these traits are the primary nonarchitectural indicators of status among these groups, which are the most socially complex in the analysis. In less socially differentiated groups like the Choctaw and Ifaluk, even though they are ranked societies with inherited leadership roles, there are few, if any, material status markers.

Perhaps most importantly, the accumulation of personal wealth was not considered to be a positive attribute in any of the analyzed groups. Chiefs and nobles at times may have accumulated more goods than others, primarily through control of trade, gift-exchange, tribute collection, or cultivation of larger plots of productive land. However, the ceremonial and social obligations of chiefs, including giving feasts and staging rituals, periodically involved the distribution of accumulated goods, thereby minimizing (but not eliminating) material differences. Thus, the absence of material indicators of status, such as in the prehistoric Eastern Tonto Basin or the Southwest in general, does not necessarily correspond with an absence of status differentiation (see also Plog 1995).

These findings are supported by an extensive study of New World middle-range societies undertaken by Feinman and Neitzel (1984). Their analysis specifically focused on the role and function of group leaders, and the authors discerned a high degree of variability in status markers, many of which would be absent or difficult to interpret archaeologically. The three most significant status markers, at least for archaeological purposes, were architecture, chiefly dress, and mortuary practices, with "special residence and dress . . . observed most frequently" (Feinman and Neitzel 1984: 57).

Chiefly dress is not usually visible in the archaeological record, except for jewelry or attachments to clothing, both of which may be difficult to interpret. Although mortuary practices are commonly used as an indicator of status, Feinman and Neitzel recorded a high degree of variability in these practices; in fact, special-

ized burials for leaders occurred in less than a third (31.4%) of the 51 analyzed groups. Furthermore, some of the specialized burials would have left little trace in the archaeological record. Leaders, in contrast to other group members, were sometimes burned, eaten, or hung from trees: "although leaders are generally differentiated during life by their dress and at death by their mortuary treatment, the absence of evidence of these differences in the archaeological record is not necessarily sufficient to conclude that social distinctions are not present" (Feinman and Neitzel 1984: 76, Table 2.9).

Feinman and Neitzel also documented a leadership structure similar to that proposed here: all groups in their study had defined positions of leadership, and "in most societies leadership roles are largely inherited," although the means of inheritance, and whether the succession was subject to constituent approval, varied. However, "purely achieved leadership positions are rare" (Feinman and Neitzel 1984: 61). In all of the historic mound-using groups examined in this analysis, status could be raised to a certain degree through achievement, but birth largely determined one's position in the social system and achieved status was rarely passed on to one's descendants.

The problems with discerning status and ranking through the artifact assemblage reemphasize the role of architecture as one of the better indicators of social differentiation (Abrams 1989, 1994; Steadman 1996; Trigger 1990). Although artifact assemblages can at times portray social distinctions, such evidence is variable and usually associated with highly ranked or stratified societies such as prehistoric Southeastern groups where copper headdresses, breastplates, earspools, and other copper emblems appear to be indicative of high status (Peebles and Kus 1977). However, most of these high status Southeastern artifacts are found in platform mound burials, and those that are not are still often associated with mound sites (Blitz 1993), further stressing the overall importance of platform mound architecture as an indication of a socially differentiated society.

The ethnographic and ethnohistoric sources revealed that, with the exception of the small residential mounds constructed by households, platform mounds were used by descent groups, that is, people who considered themselves to be of common ancestry. The notion of common ancestry was ascribed to any mound built with community labor, regardless of whether elites lived on the mounds themselves, the mounds were community structures for ceremonial and communal activities, or the mounds were primarily for mortuary practices

(Table 3.1). In this sense, mounds were corporate property, and although chiefs may have enjoyed more benefits, particularly if they lived on the mound, the mound and its attributes were essentially shared by all members of the descent group. The perception that Eastern Tonto Basin mounds were constructed and used by a descent group with a designated leader is supported not only by the historic analysis but by the size of most of the Eastern Basin mounds, which clearly required the directed labor of groups larger than a single or even several households (Craig and Clark 1994; Jacobs and Rice 1994). In small-scale societies, group organization beyond the household level was primarily through kinship, and it is likely that kinship formed the primary organizational structure of mound-building groups in the prehistoric Eastern Tonto Basin. The exact nature of the descent groups associated with construction of the mounds, that is, whether they consisted of clans, lineages, or some other organizational form, cannot be determined from the archaeological evidence.

The ethnographic and ethnohistoric accounts indicated further that platform mound-using groups were often involved with some form of ancestor worship or, at least, were concerned with descent group ancestors. This attribute existed among most of the groups examined. Abandoned mounds of all kinds, including residential, temple, and particularly burial mounds, were considered to be the homes of lineage ancestors. In Southeastern groups, there was a particular concern with lineage ancestors, and elaborate mounds were constructed to hold or bury these remains.

Ancestor worship is difficult to distinguish archaeologically, but Lindauer (1996b) derived some intriguing information from Roosevelt phase burials in the Schoolhouse Point area on this practice; it consisted of multiple burials in individual, well-defined crypts in discrete cemetery areas on Schoolhouse Mesa. Although some of the crypts contained evidence that the burials were all placed at the same time, other crypts appeared to have been periodically reopened, with the interment of new individuals partially displacing previous burials. Most significantly, the presence of a rare inherited morphological trait (fused toe phalanges) from four of the six individuals within a single crypt highlighted the possibility that repeated interments of a related social group took place here (Lindauer 1996b: 853; Ravesloot and Regan 1995: 39). It is possible that the initial burial in the crypt was that of the founding ancestor, based on the quantity of grave goods: "If the number of burial accompaniments is an indicator of social status, the bottom individual in a burial crypt was consistently the person of highest status" (Lindauer 1996b: 853). Based on a recent analysis of Zuni mortuary patterns by Howell and Kintigh (1996), the fact that discrete cemetery areas were documented at Schoolhouse Point and other sites in the Eastern Tonto Basin also may indicate the presence of individual descent groups.

Schoolhouse Point apparently did not have a platform mound during the Roosevelt phase (Lindauer 1996a), but the practice of ancestor worship may have been part of the local custom in the Roosevelt phase platform mound settlements. Although similar remains were not found at any other site in the Roosevelt Lake Project areas, the Schoolhouse Point sample represents one of the best preserved burial collections recovered from the excavations. Mortuary remains from other project sites, including those with platform mounds, were either not recovered or were thoroughly vandalized (Craig and Clark 1994; Elson 1994; Elson and Craig 1994; Jacobs 1994a; Ravesloot and Regan 1995). Therefore, although not confirmed elsewhere, the Schoolhouse Point evidence is intriguing and marks the possibility of some form of ancestor worship.

The Sequential Use of Platform Mounds

One of the most common assumptions made concerning the prehistoric use of platform mounds in the Tonto Basin and elsewhere in the Southwest is that all mounds dating to a particular 100-year or even 200-year phase were contemporaneous. Functional changes and sequential use of mounds are noted between phases, such as between the Roosevelt and Gila phases or the Soho and Civano phases, but generally not within a phase except in cases of large-scale mound remodeling.

The assumption of mound contemporaneity is a key factor in models based on competition between entrepreneurial or aggrandizing elites who controlled the mounds and vied with each other for various commodities and people (S. Fish and P. Fish 1992; Henderson 1993; Hohmann 1992; Rice 1990b; Wood 1989, 1995; Wood and Hohmann 1985). In the Eastern Tonto Basin specifically, Jacobs and Rice (1994) suggested that the mounds functioned to integrate smaller settlements within their community via feasting and food redistribution, with each contemporaneous mound possibly controlling a different ecological territory. Wood's (1995) definition of Roosevelt and Gila phase irrigation districts relied on the assumption that only one mound existed per irrigation district per phase. In an earlier model, I suggested that the Roosevelt phase mounds and villages in the Eastern Tonto Basin were integrated into a single cooperative community through ceremonial use of the mounds (Elson 1996b; Elson, Gregory, and Stark 1995; Elson and others 1996; see also Craig and Clark 1994: 196; Craig and others 1992; Gregory 1995).

In contrast to these archaeological models, information from historic mound-building groups indicates that mounds of all types were often sequentially used. This pattern appears strongest for those mounds constructed by communal labor and shared by a single descent group. Mounds were abandoned and new ones constructed (or significantly remodeled) for various reasons, including events related to both the individual life cycle and the annual calendrical cycle. The analysis of historic groups shows that group or individual life-cycle events, such as birth, puberty, marriage, death, and succession, were more common than calendrical factors in mound abandonment and renewal. Although the sample is limited, the most common factor for mound abandonment and new construction was the death of a lineage or clan chief or the succession of a new chief. This practice appeared among groups from all analyzed geographic areas and was independent of whether the chief actually inhabited the mound or not, although it was most frequent in those situations. It was particularly common among Southeastern groups (Anderson 1994): Le Petit (in the early 1700s) wrote about the Natchez, "When the great chief dies they demolish his cabin and then raise a new mound, on which they build the cabin of him who is to replace him in his dignity, for he never lodges in that of his predecessor" (in Swanton 1911: 103).

Among all historic groups in the analysis and for all mound types, including at times small residential mounds, the mounds were never completely abandoned as long as the group that constructed and used the mound remained in the territory. Platform mounds, in particular, were lineage property and remained so whether actively in use or not; they were often associated with particular ancestors, both mythic and real, and served to unify a descent group by reminding them of their common past (Dillehay 1990: 235). Abandoned mounds were visited, treated with reverence, had shrines constructed on them, often were associated with taboo and other ritual proscriptions, and were sometimes the scene of ceremonial activities.

The archaeological implication from these observations is that perhaps not all of the Roosevelt phase mounds in the Eastern Tonto Basin were contemporaneous. Rather, some of the mounds may have been used sequentially. This idea is contrary to my previous model for the use of Eastern Tonto Basin platform mounds in which I used visibility between mounds as an indication of contemporaneity. However, there may be other reasons for intervisibility.

The stated contemporaneity of Roosevelt phase platform mounds is based almost entirely on ceramic cross-dating. Unfortunately, the relatively long intervals of most Tonto Basin diagnostic ceramic types make cross-dating of limited use in discerning events of fewer than a hundred years. A century could represent two or three individual generations and even more chiefly successions if succession occurred late in the lifetime of the chief. The construction date for all Eastern Basin platform mounds stems from a single A.D. 1277vv tree-ring sample from a premound wall at the Meddler Point site, which, along with temporal ceramic information, indicated that the Meddler mound was constructed around A.D. 1280 (Craig and Clark 1994; Elson 1995). Construction of the Livingston, Pyramid Point, and Pinto Point platform mounds is also estimated at around 1280 based on the Meddler date in conjunction with supporting radiocarbon determinations and ceramic cross-dates (Elson, Gregory, and Stark 1995; Jacobs and Rice 1994; McCartney and others 1994; Rice and Lindauer 1994). The estimates for the other mounds are inconclusive, however, because of the lack of related tree-ring dates, the large standard deviations associated with radiocarbon determinations, and the limited resolution of ceramic cross-dating in the Tonto Basin. As a result, it is not certain when the mounds at Livingston, Pyramid Point, and Pinto Point were actually constructed and in use, except that it was sometime during the 100-year Roosevelt phase, between A.D. 1250 and 1350 (Fig. 1.3).

According to the frequencies of the ceramic types, the greatest overlap for all sites is in the A.D. 1250–1275 to 1325–1350 period, which is the time generally assigned to the Eastern Basin platform mound components. Meddler Point is the most securely placed, with the tree-ring date indicating mound construction after 1277 and the complete lack of Fourmile Polychrome and scarcity of Gila Polychrome supporting abandonment prior to 1325. The 1277vv date from the mound area is supported by another tree-ring date of 1273vv from a nearby residential compound (Compound 7) thought to have been directly associated with the mound (Fig. 4.11; Craig and Clark 1994; Elson 1995: 52, Table 2.5). However, reliance on a single vv-date (meaning the number of removed exterior rings cannot be estimated) from a wall built an unknown number of years prior to mound construction calls for caution even in the dating of Meddler Point.

With the overlap in the mound ceramic assemblages, it is extremely difficult to demonstrate either absolute contemporaneity or the lack thereof for the four platform mounds. The possibility that the platform mounds were not contemporaneous can be evaluated through a relative seriation using the start and end dates of diagnostic ceramic wares. The method used in this analysis was developed by Jeffery Clark (1995a: 258–263) to place in sequence the residential compounds at the Meddler Point site; a similar method was also used by Rice and Lindauer (1994: 58-60) to examine the occupations of the Pinto Point and Livingston mounds and other sites in the Livingston Project area.

Following Clark, I divided the diagnostic decorated ceramics into three temporal groups by either start date or end date (Table 5.1). In reality, the start and end dates for the ceramic types are not as discrete as the groupings suggest, but the groups are reflective of the general temporal tendencies of the included ceramic types: Group I contains pottery with an end date of approximately A.D. 1300, Group II contains pottery with a start date of approximately 1250, and Group III contains pottery with a start date of approximately 1300. None of the analyzed types date solely to the 1250 to 1300 period, and therefore no type fits into more than one category. Because the period of interest is the Roosevelt phase, between 1250 and 1350, earlier and later ceramics are not considered, although their overall number from analyzed contexts is very low.

Contexts selected for analysis from each of the sites are critical because they must be related to the use of the platform mounds. Context is particularly important at Meddler Point and Pinto Point, because both had relatively extensive premound components and much temporal mixing of remains (Craig and Clark 1994; Jacobs 1994c, 1994d). Although Pyramid Point and Livingston also had premound components, both settlements were small, were constructed quickly, and temporal mixing was much less of a problem (Elson 1994; Jacobs 1994b, 1994e). Most importantly, all of the rooms at Pyramid Point and Livingston could be directly related to the platform mound, whereas the relationships of ground floor rooms, trash areas, and outlying compounds to the platform mounds at Meddler and Pinto Point were often unclear. No platform mound fill is included in the analysis because earlier trash was often used as fill material; for example, pre-A.D. 1150 buff ware sherds were recovered from mound fill at all four sites.

Analyzed contexts from Livingston and Pyramid Point included diagnostic ceramics from the fill (excluding mound cells) and floors of all excavated rooms, including the floors of the three ground floor rooms and all elevated surfaces at Livingston (Fig. 4.15). Analyzed contexts from Pinto Point included only ceramics from the floors of the elevated mound rooms (Figure 4.16) because of the difficulty in relating premound rooms to the platform mound itself. It is unclear when these rooms were occupied and in use, so, conservatively, only the floors of the mound rooms were analyzed.

Additionally, ceramics associated with an "organic layer" deliberately, and possibly ritually, placed in the Pinto Point mound during construction (Jacobs 1994c, 1994d) were also included (but as a separate line in the analysis) to increase the potential of dating the mound construction period. Similar organic lenses have been recovered from other Roosevelt phase platform mounds, including both Meddler Point and Bass Point (Craig and Clark 1994; Lindauer 1995), but their function remains unknown.

At Meddler Point, because of the same difficulty in relating ground floor rooms with mound construction and because the mound top rooms were severely eroded and vandalized, the analyzed context consisted of ceramics from a large borrow area directly north of the platform mound (Fig. 4.11). Research by Craig and Clark (1994) and Wallace (1995a: 111–114, Fig. 4.5) has demonstrated that this area was primarily used to mine dirt for adobe used in constructing the mound and

Table 5.1. Diagnostic Pottery Types Used to Seriate Eastern Tonto Basin Platform Mounds

Group I: Types dated prior to A.D. 1300
Reserve Black-on-white
Snowflake Black-on-white
Tularosa Black-on-white
All McDonald Corrugated types
St. Johns Black-on-red
St. Johns Polychrome
Casa Grande Red-on-buff

Group II: Types dated after A.D. 1250
Pinedale Black-on-white
Pinedale Black-on-red
Pinedale Polychrome
Maverick Mountain Polychrome
Pinto Black-on-red
Pinto Polychrome

Group III: Types dated after A.D. 1300
Gila Black-on-red
Gila Polychrome
Tonto Polychrome
Cedar Creek Polychrome
Fourmile Polychrome

was subsequently trash-filled; therefore the ceramics postdate mound construction. The borrow area had a number of post-A.D. 1300 ceramics, indicating it was used for trash disposal from the time of mound construction through settlement abandonment. All analyzed contexts, then, were in use at the time of or after construction of the associated platform mound.

Figure 5.2. displays graphically the counts for the diagnostic ceramics by group for each of the four platform mounds that is presented in Table 5.2. Ceramic frequencies from all undisturbed fill and floor contexts at Locus A of the Griffin Wash site are also included in Table 5.2; they are discussed later in this chapter. Figure 5.2 shows that the Meddler Point borrow area has the highest percentage of pre-A.D. 1300 (Group I) ceramics and the lowest percentage of post-1250 (Group II) ceramics of the four mounds. These proportions support considering Meddler Point as the earliest platform mound constructed. Meddler is followed by the Livingston and Pyramid Point mounds, which are roughly similar in their percentages of pre-1300 (Group I) and post-1250 (Group II) ceramics, although Pyramid Point also has a post-1300 (Group III) component. Pinto Point was the last mound constructed, having the lowest pre-1300 (Group I) percentage and the highest post-1250 (Group II) percentage.

Figure 5.2 shows the combined counts from both the elevated floors and the organic layer at Pinto Point. If these amounts are separated, as in Table 5.2, the difference in construction date from the other platform mounds, as shown by the ceramics from the organic layer, is even more pronounced. Counts from the elevated rooms reveal that Pinto Point also has a significant post-1300 (Group III) component (8.1 percent), but it is not overly apparent when the frequencies are combined in Figure 5.2.

The temporal ordering of the four platform mounds is partially supported by the results of a similar analysis undertaken by Rice and Lindauer (1994: 58–60, Figs. 3.3 and 3.4) on the Livingston and Pinto Point mounds (using ceramic groups of pre-A.D. 1270, 1270–1320, and post-1320). Although Rice and Lindauer did not temporally order the two mounds, assigning them both to the Roosevelt phase, it is evident from the data they present that Livingston is, for the most part, earlier than Pinto Point and that Pinto Point contains a late Roosevelt or early Gila phase component.

The results of the seriation and temporal ordering are "suggestive," rather than conclusive, because of the different contexts used in analysis and the fact that the figures are from two different archaeological projects

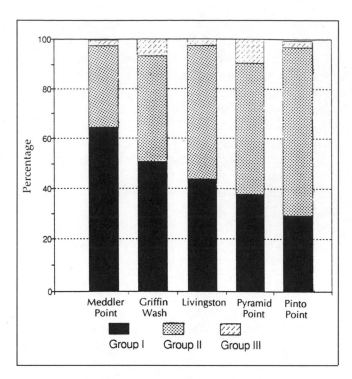

Figure 5.2. Ceramic groups from analyzed contexts at the four platform mound sites and the Griffin Wash site. Group I ceramics have an end date of A.D. 1300, Group II ceramics have a start date of A.D. 1250, and Group III ceramics have a start date of A.D. 1300.

with differing analytical methods (see Christenson 1995; Heidke 1995; Lindauer 1994b). With the relatively gross nature of the temporal groups and the small time frame that we are considering here, it is also likely that the occupations of some of the mounds overlapped. But the magnitude of difference between Meddler Point and Pinto Point strongly implies that the two mounds are not contemporaneous or, if so, only during the final years of the Meddler mound occupation and the beginning years of Pinto.

Platform Mound Function

One of the more significant findings of the analysis of historic mound-using groups, although not an unexpected one, is the extremely wide range of documented variability in platform mound function. Mounds are constructed and used for a large number of reasons. Many individual mounds are also multifunctional, serving different purposes at the same time as well as at different times in their life cycle. Perhaps most disconcerting from an archaeological perspective is the fact that mounds that are identical in appearance, both with-

SITE, Context

Ceramics	MEDDLER POINT Borrow area	LIVINGSTON All rooms without mound fill	PYRAMID POINT All rooms without mound fill	PINTO POINT Elevated floors	Organic layer	Total	GRIFFIN WASH All rooms Locus A
Group I: pre-A.D. 1300							
Reserve Black-on-white	22	0	0	0	8	8	6
Snowflake Black-on-white	130	1	4	2	1	3	27
Tularosa Black-on-white	12	6	1	5	8	13	2
McDonald Corrugated	252	25	20	7	8	15	106
St. Johns Black-on-red	1	9	0	0	7	7	1
St. Johns Polychrome	14	8	1	6	4	10	26
Casa Grande Red-on-buff	11	1	2	0	0	0	0
Group I total	442	50	28	20	36	56	168
Percent of TOTAL	*64.5*	*43.9*	*37.8*	*32.2*	*28.3*	*29.6*	*50.8*
Group II: post-A.D. 1250							
Pinedale Black-on-white	149	37	19	10	87	97	95
Pinedale Black-on-red	27	1	1	1	0	1	9
Pinedale Polychrome	5	2	1	4	0	4	2
Maverick Mountain Polychrome	2	0	4	0	0	0	0
Pinto Black-on-red	26	21	8	21	4	25	26
Pinto Polychrome	18	0	6	1	0	1	9
Group II total	227	61	39	37	91	128	141
Percent of TOTAL	*33.1*	*53.5*	*52.7*	*59.7*	*71.7*	*67.7*	*42.6*
Group III: post-A.D. 1300							
Gila Black-on-red	0	1	3	0	0	0	3
Gila Polychrome or Tonto Polychrome	8	2	0	4	0	4	3
Cedar Creek Polychrome	8	0	4	1	0	1	16
Fourmile Polychrome	0	0	0	0	0	0	0
Group III total	16	3	7	5	0	5	22
Percent of TOTAL	*2.3*	*2.6*	*9.5*	*8.1*	*0*	*2.7*	*6.7*
TOTAL	685	114	74	62	127	189	331

in and among groups, can have completely different functions. Function, then, is a highly complex characteristic that is not immediately resolvable through the ethnographic and ethnohistoric accounts.

In the Eastern Tonto Basin, prehistoric platform mounds may have had various functions and architectural style may not be directly indicative of use. The presence of attributes commonly used to indicate mound habitation, such as hearths or nearby "domestic" trash deposits, do not necessarily reflect function. Nonresidential mounds, such as the temple mounds of the Natchez and other Southeastern groups, for example, have hearths for the keeping of the "perpetual fire." And the accumulation of "domestic" trash, which usually is considered to involve deposition of eating and cooking utensils, can come from such ethnographically documented mound functions as feasting, the exact archaeological signatures of which are at present unclear or ambiguous (Hunt and Diehl 1992; Wallace 1995a: 123).

It is apparent that the age-old debate of whether specific Hohokam platform mounds contained elite residences or were unoccupied ceremonial structures cannot be conclusively answered with either historic sources or archaeological evidence. Mounds served both of these functions, and as burial locales and community centers, sometimes coincidentally and sometimes sequentially during the life of the mound. However, regardless of whether or not the mounds were occupied, the groups that used them were socially complex with a hierarchical social organization and institutionalized leadership. The degree of complexity may not be directly related to the presence or absence of residential mounds. One of the least complex groups in the historic sample, the Ifaluk, had residential mounds, whereas some of the more complex groups, such as the Mapuche, did not. The most complex groups, the Yap, Marquesans, Samoans, and Natchez, all had residential mounds, but this correlation may result from the small sample size. In the highly complex and stratified society on the island of Tonga, for example, platform mounds were not used as chiefly residences. Instead, the four different types of mounds were used as sitting or resting platforms for chiefs, for the chiefly sport of pigeon snaring, for the burial of chiefs and their lineage members, and for the burial of the *Tui Tonga* (the high chief) and his lineage members (Kirch 1990: 210). Mounds in Tonga also served as backdrops for the staging of ceremonial activities, some of which were conducted directly in front of the mound.

The archaeological models for Eastern Tonto Basin platform mounds presented in Chapter 4 list mounds as locales for ceremonies (regardless of whether or not they were residential), for resource redistribution (probably via feasting), and for managing irrigation and other subsistence activities. The mounds are also viewed as integrative features, particularly important in incorporating immigrant groups into the community. The high and low complexity models are in general agreement concerning these aspects of mound use.

The analysis of historic mound-using groups indicates that the prehistoric platform mounds in the Eastern Tonto Basin could have served all of these functions. Both redistribution and feasting are common attributes of all mound-using groups (Table 3.1), and it is likely that the Eastern Basin mounds played a similar role in this process. In Yap, Marquesa, and Samoa, the chiefs administered the collection of subsistence resources primarily from mound locales. Mounds in Yap were the focus of food redistribution, with special platforms on the mounds serving as tables for apportioning goods. In addition, the Marquesan *tohua* (a large arena surrounded by viewing and residential platform mounds), reported to hold as many as 10,000 people, was at times used jointly by several different, potentially hostile, tribes, serving to integrate these groups through mass participation and feasting. Although it is unclear whether these features functioned to integrate immigrant groups, Ferdon (1993) has noted that some of the different Marquesan tribes may have originated as migrant populations. Finally, in both their construction and use, all mounds have a ceremonial aspect, from the smallest residential mounds built by individual households to the large community mounds constructed through communal labor of the entire descent group.

Besides showing that the archaeological models are plausible, the historic sources are not overly helpful in deciphering specific activities occurring at prehistoric mound sites. The number of possible activities is simply too large and variable and the full range of behaviors is unknown. In this respect, archaeological evidence is probably most appropriate for examining specific mound use.

The possibility that prehistoric platform mounds served as physical markers for land tenure or group territories is important and supported by the analysis of historic groups. Dillehay (1990, 1992) recorded territory demarcation as one of the primary functions of platform mounds among the Mapuche. Platform mounds were also used to mark tribal territory in the Marquesas and the territory of the *tabinaw* estate in Yap. Researchers have identified a territorial function for mounds in the U.S. Southeast (Anderson 1994: 94; Hally 1996b) and in other parts of the world such as prehistoric Europe (Hodder 1985). Platform mounds are large, ostentatious features, jutting above the natural landscape; they were constructed to be seen, probably both from the immediate area and from a distance. Although some parts of the mound were hidden, such as areas behind the mounds that may have been used for ceremonial preparation and staging, for the most part mounds evince a highly public aspect.

The territorial function of platform mounds is supported by recent analyses of ethnographic data by Michael Adler and Nieves Zedeño. Adler (1996) outlines a strong correlation between increasing labor investment in subsistence activities and the presence of formalized systems of land tenure, particularly among groups practicing irrigation agriculture. Adler further proposed that environmental and social stress occurring throughout the Southwest at the same time platform mounds were first constructed in the Tonto Basin resulted in an increase in formalized land-tenure systems and restricted access to arable land. This activity was marked by an "increased permanence of the physical markers of the [labor] investment" (Adler 1996: 364). In central and southern Arizona, physical markers most likely included the construction of platform mounds. That territorial boundaries may have been highly important to Tonto Basin groups is further supported by the work of Zedeño (1997) on Hopi land use. She notes that the "living space" area, which was the core of defined Hopi territory, was demarcated by the built environment. It is reasonable, then, to suggest that another function of Tonto Basin platform mounds was to mark and define group space and territory.

ROOSEVELT PHASE SETTLEMENT IN THE EASTERN TONTO BASIN

The historic and archaeological material reviewed substantiates several ways in which platform mounds in the Eastern Tonto Basin may have been used.

1. The mounds were used by ranked descent groups with inherited and institutionalized leadership and may have been associated with descent group ancestors.

2. At least some of the mounds were used sequentially or overlapped for a part of their occupation. Meddler Point was the earliest mound constructed and Pinto Point was the latest.

3. The mounds functioned as territorial markers and were used for food redistribution, group integration, and management of irrigation and other subsistence systems; ceremony played an integral part in all mound function.

Based on these considerations, I propose the following model for Roosevelt phase settlement and platform mound use in the Eastern Tonto Basin.

Construction of the Meddler Point Platform Mound

According to the ceramic seriation, Meddler Point was the first platform mound constructed. This chronological priority makes sense, because Meddler was the first major settlement in this area, inhabited by at least A.D. 750, and by size alone dominated the Eastern Tonto Basin throughout the pre-Classic occupation. It was also situated in the best location in the Eastern Tonto Basin for irrigation agriculture and therefore had a natural resource advantage over other settlements in the local region. The estimated Colonial period (A.D. 750–950) population was small (Doelle 1995b) and at this time the Eastern Tonto Basin most likely consisted of a single, Meddler-based descent group, with small temporary and permanent farmsteads budding off from Meddler Point. During these early years all Eastern Basin settlements were probably related through kinship (Gregory 1995). Available land was plentiful, and if there were any stresses on local groups, they were not archaeologically apparent. The small size of the population probably means that the Meddler descent group was not endogamous but obtained marriage partners from other groups in the Tonto Basin and from kin-related groups in the Phoenix Basin.

By the Sedentary period, however, sometime between A.D. 950 and 1150, a permanent settlement was established at Pinto Point (see Fig. 4.6). Perhaps a small farmstead settlement had been here previously, represented by a few Santa Cruz phase sherds, but it was not until the late Sedentary period or early Classic period (around 1100–1200) that it grew to large farmstead or small hamlet size. The size of this settlement is unclear; the 15 pit houses recorded (Fig. 4.16) may not all have been contemporaneous (Jacobs 1994d), but additional structures were probably present in the hamlet. The relatively large number of Sacaton Red-on-buff (950–1150), St. Johns Black-on-red and St. Johns Polychrome (1175–1300), McDonald Corrugated (1125–1300), and Snowflake (1040–1300) and Tularosa (1175–1300) black-on-white ceramics recovered from the site may be indicative of this earlier occupation (Rice and Lindauer 1994, Table 3.2). Pyramid Point and Griffin Wash were probably settled at this time also, if not earlier, although they appear to have been substantially smaller. A small settlement was present at Eagle Ridge from at least A.D. 1000 to 1100.

The Pinto Point settlement may have been the result of a fissioning of the Meddler Point descent group (Gregory 1995) or it may represent additional migration from the Hohokam core area. Fissioning from Meddler Point is a reasonable deduction because connections with the Hohokam core area were significantly curtailed by A.D. 1050 (and possibly earlier) at the start of the Ash Creek phase (Chapter 4); demographic estimates from Meddler Point also propose a decrease in population during the Sedentary period, in contrast to the steady growth seen at all other times (Craig and Clark 1994). Fissioning is well documented in the ethnograph-

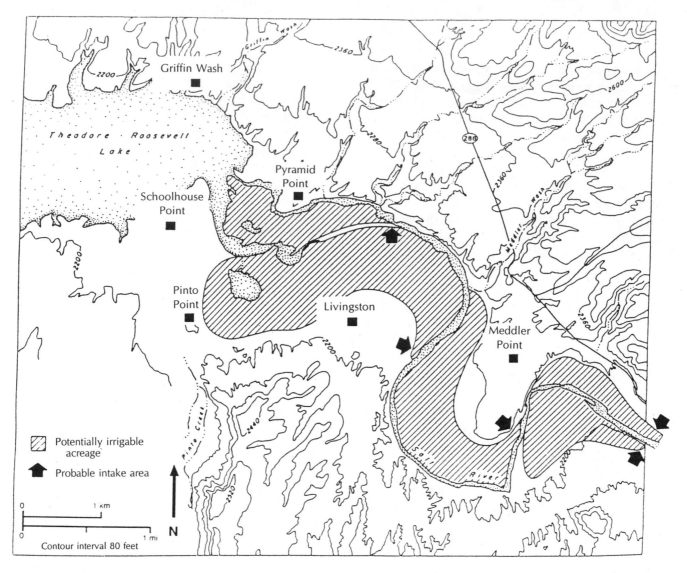

Figure 5.3. Platform mound sites in the Eastern Tonto Basin in relationship to available irrigable acreage (hatched areas) and probable canal intake locations (arrows); after Gregory 1995 (Fig. 5.12).

ic record as a common factor leading to the formation of new, independent groups, often as a result of territorial disputes or disagreements over inheritance rules or marriage practices (Johnson 1982, 1983; Keesing 1975; Zedeño 1997). It most commonly follows kinship lines and can occur at many different levels, including the household, extended household, or larger social groupings such as the clan or lineage in multilineage societies (Anderson 1994: 46–48). In contrast with Pinto Point, the much smaller settlements at Pyramid Point, Griffin Wash, and Eagle Ridge fit an interpretation of seasonal farmsteads, probably directly related to the permanent Meddler Point settlement.

I suggest, then, that the Pinto Point occupation, with the eventual addition of a few settlements on Schoolhouse Mesa in the late Sedentary period or beginning of the early Classic period (about A.D. 1150–1200), was

an independent settlement representing a descent group different from that of the settlers of Meddler Point. If the settlement was founded because of a split from Meddler Point, the two groups may have been related by kinship but antagonistic. At inception, Pinto Point was significantly smaller than Meddler Point and used a different irrigation system with canal intakes originating west of Meddler Point (Fig. 5.3; Gregory 1995; Wood 1995). The settlement was approximately 4 km (2.5 miles) from Meddler Point and located on the opposite side of the Salt River, and it was probably not a territorial threat to the dominance of the local Meddler descent group. By the time platform mound construction began during the early-to-mid Roosevelt phase (around 1280), however, Pinto Point and Schoolhouse Point had grown significantly, and each contained a number of associated compounds.

The Meddler Point platform mound was constructed for several interrelated reasons. The analysis of the historic mound-using groups revealed that one of the reasons could have been a desire to identify and solidify descent group land claims for irrigation systems. Strict territorial demarcation may not have been overly important in the Eastern Tonto Basin as long as land was plentiful, everyone was kin related, and the irrigation system was not stressed. However, beginning around A.D. 1250 and continuing to some extent into the fifteenth century, major environmental changes occurred throughout the greater Southwest (Dean 1988, 1996; Dean and others 1985; Euler and others 1979). At this time, a number of low and high frequency environmental events combined to produce significant stress throughout this area: falling alluvial water tables, increased floodplain erosion, significantly decreased precipitation (the Great Drought), low spatial and temporal climatic variability, and a major breakdown in a long term, stable precipitation pattern (Dean and Funkhouser 1995). In characterizing this period, Dean (1996: 46) noted that, "This interval was marked by far-reaching demographic and sociocultural changes that undoubtedly derive in part from major resource stress and economic uncertainties . . . ."

Environmental changes during this time affected the Tonto Basin in a number of ways, particularly during the Great Drought (around A.D. 1275–1300) when available precipitation and stream flow were significantly reduced (Altschul and Van West 1992; Craig 1995; Van West and Altschul 1994; Van West and Ciolek-Torrello 1995; Waters 1996). In the Eastern Tonto Basin, social stress was caused both by the decreased availability of water for irrigation systems and by the abandonment of the primarily dry farmed higher elevation regions by upland populations who moved into lowland riverine areas during the mid-to-late Roosevelt phase (Ciolek-Torrello and others 1994; Crary and others 1992; Germick and Crary 1992; Oliver 1994; Wood 1992, 1995). Also during this period large-scale population movement occurred throughout the greater Southwest (Cameron 1995; Dean and others 1994), and it is likely that some of these groups entered the Eastern Tonto Basin around this time, settling at places like Griffin Wash and Saguaro Muerto (Clark 1995b, 1997; Lindauer 1994a; Stark, Clark, and Elson 1995). An increasing population, the presence of immigrant groups, and a deteriorating environment resulted in significant stress on what had been for the preceding 500 years a relatively stable system.

All of these factors, but particularly the need to solidify land claims and more efficiently manage irrigation systems, may relate to the construction of the Meddler Point platform mound. The specific impetus for initial construction is perhaps unknowable, but the idea must have stemmed from the Phoenix Basin area and may have involved the transfer of some type of ideological knowledge. Evidence of contact with Phoenix Basin groups is not overtly apparent in the artifact assemblage, but some interchange must have occurred because the Meddler mound was constructed relatively quickly and from a preconceived plan, indicating some degree of familiarity with platform mounds. However, the builders made a number of significant mistakes in mound construction, demonstrated by washouts of wall sections and by buttresses built to support falling walls (Craig and Clark 1994: 182–186). They did not have a thorough knowledge of mound building techniques and the Meddler mound was most likely based on visual inspection of other mounds and not on actual construction experience. Labor and time estimates by Craig and Clark indicate that if only the Meddler Point household heads were involved in construction, providing an average of 40 to 45 person-days a year (based on ethnographic figures compiled by Erasmus, 1965), the mound itself could have been built within 1.6 to 2.6 years. But, "include just a few extra hands, such as other household members or relatives and friends from neighboring settlements, and the entire mound complex could have been completed in less than a year, probably in as little as a month or two, depending on the size of the work force involved" (Craig and Clark 1994: 194).

Mound construction was presumably under the direction of the chief or headman of the founding Meddler Point descent group. The most parsimonious explanation for the sudden adoption of a new, and in the Eastern Tonto Basin, unique labor-intensive architectural form is that construction was mandated by a powerful leader, perhaps upon ascending to the chiefly role. Only a strong leader could organize the labor and marshal the resources and food surplus necessary for mound construction. The archaeological remains suggest that the leader (or the leader's immediate household group) did not live in the mound compound itself but may have occupied nearby Compound 7 (Fig. 4.11; Craig and Clark 1994; Elson, Gregory, and Stark 1995). This compound is closest to the mound and is better constructed, with more evidence for a higher status artifact assemblage and with more elaborate storage facilities than any other compound (Craig 1995: 246). Because of the general absence of status indicators in the ethnographic record for middle-range groups, the presence of even slight status distinctions may be significant.

The primary use of the platform mound itself was probably ceremonial. A staging area on the front side of the mound, facing into the Eastern Tonto Basin, perhaps served as a locus for public performance and display; the rear of the mound, which was restricted to general access by a series of partitioning walls and check-points, may have been used for preparation and other private ritual activities (see Figs. 4.3 and 4.4; Craig and Clark 1994). Obviously, the exact nature of the ceremonies cannot be reconstructed from archaeological remains, but the ethnographic and ethnohistoric sources support the idea that they involved glorification of the descent group and some form of ancestor worship.

Construction of the Livingston Platform Mound by the Meddler Point Descent Group

Based on the ceramic seriation, the Livingston platform mound was the next mound constructed (Fig. 5.2). There are some architectural differences between the Livingston and Meddler Point mounds (the use of pillars and the presence of a few additional small rooms on top of the mound at Livingston), but the Livingston mound is similar enough to have been built by the same group that constructed the Meddler Point mound (Doelle and others 1995, Figure 13.10).

The two most similar in their composition and arrangement are those of Meddler Point and Livingston. In each case, two large rectangular, contiguous rooms of similar dimensions were constructed atop the mounds, both having doorways opening in the same direction. . . . Both rooms had two large, main roof-support posts along the midline of the long axis. At Livingston, an additional room [or several rooms] was attached to the south side of the two east-facing rooms (Doelle and others 1995: 404).

Significantly, Livingston is located in relative isolation; the closest residential compound is 400 m distant and the only other residential settlements in possible association are between 700 m and 900 m away (Fig. 4.7). This settlement arrangement is unique in the Eastern Tonto Basin, although present at a few other mound sites in the Lower Basin. The mound's isolation and the fact that both the artifact and subsistence assemblages portray a short term and limited occupation (Jacobs 1994a; Spielmann 1994) have puzzled archaeologists, but all agree that the site was nonresidential. Wood

(1995: 35), for example, suggested that the Livingston mound was never completed and therefore never used (see Doelle and others 1995; Gregory 1995; Jacobs and Rice 1994).

The function of the Livingston mound becomes clear if its spatial setting is examined (Fig. 5.3). The mound is almost exactly halfway between Meddler Point and Pinto Point: it is 2.0 km (1.2 miles) from Meddler Point to Livingston, and 2.1 km (1.3 miles) from Livingston to Pinto Point. The Livingston mound is also situated between the Pinto Point mound and the first potential location for an intake canal west of Meddler Point. Based on these relationships, I suggest that construction of the Livingston mound represents an attempt by the Meddler Point descent group to consolidate this area of irrigable land under their territorial domain. The mound was purposely placed in a previously unoccupied area with the expectation that settlement of this area would increase, resulting in more complete control of the irrigation system. The Livingston mound itself may have been built by the Meddler Point leader, or possibly by close kin of the leader, and, considering the architectural similarities, it was probably meant to function in a similar manner.

It appears that Meddler Point and Livingston were partly contemporaneous, and that Livingston was constructed after Meddler. If we accept the A.D. 1280 date for Meddler mound construction, Livingston may have been built just prior to 1300. Both mounds were abandoned at approximately the same time, probably around or just after 1300 based on the low frequency of Cedar Creek Polychrome (1300–1350) at Meddler Point and the lack of Cedar Creek at Livingston; Fourmile Polychrome (1325–1375) is absent from both sites as well.

Pyramid Point and Griffin Wash

The chronological placement of Pyramid Point in this developmental sequence is somewhat problematic. The settlement was small, containing perhaps 30 residents, with a small platform mound that probably functioned primarily as a tower. Construction, dated by the ceramic seriation, must have coincided with that at Livingston and later occupation overlapped with that at Pinto Point. Fitting Griffin Wash into the model is also problematic. It was settled by migrant groups who joined a small local population sometime during the Roosevelt phase, but the exact timing of this migration is uncertain. Again, the ceramic seriation (Fig. 5.2) seems to indicate that Locus A, the migrant-related settlement, was earlier than Livingston but later than Meddler Point, although it may have overlapped with both.

One of the functions of the Pyramid Point tower may have been specifically to link the Griffin Wash and Meddler Point settlements. The Pyramid tower was visible to all major settlements in the Eastern Tonto Basin, but the only large Roosevelt phase settlements that were not visible to each other were Meddler Point and Griffin Wash, and Pyramid Point could have provided that line-of-sight connection. Meddler Point, Livingston, and Pinto Point were all intervisible from the tops of their respective platform mounds and there was no need for Pyramid Point to connect them; furthermore, this intervisibility may have had more to do with the open physiographic layout of the Eastern Basin (the mound settlements were all situated on ridges overlooking the floodplain) than to a desire to be visibly connected.

The botanical remains recovered from the Meddler Point platform mound indicate that Griffin Wash and Meddler Point were related and, therefore, that Pyramid Point may have served to connect the two settlements. There were two rooms on top of the Meddler Point platform mound, and one had a "high elevation" construction wood assemblage (Douglas-fir, white fir, ponderosa pine, and no mesquite) that was identical to the construction wood assemblages found in more than half of the excavated Griffin Wash structures (Miksicek 1995). The use of high elevation species was extremely rare in the Eastern Tonto Basin; almost all other excavated structures were built from "low elevation," locally available species (mesquite, palo verde, and juniper). I suggested elsewhere that the differential use of these resources may symbolize the integration, via the Meddler Point platform mound, of the migrant Griffin Wash population with the local Meddler Point descent group (Elson, Gregory, and Stark 1995: 457; Elson and others 1996).

The positioning of the Griffin Wash migrants on the far western edge of the Eastern Basin community (Fig. 4.7) may represent use of the migrants as a buffer against unwanted intrusions from that direction (Gregory 1995), perhaps in a manner similar to the positioning of the Tewa (at Hano Village) by the Hopi (Connelly 1979: 540; Dozier 1966: 17). In this sense, integration of Griffin Wash settlers would have been advantageous to the Meddler Point mound builders. The local Meddler population would have benefited from increased labor to construct and maintain canal systems and to bolster defense against real or perceived threats. Benefits to the immigrant population would have been related to the reason for migration in the first place.

Without the security of kinship relations, integration with the local population was the only way short of conquest to ensure a permanent place of residence and a dependable food supply for those moving from an environmentally (and probably socially) stressed region into an already land tenured system.

The next settlement system downriver (west) from the Eastern Tonto Basin was at Armer Ranch Ruin (Fig. 4.5), separated from Griffin Wash by 3 km (nearly 2 miles) of largely uninhabited terrain. During periods of low precipitation, which at least partially coincided with the period when the mounds were first constructed, the Meddler and Pinto Point irrigation systems would have drained water away from the settlement at Armer and impacted its ability to successfully irrigate (Elson, Gregory, and Stark 1995: 459; Gregory 1995). Conflict, then, could have come from this direction. Pyramid Point perhaps acted as a watch-tower that directly linked the Griffin Wash outpost with Meddler Point and Livingston. If Griffin Wash had been attacked, the Pyramid Point populace would have had a direct view and could have warned the other settlements in the Meddler descent group.

Recent research indicates that the period after A.D. 1250 was one of increasing intergroup conflict (Wilcox and Haas 1994), undoubtedly related to widespread environmental stress, population dislocation, and competition for resources (Dean 1996). Prior to the Roosevelt phase, there is scant evidence from the Eastern Tonto Basin, or the Tonto Basin in general, of any form of conflict, except for an occasional burned structure (which may or may not represent conflict; see Cameron 1990). This sense of peaceful accommodation changed during the Roosevelt phase, when for the first time settlements were located in apparently defensive positions (for example, Griffin Wash Locus C; see Fig. 4.12) and there was widespread burning of structures, many with floor artifacts in place. Full-standing and well-built compound walls were constructed around many settlements, and, as additional evidence, three adult males were found "sprawled" across the floors of two burned rooms at a Roosevelt phase site (AZ U:8: 221) located approximately 5 km (3 miles) west of the Eastern Tonto Basin (Shelley and Ciolek-Torrello 1994: 254–255).

Therefore, I suggest that at least initially, Pyramid Point and Griffin Wash were linked to Meddler Point, either directly through kinship with the Meddler descent group or indirectly in some (possibly fictive) manner. Solidification of this relationship may have been accomplished through ritually focused platform mound activities, including resource redistribution and feasting. The Meddler Point platform mound was no more than an easy two-hour walk from the Griffin Wash settlement (Fig. 4.7). The presence at both Pyramid Point and Griffin Wash of a few Santa Cruz and Sacaton phase pit houses (and possibly even earlier Gila Butte phase pit houses), perhaps represents early, probably seasonal, farmstead settlements closely related to the primary occupation at Meddler Point.

The social reconstruction described here, then, sets up an opposition between two different descent groups on opposite sides of the Salt River (Figs. 4.7 and 5.3). On the north bank was the Meddler descent group, centered around the founding Gila Butte phase (A.D. 750–850) lineage at the long occupied Meddler Point settlement. Included in the Meddler descent group were the inhabitants of Pyramid Point, Griffin Wash, and other north bank Roosevelt phase settlements. On the south bank was the Pinto Point–Schoolhouse Point descent group, probably founded sometime in the Sedentary period (950–1150). The Pinto Point–Schoolhouse settlements were built by dissatisfied members of the Meddler descent group, who left Meddler Point to establish a new settlement using a different irrigation system on the other side of the river. Territorial boundaries of historic groups frequently coincided with major geographic features, and although the Salt River was probably crossable except during high floods, it is the largest and most obvious geographic landmark in the Tonto Basin. The establishment of the Livingston platform mound by the Meddler descent group was a transgression of established territorial boundaries, even though into unsettled territory, and an attempt by the Meddler group to claim additional irrigable land in a time of increasing environmental and social stress.

Construction of the Pinto Point Platform Mound

To continue this reconstruction, I suggest that the Pinto Point platform mound was built in response to the construction of the Livingston mound. Although Doelle and others (1995: 403) characterize the Pinto Point mound as belonging to the same general class as Meddler Point and Livingston, it was sufficiently distinct in architectural layout to have had a different, but possibly related, origin (compare Figs. 4.3 and 4.11 with Figs. 4.16 and 4.17). The most significant difference was the residential occupation of the Pinto mound compound, unlike the platform mound compound at either Meddler or Livingston (Jacobs and Rice 1994: 924).

The exact time of mound construction is unclear; the ceramic seriation indicates only that it probably happened after construction of the mounds at Meddler Point and Livingston (Fig. 5.2). I suggest, however, that it occurred during the life of the Meddler and Livingston mounds as a means to solidify territorial land claims in response to the potential threat from Livingston. Pinto Point mound construction conceivably could have represented the ascension of a particularly strong or powerful lineage head who was able to muster the necessary manpower and resources to build a mound. There is no doubt that the Pinto Point mound lasted into the late Roosevelt or early Gila phase (Rice and Lindauer 1994), possibly some 20 to 30 years beyond the abandonment of Meddler Point and Livingston. Although the Pinto Point mound was probably used in a primarily ceremonial manner, occupation within the mound compound itself denoted a change in mound function and increasing social differentiation, perhaps reflecting control by a powerful leader. The mound was the focal point in the integration of the residential compounds dispersed along the Pinto Point ridge as well as the numerous compounds on Schoolhouse Mesa (Fig. 4.7).

The construction of the Pinto Point mound may have formalized a competitive relationship between the two descent groups that had been brewing for years. Competition between clans and lineages, often in just the social arenas of prestige or status, was documented in all the historic multilineage groups examined in this analysis. Competition may have been particularly keen if Pinto Point was, in fact, established through the fissioning of the Meddler descent group. Before then, there is no doubt that the larger and longer-lived Meddler Point descent group dominated the relationship. The construction of the Pinto Point mound represented the first tangible threat to Meddler Point dominance in the Eastern Tonto Basin.

Relatively soon after the construction of the Pinto Point mound, most of the settlements associated with the Meddler descent group were abandoned. The Meddler Point and Livingston platform mounds, the residential compounds along Meddler Point, and many of the settlements on the north bank of the Salt River became depopulated around or just after A.D. 1300. The abandonment of the Meddler Point mound and settlement meant the relinquishment of power in the Eastern Tonto Basin. Both structures on top of the platform mound were burned, as were the majority of excavated Roosevelt phase structures in the settlement (Craig and Clark 1994). However, few of these structures contained intact floor assemblages; most had only a scattering of miscellaneous pieces of ground stone and other non-portable goods. Conversely, at Livingston, the only feature that burned was a single ground floor room (Feature 14) located in the mound compound but not directly associated with the mound itself (Jacobs 1994b).

There are several ways of interpreting the remains from the Meddler and Livingston settlements. One is that the burning resulted from conflict, inflicted by either Pinto Point or other groups, and that the Meddler inhabitants were warned of the attack by those at Pyramid Point in enough time to remove most of their portable artifacts and flee the settlement. A second possibility is that Meddler Point was attacked, but the inhabitants did not have enough time to remove their goods, which were subsequently taken by the invaders prior to burning the village. Alternatively, the burning, particularly of the mound rooms, may have been ritually related, perhaps associated with the death of the lineage head responsible for the construction of the Meddler Point mound. Burning structures when the household head dies has been reported ethnographically for O'odham groups (Castetter and Bell 1942: 130; Russell 1908) and has been suspected in certain Hohokam archaeological contexts, particularly at Tucson Basin sites (Doelle 1985; Elson 1986; Wallace 1995b).

Ritual burning may have been even more widespread on the death of a powerful lineage head. Perhaps Livingston was simply abandoned and not burned because it lacked any concentrated population or because it was more directly associated with a close relative of the lineage head rather than the head himself. Ritual burning of entire villages is not documented in the Southeastern ethnohistoric record, but groups burned mound structures on the death of powerful chiefs or near relatives (Anderson 1994; Blitz 1993) and occasionally practiced associated human sacrifice (Swanton 1946).

The ceramic remains, and their seriation, indicate that both Pyramid Point and Griffin Wash continued to be occupied after the abandonment of Meddler Point (Table 5.2). These settlements may have moved into an affiliation with Pinto Point, or they may have remained independent. It is possible that Pyramid Point functioned as a watch-tower in the Pinto Point community as it did in the Meddler Point community. Except for Pyramid Point and Griffin Wash, most of the small habitation settlements along the north bank of the Salt River were abandoned about the same time as Meddler Point (Elson and Swartz 1994).

Eventually, within the next 20 to 30 years, Pyramid Point, Griffin Wash, and Pinto Point were abandoned, along with most of the small habitation settlements on Schoolhouse Mesa, and power was transferred to the aggregated settlement and platform mound at Schoolhouse Point (Lindauer 1996a, 1997a). This settlement change, too, may have been related to continued social and environmental stress. The majority of excavated structures at Griffin Wash were burned, many containing large floor assemblages (Swartz and Randolph 1994), again raising the possibility of conflict. Curiously, Pyramid Point was not burned (Elson 1994).

Environmental variability, including a series of severe floods in the early A.D. 1300s that could have destroyed canal systems, may have been a causal factor in this abandonment and subsequent aggregation (Craig 1995: 241–242; Waters 1996). With the prior abandonment of Meddler Point and settlements along the north bank of the Salt River, most of the population had probably already left the Eastern Tonto Basin by this time (Doelle 1995b); those that remained may have then aggregated at Schoolhouse Point.

EASTERN TONTO BASIN SETTLEMENT SYSTEMS

The model presented above postulates that the life-span of the platform mounds was extremely short, each mound lasting no more than 30 years. Roosevelt phase mounds were constructed around A.D. 1280 and probably ceased functioning as mounds by 1330 or 1340. Within this time period, three mounds were constructed in the Eastern Tonto Basin (excluding Pyramid Point). The estimated span of each mound corresponds, more-or-less, to one, or at most, two generations. The impetus for building a platform mound, then, could have been related to the ascension of a particularly powerful chief who was able to accumulate the resources and food surplus necessary for mound construction. If mounds were associated with particular leaders, their abandonment and the collapse of the surrounding settlement may have been at least partially related to the leader's death. Other factors, such as increasing conflict and environmental stress were probably also involved in settlement abandonment.

A similar model has been proposed by David Anderson for prehistoric platform mound-using groups in the Southeastern United States. Anderson (1994: 72) uses the ethnohistoric record to document what he calls "political cycling" or the "rising fortunes and decline" of Southeastern chiefdoms, and he notes that within very brief periods of time, local communities can, and often do, move through different stages of hierarchical and political organization. Furthermore, unlike many common archaeological models, movement is not always in a "step-like" forward direction from low to high complexity, but rather the system continually cycles, with movement occurring in both directions (Anderson 1994: 330).

As an example, Anderson describes the sixteenth-century platform mound village of Coosa, which fluctuated between the time of de Soto's visit in 1540, when it was a powerful regional chiefdom, to de Luna's visit in 1560, when "the chiefdom had apparently fragmented and nearby towns were refusing [to pay] tribute" (Anderson 1994: 72). European contact and disease may have been partly responsible (Hally 1994; Hudson 1976), but Anderson (1994) and other archaeologists (DePratter 1994) argue that disease was probably not a determining factor. By the late 1560s, Coosa apparently regained its regional authority. The situation documented in the less socially complex Eastern Tonto Basin is slightly different, with the platform mound settlements rising in power and then being permanently abandoned. However, the basic mechanisms suggested by Anderson are plausible and the patterns documented here may represent a similar situation.

Platform mounds in the Eastern Tonto Basin were most likely based on descent groups and they benefited the entire group rather than a few elite leaders. As in all middle-range groups, leaders may have enjoyed greater privileges and accumulated greater quantities of goods, but the platform mounds functioned primarily as corporate rather than individual features. As I discuss in the following chapter, I believe this to be also true in the much more socially differentiated Phoenix Basin, although there the mounds may have benefited an elite descent group rather than all of the descent groups in the community.

Theory needed to understand archaeological signatures of a descent group, or to distinguish two different descent groups like those at Meddler Point and Pinto Point, is unfortunately not well developed. Limited research along these lines has been undertaken, influenced by the New Archaeology of the 1960s, through analyses of architectural, ceramic, and mortuary remains (Hill 1970; Kent 1990; Lipe and Hegmon 1989; Longacre 1970; Reid 1989; Rice 1992; Shennan 1989; Whittlesey 1978). These efforts, while commendable, have for the most part been unconvincing, causing the near abandonment of a once promising field. In fact, as recently noted by Howell and Kintigh (1996: 537), most archaeologists have left kinship or descent group studies largely to the ethnographer, even though "kinship is such an important structuring force, particularly in nonstate societies, that it is impossible to ignore." This may be changing; several recent analyses suggest that archaeological investigations of kinship systems and social boundaries are not only possible, but essential for understanding the organization of prehistoric groups (for example, Abbott 1994b; Howell 1996; Howell and Kintigh 1996; Stark 1998).

How the model for the Eastern Tonto Basin applies to other platform mounds in the Tonto Basin is unclear. The basin is divided into nine local settlement systems containing 21 primary riverine platform mounds (Fig. 4.5). Some of the settlement systems contain several mounds, whereas others contain only one; none have as many mounds as the Eastern Tonto Basin. Most of the mounds in the other settlement systems are unexcavated and dated primarily from surface ceramics. The Roosevelt Lake Project proved unequivocally that excavation is necessary to accurately date and interpret these features; prior to this project, for example, both Meddler Point and Pinto Point were believed to date primarily to the Gila phase.

The association of most Tonto Basin platform mounds with irrigable land and with geographic features suitable for canal systems suggests that the mounds played at least some role in irrigation management. However, as this and other research has shown, each local settlement system is structured by its own developmental history (Anderson 1994; Doelle and others 1995). Although platform mounds in other Tonto Basin systems may have functioned in ways similar to the Eastern Tonto Basin and been used by similar groups, the nature of other settlement systems cannot be thoroughly understood without additional archaeological investigations.

What is crystal clear from this research, however, is the dynamic nature of the Eastern Tonto Basin settlement system, which involved the rise and fall of platform mounds and the shifting of social and political power within a surprisingly brief time and small area, encompassing no more than 50 or 60 years and 30 square kilometers. It is likely that similar dynamics characterized other settlement systems, both in the Tonto Basin and in other platform-mound building regions of the Southwest.

CHAPTER SIX

An Ethnographic Perspective on Hohokam Platform Mounds

The function of prehistoric platform mounds has been the subject of archaeological debate in the American Southwest for more than a century. By defining common attributes of historic mound-using groups, this study provides support for some archaeological models and challenges others. Significantly, the research documented variability in both the social organization of middle-range mound-using groups and the manner in which platform mounds were used. Several ethnographic correlates derived from the historic analysis have important archaeological implications.

1. Platform mounds are constructed and used by ranked descent groups with well-defined, inherited leadership positions.
2. The greater the diversity in platform mound type and function, and the larger the size of the mounds, the greater the social complexity and the authority of the chiefs or religious leaders.
3. Platform mounds are often multifunctional and the specific use of a mound may change over its lifetime; architecture and morphology are not necessarily directly indicative of mound function.
4. Platform mounds built by suprahousehold labor generally have a territorial function and are important in marking descent group land claims.
5. Ceremonial activities, often involving ancestor worship and the glorification of the descent group, are involved with all aspects of mound construction and use.

It is important to stress that *only* groups defined as middle range were included in the historic analysis in Chapter 2, and that the defined attributes are not necessarily applicable to groups with higher levels of social complexity. In state-level societies, for example, status, class, and role differentiation are much more pronounced and platform mounds may have functioned in a different manner. A consideration of scale is important in any analysis of prehistoric Southwestern societies (Johnson 1989). That is, even when archaeologists talk about high complexity in the Southwest, they are still dealing with groups of relatively low complexity on a worldwide scale. To conclude this analysis, I go out on the proverbial limb, so to speak, and, using the information from the historic study of mound-using groups, I discuss the manner in which platform mounds in the Phoenix Basin and in other areas of the Hohokam region may have been operating.

REGIONAL COMPARISONS OF HOHOKAM PLATFORM MOUNDS

As part of the Roosevelt Community Development Study, archaeologists at Desert Archaeology comprehensively reviewed platform mounds throughout the Hohokam region (Doelle 1995a; Doelle and others 1995). Doelle and his colleagues identified seven platform mound clusters in central and southern Arizona: the lower Salt River of the Phoenix Basin, the middle Gila River of the Phoenix Basin, the Tonto Basin, the Tucson Basin, the lower San Pedro River, the eastern Papaguería, and a somewhat diffuse cluster in the northern Tucson Basin–Picacho Peak area (Fig. 1.1, Table 1.1). Their compilation of descriptive information for each cluster, including maps and available metric data for each mound, is a valuable contribution for comparative analyses of the different mound groupings. Such a compilation was not possible until the 1990s, with the recording of mound sites in the Papaguería and San Pedro regions and the detailed descriptions of mounds in the Tonto Basin. Although variability in platform mounds was recognized before this time, particularly at sites outside the Phoenix Basin (S. Fish and others 1992; Gregory 1987), a Phoenix Basin prototype was still the standard by which all mounds were judged and generally modeled in both form and function.

With the exception of the northern Tucson Basin–Picacho Peak area, the mound clusters were relatively discrete: platform mounds within clusters were more similar in form, and possibly function, than those between clusters, suggesting that the mounds most likely had a primarily local, rather than regional, orientation. Doelle and his co-authors (1995: 433) noted that the clearest difference that emerged from a comparative view was that the Salt and Gila mound clusters in the Phoenix Basin were earlier, with larger and greater numbers of mounds and significantly higher prehistoric populations than the other clusters. This means that the use of the Phoenix Basin as a model for the other areas is most likely insupportable. No other area had a developmental history like the Phoenix Basin, with platform mound use extending from the pre-Classic to well into the Classic period. Even without the pre-Classic portion of this sequence, the massive rectangular Classic period mound form was apparently earlier in the Phoenix Basin than in the other areas, appearing sometime between A.D. 1200 and 1250 (Doelle and others 1995:437). In the other mound clusters, with the possible exception of the northern Tucson Basin Marana mound, platform mounds appeared relatively suddenly, sometime around or after A.D. 1250. In the Tonto Basin, which is now one of the best dated areas, tree-ring, ceramic, and radiocarbon dates are in accord, suggesting that the platform mounds were initially constructed at about A.D. 1280 (Elson 1995; McCartney and others 1994).

Graphing the size of the platform mounds by surface area shows that mounds in the Salt and Gila basins were significantly larger than mounds in the other areas, by a factor of more than two (Doelle and others 1995, Fig. 13.26). Mound sizes of the seven clusters are summarized in Table 6.1. Although the number of measured mounds is small (33.3%) and some clusters, like the Salt River, are heavily skewed by a few very large mounds (hence the large standard deviation), the figures are believed to be generally representative.

There is almost no overlap in size between the smallest Phoenix Basin mounds and the largest mounds in the other clusters. This size differential has important implications for platform mound function and the organization of the social groups who constructed the mounds. First of all, facilities on top of Phoenix Basin mounds could have held significantly greater numbers of people, including large residential groups (Doelle and others 1995:435). Although it is possible that smaller residential groups occupied mound tops in other areas

Table 6.1. Platform Mound Systems in Central and Southern Arizona

System	No. of mounds	No. of mounds measured	Range (m³)	Average (m³)	Standard deviation
Lower Salt	43	4	1,584–14,000	8,063	5,949.4
Middle Gila	13	4	1,056–4,050	2,119	1,145.0
Tonto Basin	26	7	300–2,142	864	578.0
Tucson Basin	7	3	257–892	512	335.3
Lower San Pedro	14	10	111–538	316	165.7
Papaguería	8	7	130–476	230	116.9
N. Tucson Basin–Picacho Peak	6	4	788–2,360	1,617	709.2

NOTE: Platform mounds of less than 100 cubic meters, which may have been tower mounds, are excluded.
SOURCES: Doelle 1995a; Doelle and others 1995.

(as has been suggested for example, at the Marana mound), the size variation does indicate that the individual mound clusters probably differed in their forms of social organization and possibly in the functions of the mounds themselves. Second, considering the substantially greater area and volume of Phoenix Basin mounds, the size of the mound construction groups had to be much larger than groups in other areas, or they had to expend much more time in construction, or both, again underscoring differences in social organization and particularly methods of labor recruitment and control. Also, in terms of resource acquisition, a greater amount of surplus food was needed to feed workers not directly involved in subsistence-related tasks.

To better understand the magnitude of the differences between the various regions, I turn again to the labor cost (energy expenditure) measures discussed in Chapter 5. Craig and Clark (1994: 188–194) analyzed the comparative labor costs involved in building the Tonto Basin Meddler Point platform mound (volume of 966 cubic meters with a surrounding compound measuring 3,021 square meters) and the Phoenix Basin Mesa Grande platform mound (volume of 14,000 cubic meters with a compound measuring 9,100 square meters). Using labor estimates experimentally derived by Charles Erasmus (1965) for earth- and stone-moving activities in Mesoamerica under simulated prehistoric conditions, Craig and Clark estimated that construction of the Meddler mound and compound would have taken 3,806 person-days and the Mesa Grande mound and compound more than 50,000 person-days. Mesa Grande (along with the similarly sized Pueblo Grande) is the largest mound remaining in the Hohokam region. The energy needed to build the Mesa Grande mound and compound is impressive, involving more than 10 times the amount of labor that went into the Meddler Point mound. To put these figures in more comprehensible terms, a crew of 30 laborers working full-time could have constructed the Meddler Point platform mound and compound in a little more than four months. This same crew would have taken more than four and a half years to build the Mesa Grande mound and compound. With the Classic period Meddler Point population estimated to have been around 100 to 150 individuals (Craig and Clark 1994:194), 30 full-time laborers may be unrealistic, but this simple exercise underscores the magnitude of difference between the two mounds.

The Salt River cluster is by far the largest in the Hohokam region (Table 6.1). Although it does not cover as much physical area as the Middle Gila and the Tonto Basin clusters (Table 1.1), the Salt River cluster contains more platform mound sites (30) with more mounds (43) than any other. This number would likely be greater if Phoenix had not undergone extensive agricultural and urban development at a relatively early time. The two largest mounds, Pueblo Grande and Mesa Grande, surpass by more than three times the next largest existing Southwestern mound, Adamsville (4,050 cubic meters) on the Gila River.

The mounds along the Gila River are next in size, followed by the northern Tucson Basin–Picacho Peak area and the Tonto Basin; the mounds in the other three clusters are significantly smaller (note the ranges in Table 6.1). The platform mound clusters were separated from each other by great enough distances (with the exception of the Salt and Gila clusters) that probably only limited interaction took place between them, and therefore each cluster may have functioned in a largely independent manner (Doelle and others 1995). It is possible, then, that the groups in each area used the mounds in a number of different, and perhaps unrelated, ways.

The Phoenix Basin portion of the Salt River is unique in terms of the number and size of its prehistoric remains. The Gila River area is also distinct from the other clusters. The ethnohistoric and ethnographic information on mound size and diversity supports the probability, noted by other archaeologists (Chapter 1), that higher social complexity was present in groups along the Salt River (and possibly along the Gila River) than in the rest of the Hohokam region. Although archaeological evidence from the mounds along the Salt River is not sufficient to conclusively argue for mound diversity, at least three different types have been recognized:

platform mounds, tower mounds, and Great Houses (Doelle and others 1995). Mound diversity is also indicated by the range in mound size (Table 6.1). Therefore, it is likely that Salt River groups were highly ranked, at least at Pueblo Grande and Mesa Grande, and that stratification may have been present with elite leaders having coercive power over those in the lower classes.

The estimated 50,000 person-days of labor needed to build the Mesa Grande platform mound is substantial, and this figure would probably increase if more excavation revealed actual construction patterns. The 14,000-cubic-meter volume of the Mesa Grande and Pueblo Grande mounds is comparable to platform mounds in the Southeast, such as those along the Tombigbee River or in the Savannah River Valley (Anderson 1994; Blitz 1994), and to *heiau* on the islands of Maui and Molokai in Hawaii (Kirch 1990; Kolb 1994), although both areas also contained even larger mounds (Fig. 5.1). The Southeast and Hawaii have long been characterized by anthropologists and archaeologists as the homes of highly ranked or stratified chiefdoms. Of the five excavated Maui *heiau* measured by Kolb (1994, Table 1), which included only residences, refuges, and war temples (and not the smaller agricultural enclosures), only one residence had a greater platform volume than Pueblo Grande or Mesa Grande (Fig. 5.1). When these constructions are translated into energy measures, only two *heiau* (the residence noted above and a refuge) had greater than 50,000 person-days of expended labor (Kolb 1994, Table 2). These comparisons, although not conclusive, further argue that Phoenix Basin groups were highly ranked and probably stratified.

Some of the differences between the Phoenix Basin and the other platform mound clusters in the Hohokam region undoubtedly relate to the much greater amounts of water and irrigable land available along the Salt and Gila rivers. These geographic attributes contributed to a higher prehistoric population density here than in the other areas (Dean and others 1994; Doelle 1995b, Fig. 7.8). Demographic reconstructions reveal that the Salt and Gila populations were already larger than other Hohokam areas by around A.D. 750 and that differences increased significantly after 950 (Doelle 1995b). At that time, populations along the Salt continued to increase and diverged from those along the Gila, which remained constant. Greater population and longer developmental histories resulted in a higher density of platform mounds in these river valleys. The time depth and the information derived from the ethnographic and ethnohistoric analysis obviously support sequential use of the mounds. It is likely that the mounds at Las Colinas were not all contemporaneous, but instead represent repeated construction events. The major remodeling episodes at Mound 8 of Las Colinas (Gregory 1988a) may also be indicative of this process, similar to assessments by Blitz (1993) on prehistoric mounds in the Southeast.

Based on distributional patterns, Gregory (1987, 1988a, 1991; Gregory and Nials 1985) has convincingly argued that platform mounds in the Phoenix Basin were strongly associated with irrigation systems. The strength of this pattern was confirmed by Rice (1992), who observed that platform mounds were almost exclusively confined to the Sonoran Desert where irrigation agriculture was necessary for the survival of any large, permanent settlement. Mound sites in both the Salt and Gila areas are located approximately every 5 km to 8 km (3 to 5 miles) along irrigation canals (Gregory 1991: 170–174). Irrigation systems and primary villages were established long before the construction of platform mounds; along the Gila (and almost certainly the Salt) all available irrigable niches appear to have been occupied by the end of the Colonial period at around A.D. 950 (Gregory and Huckleberry 1994). As a result, land tenure principles must have been active prior to the major period of mound construction at the start of the Classic period and Phoenix Basin platform mounds probably did not function to solidify descent group land claims. Still, the mounds themselves likely served as territorial markers, perhaps as physical symbols of boundaries. Sounding a cautionary note, however, is the fact that the relationship between the major mound sites and their placement along the canals was not entirely straightforward. Pueblo Grande, for example, was at the head of Canal System 2, which terminated at Las Colinas. Mesa Grande, on the other hand, was positioned at the approximate center or toward the end of the Lehi Canal System, and Casa Grande on the Gila River was at the end of its canal system (Howard and Huckleberry 1991).

The fact that the major platform mounds were not necessarily associated with canal intake locations, where they would have had the most direct control of water allocation, means that each canal system probably represented an integrated community. Gregory (1991: 173) wrote, "The inference that irrigation communities functioned at some level as a single social and political unit is strongly supported by their association with the same canal system. All were dependent on the same intakes, and a minimal amount of cooperation would have been necessary for maintenance and repair not only of intakes but of the canals themselves." The irrigation community concept is supported by data from the utilitarian ceramic assemblages, which suggest that greater interaction occurred within than between canal systems (Abbott 1994a: 408), particularly in the early part of the Classic period when many of the platform mounds were first constructed.

The archaeological evidence indicates, and the historic perspectives support, the strong likelihood that each separate canal system along the Salt and Gila rivers was occupied by a single, large descent group, composed of a number of smaller kin groups or lineages that were all related through descent from a common (and most likely semimythical) ancestor. In all multi-lineage groups examined in the historic analysis, the lineages themselves were ranked; some lineages had chiefly titles and greater privileges, whereas other lineages were composed of lower ranked chiefs or commoners. I suggest, then, that the mound settlements within each separate canal system represented the domain of an elite descent group, with the higher ranked elites within the descent group associated with the larger mounds and the lower ranked elites associated with the smaller mounds. The non-elite members of the descent group, who comprised the majority of the population, lived in the habitation areas of the mound villages and in the small hamlets and farmsteads along the canal system. Whether the mounds themselves were inhabited by the elites is unclear and the subject of continuing debate (Chapter 1), although the Phoenix Basin probably has the best evidence for actual mound-top occupation (Doelle and others 1995: 439).

This form of social organization is most apparent during the late Classic period when social differentiation was pronounced and lineage leaders of a canal system may have competed with leaders of other canal systems for both prestige goods and possibly followers. In the early Classic period, elite lineages probably still occupied the mound settlements of a canal system and benefited from their higher status, but social differentiation was not as great and the mounds may have functioned in a much more communal or corporate manner. These patterns are tentatively supported by Phoenix Basin ceramic assemblages, which indicate that early Classic canal systems were internally focused, with fewer goods coming from the other canal systems, whereas late Classic assemblages contained a greater diversity of wares, including higher frequencies of the more expensive red wares (Abbott 1994a: 419). Most importantly, significantly greater quantities of late Classic red wares were recovered from several discrete domestic units at Pueblo Grande (Abbott 1994b), suggesting increasing social differentiation that may have been fostered in part by individual or lineage control of exchange networks outside of the canal system. This change in social organization can be phrased in terms of a model recently proposed by Feinman (1995) and Blanton and others (1996) as a shift from a largely corporate political-economic system to one with greater influence from leader-initiated network or exclusionary strategies.

The social organization of Phoenix Basin groups, therefore, may have been like that of the Natchez, and the relationship between the Great Sun, who lived in the main village, and other members of the Sun class who ruled the smaller, outlying villages (Swanton 1946). Only members of the Sun lineage were allowed to occupy the platform mounds, even though the mounds served the entire Natchez people as a whole. In this respect, Phoenix Basin mounds may have benefited a class of kinship-related elite leaders, that is, a highly ranked kin group or lineage within the larger descent group, to a much greater degree than the mounds in the Tonto Basin, where the entire descent group was associated with the platform mound.

The other mound clusters in the Hohokam region probably functioned in a corporate manner more similar to that proposed for the Tonto Basin. In these systems, ranked leaders were present but social differentiation was not as extreme as in the Phoenix Basin, and the mounds were primarily the property of the entire descent group rather than of a single sublineage. This is true for both the early and late Classic periods, even though there is some evidence for increasing social differentiation through time. Leaders had higher status, may have been deferred to, accumulated greater resources than others, and probably controlled the distribution of some goods but otherwise were probably not much different from the rest of the group. Evidence from the excavation of the Marana platform mound in the northern Tucson Basin–Picacho Peak area can be interpreted this way (Bayman 1994; P. Fish and others 1992; S. Fish and others 1992). In some of the other mound clusters, like the Papaguería, the platform mounds are so small (averaging under 200 square meters in surface area and just over a meter in height) and the associated population so limited that they perhaps functioned quite differently.

Unlike Phoenix Basin mounds, which were used and remodeled over relatively long periods of time (Doyel 1981; Gregory 1988a), the majority of mound sites investigated in the other clusters were short-lived, with little evidence of extensive remodeling. They were built significantly later than the Phoenix Basin mounds; available chronometric dates indicate a lag time of 50 to 100 years between the construction of Classic period mound forms in the Phoenix Basin and the appearance of similar mounds in the outlying clusters (Doelle and others 1995:437). This pattern strongly indicates that platform mounds in the outlying clusters were at least physically based on a Phoenix Basin model and on some form of emulation.

There is an interesting relationship between the initial construction of platform mounds in some of the outlying clusters, particularly in the Tonto Basin and possibly in the San Pedro River area, and the onset of environmental disturbances that affected the greater Southwest after A.D. 1250. Environmental and social stress in the Southwest at this time was a causal factor in large-scale population movement, including immigration of northern pueblo groups to points south (Cameron 1995; Clark 1997). Platform mounds in the outlying clusters may have played important roles in the marking and consolidation of descent group territory, particularly irrigable lands, as competition between groups increased for control of critical resources. The mounds probably also served to integrate immigrant groups into the community and as areas for feasting and resource redistribution.

Therefore, emulation of the Phoenix Basin mounds seemingly took place (1) when environmental conditions and the resulting social stress demanded new methods of group integration and solutions to competition for resources and (2) when, as a result, leaders of the descent group were able to marshall the necessary power and resources for mound construction. The simplest explanation for the rapid adoption of a new, labor-intensive architectural form that required some form of social control and organization is that construction was mandated by a particularly powerful leader.

Each mound cluster had its own unique settlement history that strongly influenced platform mound construction and the nature of the groups that used them. For example, there were certain similarities in the nature of mound use and the degree of social complexity in the Eastern Tonto Basin and in the Marana area of the northern Tucson Basin–Picacho Peak cluster, but differences between them still existed: Tonto Basin mounds probably did not function to integrate settlements in diverse resource zones, as the Marana model proposes, and the control of irrigation agriculture was probably more important in the Tonto Basin than in the northern Tucson Basin–Picacho Peak area. The research on historic groups demonstrated that morphological similarities in platform mounds did not necessarily indicate functional or processual similarities. Our perceptions of these aspects of platform mounds will be sharpened enormously when platform mound sites are excavated in the San Pedro and Papaguería and when additional investigations are undertaken in the Tucson, Tonto, and Phoenix basins.

SOCIAL COMPLEXITY AND PLATFORM MOUNDS

Because the above analysis relied on case studies from seven historic groups, this research has only sampled the degree of variability in platform mounds and mound-using groups. Yet information from even this limited sample indicates that many previous models for prehistoric Southwestern platform mounds, my own and others, are overly simplistic. Most of these models are based almost exclusively on archaeological evidence, accounting, at least in part, for their limitations.

When I began this research, I was of the opinion that most Hohokam platform mounds, and particularly those in the Tonto Basin, were largely uninhabited ceremonial features used by groups of relatively low social complexity. I am now convinced that I was wrong. Although all prehistoric platform mounds had a strong ceremonial component, their functions were highly variable: it is likely that some mounds were inhabited, whereas others were not. Furthermore, it is also likely that some mounds functioned in a manner of which we are currently unaware. Unfortunately, considering the range of documented variation in the use of historic platform mounds, the poor state of preservation of most remaining mounds, and the ambiguity of interpreting archaeological remains, excavation alone may not resolve the question of specific mound function.

Much time and energy has been spent arguing whether or not groups resided on top of the platform mounds, and archaeologists are still debating the same basic functions suggested by Cushing in 1892, by Bandelier in 1892, and by Fewkes in 1912. We may spend the next hundred years arguing without reaching substantive archaeological resolution. What is clear is that regardless of whether mounds were inhabited, the groups that used the mounds were socially complex; in the Southwest it is likely that these groups were ranked and, possibly in the Phoenix Basin, stratified, and all mound-using groups had inherited and institutionalized leadership positions.

This analysis of historic platform mound-building groups has opened up new and, I think, exciting avenues of exploration. Above all, this study suggests that it is time to critically reexamine both the questions we have been asking and the tools we use to answer them. The variability that archaeologists discern in prehistoric material culture and architecture is but a thin reflection of the total variability in human behavior. But, by looking more closely at the ethnographic and ethnohistoric record and judiciously applying what we learn to archaeological contexts, we can better understand the social dynamics that guided the individuals and groups of prehistory. By examining the past in this manner we can effectively expand our view beyond the ruined remains on the mound tops.

Primary Reports from the Bureau of Reclamation Archaeological Projects around Roosevelt Lake, Arizona

The majority of archaeological investigations in the United States today are conducted under the mandate of cultural resource legislation and are funded by various government agencies and the private sector. The Roosevelt Lake research described in this volume was funded by the United States Bureau of Reclamation, and it exemplifies the important role government agencies have played in preserving our national heritage and supporting archaeological studies. As Thomas Lincoln (1998: 7) recently noted, during the past 12 years the work undertaken for the Bureau in the state of Arizona alone has resulted in the organization of 12 symposia at professional meetings, 115 presented papers, 34 articles in major journals and edited books, 11 books or monographs published by university or independent presses, 7 Ph.D. dissertations, and 3 Masters theses. This total does not include the more than 50 volumes published by the individual contracting firms and submitted to the Bureau as part of project reports.

More than 20 years ago the Phoenix Projects Office of the Bureau of Reclamation designed the Roosevelt Lake studies to offset the potential damage to archaeological resources caused by increasing the height of the dam at Roosevelt Lake around 80 feet to provide better flood control for the rapidly growing city of Phoenix (Pedrick 1992). When the dam and Roosevelt Lake were created in 1911, hundreds of archaeological sites were undoubtedly inundated. By raising the dam, the maximum extent of the lake would be further increased, particularly during years of heavy rain and mountain snowfall when the lake reached its full capacity.

The Tonto Basin is abundantly rich in archaeological remains. Pedestrian surveys made for the Roosevelt Project recorded more than 750 prehistoric and historic sites within the boundaries of the projected maximum floodpool (Ahlstrum and others 1991; Fuller and others 1976; Rice and Bostwick 1986). Obviously, no project, no matter how well funded, could reasonably excavate and study fully all 750 sites, and a sampling program was designed by an interagency team of archaeologists from the Bureau of Reclamation, Tonto National Forest, and the Arizona State Historic Preservation Office. This team established a set of specific research goals and selected about 150 prehistoric sites for investigation. The Bureau further divided the research into three separate but overlapping areas and in the early 1990s entered into contractual agreements with three archaeological firms to undertake testing and excavation programs.

This Appendix lists the Roosevelt Project reports by volume with chapter titles and authors, and the volumes are arranged by the three archaeological firms responsible for the majority of the work: Desert Archaeology, Inc. and Statistical Research, Inc. in Tucson and the Office of Cultural Resource Management at Arizona State University in Tempe. In addition to this material, the archaeologists involved with the various Roosevelt studies have presented numerous papers at scientific meetings and published articles in various journals and edited books. More information and artifact data tables from these projects may be found on the internet at Arizona State University's Archaeological Research Institute website (http://archaeology.la.asu.edu).

DESERT ARCHAEOLOGY

Anthropological Papers 12

Doelle, William H., Henry D. Wallace, Mark D. Elson, and Douglas B. Craig
   1992   Research Design for the Roosevelt Community Development Study. *Anthropological Papers* 12. Tucson: Center for Desert Archaeology.

   1. Introduction, *William H. Doelle*
   2. Environmental Setting and Prehistoric Subsistence, *Mark D. Elson and William H. Doelle*
   3. Previous Research and Culture History, *Stephen H. Lekson, Mark D. Elson, and Douglas B. Craig*
   4. The Role of Formation Process Studies in Prehistoric Research, *Douglas B. Craig and Henry D. Wallace*
   5. Tonto Basin Temporal Patterns and Methods for Chronological Refinement, *Mark D. Elson and Henry D. Wallace*
   6. Prehistoric Demography in the Tonto Basin, *William H. Doelle and Douglas B. Craig*
   7. Production, Distribution, Consumption, and Interaction, *Henry D. Wallace, Mark D. Elson, and James M. Heidke*
   8. The Question of Cultural Identity, *Henry D. Wallace, Mark D. Elson, and Miriam T. Stark*
   9. A Framework for Studying Prehistoric Communities, *William H. Doelle, Henry D. Wallace, and Douglas B. Craig*
   10. Sampling Design and Field Methods, *William H. Doelle, Douglas B. Craig, and Henry D. Wallace*
References Cited

Anthropological Papers 13, Volume 1

Elson, Mark D., and Deborah L. Swartz
   1994   The Roosevelt Community Development Study, Vol. 1: Introduction and Small Sites. *Anthropological Papers* 13(1). Tucson: Center for Desert Archaeology.

   1. Introduction, *Mark D. Elson*
   2. Project Methods, *Mark D. Elson and Douglas B. Craig*
   3. The Eagle Ridge Site, AZ V:5:104/1045 (ASM/TNF), *Mark D. Elson and Michael Lindeman*
   4. The Hedge Apple Site, AZ V:5:189/1605 (ASM/TNF), *Deborah L. Swartz and Brenda G. Randolph*
   5. The Porcupine Site, AZ V:5:106/217 (ASM/TNF), *Mark D. Elson and Brenda G. Randolph*
   6. Tested Sites, *Deborah L. Swartz and Mark D. Elson*
References Cited

Anthropological Papers 13, Volume 2

Elson, Mark D., Deborah L. Swartz, Douglas B. Craig, and Jeffery J. Clark
   1994   The Roosevelt Community Development Study, Vol. 2: Meddler Point, Pyramid Point, and Griffin Wash Sites. *Anthropological Papers* 13(2). Tucson: Center for Desert Archaeology.

   7. The Meddler Point Site, AZ V:5:4/26 (ASM/TNF), *Douglas B. Craig and Jeffery J. Clark*
   8. The Pyramid Point Site, AZ V:5:1/25 (ASM/TNF), *Mark D. Elson*
   9. The Griffin Wash Site, AZ V:5:90/96 (ASM/TNF), *Deborah L. Swartz and Brenda G. Randolph*
Appendix A: Archaeomagnetic Laboratory Results for the Roosevelt Community Development Study, *Jeffrey L. Eighmy*
References Cited

Volume 2 Supplement: Meddler Point Map Packet (bound separately)
   James P. Holmlund, Jeffery J. Clark, and Douglas B. Craig

Anthropological Papers 14, Volume 1

Elson, Mark D., and Jeffery J. Clark (Editors)
   1995   The Roosevelt Community Development Study, Vol. 1: Stone and Shell Artifacts. *Anthropological Papers* 14(1). Center for Desert Archaeology, Tucson.

   1. The Chipped Stone Assemblage, *Michael Lindeman*

Anthropological Papers **14, Volume 1** (*continued*)

Anthropological Papers **14, Volume 2**

Heidke, James M., and Miriam T. Stark (Editors)
   1995 The Roosevelt Community Development Study, Vol. 2: Ceramic Chronology, Technology, and Economics. *Anthropological Papers* 14(2). Tucson: Center for Desert Archaeology.

Anthropological Papers **14, Volume 3**

Elson, Mark D., and Jeffery J. Clark (Editors)
   1995 The Roosevelt Community Development Study, Vol. 3: Paleobotanical and Osteological Analyses. *Anthropological Papers* 14(3). Tucson: Center for Desert Archaeology.

Anthropological Papers **15**

Elson, Mark D., Miriam T. Stark, and David A. Gregory (Editors)
- 1995   The Roosevelt Community Development Study: New Perspectives on Tonto Basin Prehistory. *Anthropological Papers* 15. Tucson: Center for Desert Archaeology.

1. Introduction, *Miriam T. Stark and Mark D. Elson*
2. Assessment of Chronometric Methods and Dates, *Mark D. Elson*
3. Tonto Basin Chronology and Phase Sequence, *Mark D. Elson and David A. Gregory*
4. Ceramic Accumulation Rates and Prehistoric Tonto Basin Households, *Henry D. Wallace*
5. Prehistoric Settlement Patterns in the Eastern Tonto Basin, *David A. Gregory*
6. Western Apache and Yavapai Settlement in the Tonto Basin, *Alan Ferg*
7. Tonto Basin Demography in a Regional Perspective, *William H. Doelle*
8. The Social Consequences of Irrigation Agriculture: A Perspective from Meddler Point, *Douglas B. Craig*
9. Domestic Architecture in the Early Classic Period, *Jeffery J. Clark*
10. Commodities and Interaction in the Prehistoric Tonto Basin, *Miriam T. Stark*
11. Social Boundaries and Cultural Identity in the Tonto Basin, *Miriam T. Stark, Jeffery J. Clark, and Mark D. Elson*
12. The Role of Migration in Social Change, *Jeffery J. Clark*
13. Classic Period Platform Mound Systems in Southern Arizona
     William H. Doelle, David A. Gregory, and Henry D. Wallace
14. New Perspectives on Tonto Basin Prehistory, *Mark D. Elson, David A. Gregory, and Miriam T. Stark*

Appendix A: Mixture Model and Additional Ceramic Data, *Henry D. Wallace*
Appendix B: Terminology, Methodologies for Measurement, and Comparative Data for Tonto Basin Architectural Units
     David A. Gregory
Appendix C: Excavation of a Protohistoric Western Apache Activity Area at the Eagle Ridge Site Locus D, *Alan Ferg*
Appendix D: A Method for Estimating Regional Population, *William H. Doelle*
Appendix E: Raw Data Used in Meddler Point Agricultural Productivity Analysis, *Douglas B. Craig*
Appendix F: Regional Platform Mound Systems: Background and Inventory, *William H. Doelle*
References Cited

STATISTICAL RESEARCH

Technical Series **28, Volume 1**

Ciolek-Torrello, Richard S., Steven D. Shelley, Jeffrey H. Altschul, and John R. Welch
- 1990   The Roosevelt Rural Sites Study, Vol. 1: Research Design. *Technical Series* 28(1). Tucson: Statistical Research.

Introduction
Section One - Regional Background
Section Two - Research Design
Section Three - Methodology
Section Four - Concluding Thoughts
References
Appendix: Inventory Number Concordance for the Roosevelt Rural Sites Study

Technical Series **28, Volume 2**

Ciolek-Torrello, Richard S., Steven D. Shelley, and Su Benaron (Editors)
- 1994   The Roosevelt Rural Sites Study, Vol. 2: Prehistoric Rural Settlements in the Tonto Basin. *Technical Series* 28(2). Tucson: Statistical Research.

PART 1, bound separately
1. Introduction, *Richard S. Ciolek-Torrello*
2. Cholla Recreation Area, *Steven D. Shelley*

ARIZONA STATE UNIVERSITY

Roosevelt Monograph Series **1**, *Anthropological Field Studies* **22**

Rice, Glen E. (Editor)
   1990   A Design for Salado Research. *Roosevelt Monograph Series* 1, *Anthropological Field Studies* 22. Tempe: Office of Cultural Resource Management, Arizona State University.

   1. Toward a Study of the Salado of the Tonto Basin, *Glen E. Rice*
   2. An Intellectual History of the Salado Concept, *Glen E. Rice*
   3. Variability in the Development of Classic Period Elites, *Glen E. Rice*
   4. Implementing the Field Research, *Glen E. Rice, Charles L. Redman, and John C. Ravesloot*
   5. Overview of the Analysis, *Arleyn W. Simon, Keith W. Kintigh, and Glen E. Rice*
   6. An Integrated Approach to the Roosevelt Lake Ceramics, *Arleyn W. Simon and Charles L. Redman*
   7. Ceramic Chronometric and Spatial Issues, *Glen E. Rice and Owen Lindauer*
   8. Gila Polychrome: An Investigation of the Hallmark of the Salado Tradition
        Glen E. Rice, Owen Lindauer, and John C. Ravesloot
   9. Analysis of Stone Artifacts, *Glen E. Rice and John C. Ravesloot*
   10. Shell Analysis, *Carol A. Griffin and Glen E. Rice*
   11. Prehistoric Use of the Tonto Basin Landscape: Toward a Synthetic Overview, *Paul E. Minnis and Glen E. Rice*
   12. Diet and Subsistence Studies, *Katherine A. Spielmann*
   13. Geoarchaeological Studies in the Roosevelt Study Area, *Michael R. Waters*
   14. The Biology of the Salado People, *Christy G. Turner II, Marcia H. Regan, and Joel D. Irish*
   15. Burial Studies, *John C. Ravesloot*
   16. Summary Thoughts, *Glen E. Rice and John C. Ravesloot*
References Cited
Appendix A: Concordance of Roosevelt Platform Mound Study Site Numbers

Roosevelt Monograph Series **2**, *Anthropological Field Studies* **26**

Redman, Charles L., Glen E. Rice, and Kathryn E. Pedrick (Editors)
   1992   Developing Perspectives on Tonto Basin Prehistory. *Roosevelt Monograph Series* 2, *Anthropological Field Studies* 26. Tempe: Office of Cultural Resource Management, Arizona State University.

   1. Introduction, *Kathryn E. Pedrick*
   2. Pursuing Southwestern Social Complexity in the 1990s, *Charles L. Redman*
   3. Modeling the Development of Complexity in the Sonoran Desert of Arizona, *Glen E. Rice*
   4. Factors Affecting Prehistoric Salado Irrigation in the Tonto Basin, *J. Scott Wood, Glen E. Rice, and David F. Jacobs*
   5. Centralized Storage: Evidence from a Salado Platform Mound, *Owen Lindauer*
   6. Increasing Ceremonial Secrecy at a Salado Platform Mound, *David F. Jacobs*
   7. Patterns of Production and Distribution of Salado Wares as a Measure of Complexity
        Arleyn W. Simon, Jean-Christophe Komorowski, and James H. Burton
   8. The Inference of Social Complexity from Distributions of Exotic Artifacts in the Tonto Basin
        Carol A. Griffith, Keith W. Kintigh, and Mary S. Carroll
   9. Artiodactyl Exploitation by Prehistoric Horticulturists in the Roosevelt Lake Area, Arizona, *Judi L. Cameron*
   10. Issues and Challenges in the Design of a Computerized Database, *Mary S. Carroll and Peter H. McCartney*

Roosevelt Monograph Series **3**, *Anthropological Field Studies* **32**

Jacobs, David F.
   1994   Archaeology of the Salado in the Livingston Area of Tonto Basin: Roosevelt Platform Mound Study, Report on the Livingston Management Group, Pinto Creek Complex. *Roosevelt Monograph Series* 3, *Anthropological Field Studies* 32. Tempe: Office of Cultural Resource Management, Arizona State University.

PART 1, bound separately
Preface: The Roosevelt Platform Mound Study, *Glen E. Rice, Owen Lindauer, and David F. Jacobs*
   1. The Livingston Site Group, *David F. Jacobs and Glen E. Rice*
   2. Chronological Methods, *Peter H. McCartney, Owen Lindauer, Glen E. Rice, and John C. Ravesloot*

Roosevelt Monograph Series 3, Anthropological Field Studies 32 *(continued)*

3. Phase Chronology, *Glen E. Rice and Owen Lindauer*
4. Gila Pueblo Collections from the Livingston Sites, *John C. Ravesloot*
5. The Excavation and Description of V:5:76/700, *David F. Jacobs*
6. The Architecture and Chronology of V:5:76/700, *David F. Jacobs*
7. The Excavation and Description of V:5:66/15a, *David F. Jacobs*
8. The Architecture and Chronology of V:5:66/15a, *David F. Jacobs*
9. Artifact Assemblages from V:5:66/15a and V:5:76/700, *Glen E. Rice, Peter H. McCartney, and David F. Jacobs*
10. V:5:119/997, A Roosevelt Phase Compound, *David F. Jacobs*
11. V:5:112/995, The Sand Dune Site, *David F. Jacobs*
12. Site V:5:128/1011, Saguaro Muerto, *Owen Lindauer*
13. V:5:121/999, A Roosevelt Phase Compound, *David F. Jacobs*
14. Sample Excavations at Livingston Sites: V:5:141/1013, V:5:130/1015, V:5:120/998, V:5:125/1007, and V:5:139/15b
    David F. Jacobs
15. Pre-classic Sites in Livingston: V:5:111/994, V:5:117/993, and V:5:140/1012, *David F. Jacobs*
16. Architectural Patterns in the Livingston Management Group Sites, *David F. Jacobs*

PART 2, bound separately
17. Systematics of Decorated Wares, *Owen Lindauer*
18. Analysis of Plain Ware Ceramic Assemblages, *Arleyn W. Simon*
19. Compositional Analysis of the Livingston Ceramic Assemblage, *Arleyn W. Simon*
20. Performance Analysis of the Livingston Ceramic Assemblage, *Arleyn W. Simon*
21. Ceramic Evidence for Room Function, *Arleyn W. Simon*
22. Lithic Evidence for Room Function, *Glen E. Rice*
23. Projectile Points, Bifaces, and Drills, *Glen E. Rice*
24. Lithic Assemblage Analysis, *Arleyn W. Simon, Peter H. McCartney, and M. Steven Shackley*
25. Ceramic Disks, Whorls, and Unusual Forms, *Arleyn W. Simon and Kim S. Savage*
26. Ground-stone Artifacts of the Livingston Sites, *Arleyn W. Simon and Peter H. McCartney*
27. Shell Artifacts from the Livingston Area, *Carol A. Griffith and Peter H. McCartney*
28. The Distribution of Special Artifacts, *Glen E. Rice*
29. Physical Anthropology of the Roosevelt Lake Livingston Study Area
    Christy G. Turner II, Marcia H. Regan, and Joel D. Irish
30. Burial Practices in the Livingston Area, *John C. Ravesloot*
31. Pollen Results from the Livingston Management Group, *Suzanne K. Fish*
32. Plant Remains from Six Roosevelt and Gila Phase Sites, *J. Phil Dering*
33. Archaeofaunal Remains from the Livingston Area, *Judi L. Cameron*
34. Subsistence Patterns at the Livingston Sites, *Katherine A. Spielmann*
35. Summary, *David F. Jacobs and Glen E. Rice*
Data Appendix
References Cited
Concordance of Sites

Roosevelt Monograph Series 4, Anthropological Field Studies 33

Lindauer, Owen
1995   Where the Rivers Converge: Roosevelt Platform Mound Study, Report on the Rock Island Complex. *Roosevelt Monograph Series* 4, *Anthropological Field Studies* 33. Tempe: Office of Cultural Resource Management, Arizona State University.

Preface: The Roosevelt Platform Mound Study, *Owen Lindauer and Glen E. Rice*
1. Introduction to the Rock Island Complex, *Owen Lindauer*
2. Investigations at Bass Point Mound, U:8:23/177, *Owen Lindauer*
3. Bass Point Mound Room Feature Descriptions, *Owen Lindauer*
4. Non-room Features at Bass Point Mound, U:8:23/177, *Owen Lindauer*
5. Bass Point Mound Chronology, *Owen Lindauer and Peter H. McCartney*

Roosevelt Monograph Series **4,** *Anthropological Field Studies* **33** (*continued*)

6. Bass Point Mound Architecture, *Owen Lindauer*
7. Three Small Sites in the Rock Island Area: U:8:391/970, U:8:400/863, and the North Locus of U:8:23/177
     David F. Jacobs
8. Petroglyphs, Grinding Slicks, and Cupules of the Rock Island Complex, *Chris Loendorf, David F. Jacobs, and Glen E. Rice*
9. Plain, Red, and Other Ceramic Wares from the Rock Island Complex, *Owen Lindauer and Arleyn W. Simon*
10. Flaked- and Carved-stone Assemblages of the Rock Island Complex
     Glen E. Rice, Peter H. McCartney, and Arleyn W. Simon
11. Ground-stone Artifacts from the Rock Island Complex, *Peter H. McCartney and Arleyn W. Simon*
12. Special Artifacts and Evidence for the Differentiation of Residential and Ritual Rooms at the Bass Point Mound
     Glen E. Rice
13. Shell Artifacts from the Bass Point Mound, U:8:23/177, *Peter H. McCartney*
14. Plant Remains from Bass Point Mound, a Classic Period Site in the Tonto Basin, *J. Phil Dering*
15. Pollen Results from Bass Point Mound, U:8:23/177, *Suzanne K. Fish*
16. Faunal Remains from Bass Point Mound, U:8:23/177, *Judi L. Cameron*
17. Burial Features at the Bass Point Mound, U:8:23/177, *Chris Loendorf, Owen Lindauer, and John C. Ravesloot*
18. Physical Anthropology of the Rock Island Complex, Roosevelt Platform Mound Study
     Marcia H. Regan, Joel D. Irish, and Christy G. Turner II
19. Understanding the Salado through Work at Bass Point Mound, U:8:23/177, *Owen Lindauer*
Data Appendix
References Cited
Concordance of Sites

Roosevelt Monograph Series **5,** *Anthropological Field Studies* **34**

Oliver, Theodore J.
1994   Classic Period Settlement in the Uplands of the Tonto Basin, Report on the Uplands Complex: Roosevelt Platform
          Mound Study (1994 Draft). *Roosevelt Monograph Series* 5, *Anthropological Field Studies* 34. Tempe: Office of
          Cultural Resource Management, Arizona State University.

Preface: The Roosevelt Platform Mound Study, *Theodore J. Oliver and Glen E. Rice*
1. Introduction to the Uplands Complex, *Theodore J. Oliver and Peter H. McCartney*
2. The Research Setting of the Uplands Complex, *Theodore J. Oliver*
3. Chronology of Sites in the Uplands Complex, *Theodore J. Oliver and Peter H. McCartney*
4. Investigations at Sites in Unit 3, *Theodore J. Oliver*
5. Investigations at Sites in Unit 11, *Theodore J. Oliver*
6. Investigations at Sites in Unit 22, *Theodore J. Oliver*
7. Investigations at Compounds and Small Sites in Unit 27, *Theodore J. Oliver*
8. U:8:530/106, A Gila Phase Platform Mound Site in Unit 27, *Theodore J. Oliver*
9. A Supplemental Survey near Armer Wash, *Theodore J. Oliver*
10. Analysis of Ceramic Assemblages from Sites in the Uplands Complex, *Arleyn W. Simon and Owen Lindauer*
11. Flaked- and Carved-stone Assemblages from Sites in the Uplands Complex, *Glen E. Rice and Arleyn W. Simon*
12. Ground-stone Artifacts from Sites in the Uplands Complex, *Peter H. McCartney and Arleyn W. Simon*
13. Shell and Special Artifacts from Sites in the Upland Complex, *Glen E. Rice and Ronna J. Bradley*
14. Pollen Results from Sites in the Uplands Complex, *Suzanne K. Fish*
15. Plant Remains from the Upland Sites, Roosevelt Platform Mound Study, *J. Phil Dering*
16. Archaeofaunal Remains from the Uplands Complex, *Judi L. Cameron*
17. Classic Period Subsistence and Settlement in the Uplands of Tonto Basin, *Theodore J. Oliver*
Data Appendix
References Cited
Concordance of Sites

Roosevelt Monograph Series **6,** *Anthropological Field Studies* **35**

Lindauer, Owen
   1996   The Place of the Storehouses: Roosevelt Platform Mound Study, Report on the Schoolhouse Point Mound, Pinto Creek

Roosevelt Monograph Series 6, Anthropological Field Studies 35 (*continued*)

Complex. *Roosevelt Monograph Series 6, Anthropological Field Studies* 35. Tempe: Office of Cultural Resource Management, Arizona State University.

PART 1, bound separately
1. The History and Setting of the Schoolhouse Point Mound, U:8:24/13a, *Owen Lindauer*
2. Investigations at Schoolhouse Point Mound, U:8:24/13a, *Owen Lindauer*
3. Room Feature Descriptions at the Schoolhouse Point Mound, U:8:24/13a, *Owen Lindauer*
4. Midden and Plaza Descriptions, Schoolhouse Point Mound, U:8:24/13a, *Owen Lindauer*
5. Room and Platform Mound Architecture at Schoolhouse Point Mound, U:8:24/13a, *Owen Lindauer*
6. The Developmental Sequence and Site Chronology of Schoolhouse Point Mound, U:8:24/13a
    Peter H. McCartney and Owen Lindauer

PART 2, bound separately
7. Plain, Red, and Other Ceramic Wares from the Schoolhouse Point Mound, U:8:24/13a, *Arleyn W. Simon*
8. Flaked- and Carved-stone Artifacts from Schoolhouse Point Mound, U:8:24/13a, *Glen E. Rice and Arleyn W. Simon*
9. Ground-stone Artifacts from the Schoolhouse Point Mound, U:8:24/13a, *Arleyn W. Simon and Glen E. Rice*
10. Shell Artifacts from the Schoolhouse Point Mound, U:8:24/13a, *Ronna J. Bradley and Glen E. Rice*
11. The Distribution of Special Artifacts at Schoolhouse Point Mound, U:8:24/13a, *Glen E. Rice*
12. Plant Remains from the Schoolhouse Point Mound, U:8:24/13a, *J. Phil Dering*
13. Pollen Results from Schoolhouse Point Mound, U:8:24/13a, *Suzanne K. Fish*
14. Faunal Remains from the Schoolhouse Point Mound, U:8:24/13a, *Judi L. Cameron*
15. Burial Practices at the Schoolhouse Point Mound, U:8:24/13a, *Chris Loendorf*
16. Painted Wooden Artifacts from Burials at Schoolhouse Point Mound, U:8:24/13a, *Chris Loendorf*
17. Quantitative Analysis of the Burial Assemblage from Schoolhouse Point Mound, U:8:24/13a, *Chris Loendorf*
18. Physical Anthropology of the Schoolhouse Point Mound, U:8:24/13a
    Marcia H. Regan, Christy G. Turner II, and Joel D. Irish
19. Understanding the Salado through Work at the Schoolhouse Point Mound, U:8:24/13a, *Owen Lindauer*
Data Appendix Tables
References Cited
Profile Appendix
Concordance of Sites

Roosevelt Monograph Series 7, Anthropological Field Studies 36

Jacobs, David F.
1997   A Salado Platform Mound on Tonto Creek: Roosevelt Platform Mound Study, Report on the Cline Terrace Mound, Cline Terrace Complex. *Roosevelt Monograph Series 7, Anthropological Field Studies* 36. Tempe: Office of Cultural Resource Management, Arizona State University.

Preface: The Roosevelt Platform Mound Study, *Owen Lindauer, Glen E. Rice, and David F. Jacobs*
1. U:4:33/132, The Cline Terrace Mound, *David F. Jacobs*
2. U:4:33/132, Setting and Archaeological Investigations, *David F. Jacobs*
3. Elevated Features at U:4:33/132, The Cline Terrace Mound, *David F. Jacobs*
4. Ground-level Features at U:4:33/132, The Cline Terrace Mound, *David F. Jacobs*
5. Features Outside the Compound Wall at U:4:33/132, The Cline Terrace Mound, *David F. Jacobs*
6. Architecture and Construction Chronology of U:4:33/132, The Cline Terrace Mound, *David F. Jacobs*
7. Chronological Studies at U:4:33/132, The Cline Terrace Mound, *Peter H. McCartney*
8. Plain, Red, and Decorated Ceramics at U:4:33/132, The Cline Terrace Mound, *Arleyn W. Simon*
9. Flaked- and Carved-stone Assemblages from U:4:33/132, The Cline Terrace Mound, *Theodore J. Oliver*
10. Ground-stone Artifacts from U:4:33/132, The Cline Terrace Mound, *Sheldon T. Watson*
11. Special Artifacts as a Measure of Room Function at U:4:33/132, The Cline Terrace Mound
    Glen E. Rice and David F. Jacobs
12. Shell Artifacts from U:4:33/132, The Cline Terrace Mound, *Ronna J. Bradley and Glen E. Rice*
13. Burial Practices at U:4:33/132, The Cline Terrace Mound, *Chris Loendorf*

Roosevelt Monograph Series 7, *Anthropological Field Studies* 36 (*continued*)

14. Physical Anthropology and Human Taphonomy of U:4:33/132, The Cline Terrace Mound
       Christy G. Turner II and Marcia H. Regan
15. Plant Remains from U:4:33/132, The Cline Terrace Mound, *J. Phil Dering*
16. Pollen Results from U:4:33/132, The Cline Terrace Mound, *Suzanne K. Fish*
17. Faunal Remains from U:4:33/132, The Cline Terrace Mound, *Judi L. Cameron*
18. The Function of U:4:33/132, The Cline Terrace Mound, *David F. Jacobs and Glen E. Rice*
Data Appendix Tables
References Cited
Concordance of Sites

Roosevelt Monograph Series 8, *Anthropological Field Studies* 37

Lindauer, Owen
   1997   The Archaeology of Schoolhouse Point Mesa: Roosevelt Platform Mound Study, Report on the Schoolhouse Point
            Mesa Sites, Schoolhouse Management Group, Pinto Creek Complex. *Roosevelt Monograph Series* 8, *Anthropological
            Field Studies* 37. Tempe: Office of Cultural Resource Management, Arizona State University.

Preface: The Roosevelt Platform Mound Study, *Owen Lindauer and Glen E. Rice*
   1. Introduction to the Schoolhouse Point Mesa, *Owen Lindauer*
   2. Schoolhouse Management Group Investigations, *Owen Lindauer*
   3. Chronology of Sites on Schoolhouse Point Mesa, *Peter H. McCartney and Owen Lindauer*
   4. Excavations on Upper Schoolhouse Point Mesa at U:8:25/14a and U:8:450/14b, *Owen Lindauer*
   5. Excavations on Upper Schoolhouse Point Mesa, *Owen Lindauer*
   6. Sample Excavations on Lower Schoolhouse Point Mesa, *Owen Lindauer*
   7. Sample Excavations of Four Sites West of Schoolhouse Point Mesa, *Owen Lindauer*
   8. Plain, Red, and Other Ceramic Wares from the Schoolhouse Point Mesa Sites, *Arleyn W. Simon*
   9. Flaked- and Carved-stone Assemblages from the Schoolhouse Point Mesa Sites, *Theodore J. Oliver and Arleyn W. Simon*
  10. Ground-stone Artifacts from the Schoolhouse Point Mesa Sites, *Sheldon T. Watson*
  11. Shell Artifacts from the Schoolhouse Point Mesa Sites, *Ronna J. Bradley*
  12. The Distribution of Special Artifacts at the Schoolhouse Mesa Sites, *Glen E. Rice*
  13. Pollen Results from the Schoolhouse Point Mesa Sites, *Suzanne K. Fish*
  14. Plant Remains from the Schoolhouse Point Mesa Sites, *J. Phil Dering*
  15. Faunal Remains from the Schoolhouse Point Mesa Sites, *Judi L. Cameron*
  16. Burial Practices at the Schoolhouse Point Mesa Sites, *Chris Loendorf*
  17. Physical Anthropology and Human Taphonomy of the Schoolhouse Point Mesa Sites
         Marcia H. Regan and Christy G. Turner II
  18. Understanding the Salado through Work at Schoolhouse Point Mesa, *Owen Lindauer*
References Cited
Concordance of Sites

Roosevelt Monograph Series 9, *Anthropological Field Studies* 38

Oliver, Theodore J., and David F. Jacobs
   1996   Salado Residential Settlements on Tonto Creek: Roosevelt Platform Mound Study, Report on the Cline Mesa Sites,
            Cline Terrace Complex (1996 Draft). *Roosevelt Monograph Series* 9, *Anthropological Field Studies* 38. Tempe: Office
            of Cultural Resource Management, Arizona State University.

PART 1, bound separately
Preface: The Roosevelt Platform Mound Study, *Owen Lindauer and Glen E. Rice*
   1. Introduction to the Cline Mesa Sites, *Theodore J. Oliver and David F. Jacobs*
   2. Chronology of the Cline Mesa Sites, *Peter H. McCartney*
   3. The Excavation of U:3:128/758, *David F. Jacobs*
   4. Intensively Sampled and Tested Sites in the Vicinity of Casa Bandolero, *David F. Jacobs*
   5. Intensively Sampled and Tested Sites in the Vicinity of U:4:33/132, The Cline Terrace Mound, *David F. Jacobs*
   6. The Excavation and Description of the Indian Point Community, *Theodore J. Oliver*

Roosevelt Monograph Series **9**, *Anthropological Field Studies* **38** (*continued*)

7. Architecture, Chronology, and Interpretation of the Indian Point Locality, *Theodore J. Oliver*
8. The Excavation and Description of U:4:9/295, A Multicomponent, Residential Site, *Theodore J. Oliver*
9. Intensively Sampled and Tested Sites near Indian Point, *Theodore J. Oliver*

PART 2, bound separately
10. Plain, Red, and Other Ceramic Wares from the Cline Mesa Sites, *Arleyn W. Simon*
11. Flaked- and Carved-stone Assemblages from the Cline Mesa Sites, *Chris Loendorf and Arleyn W. Simon*
12. Ground-stone Artifacts from the Cline Mesa Sites, *Sheldon T. Watson*
13. Shell Artifacts from the Cline Mesa Sites, *Ronna J. Bradley*
14. The Distribution of Special Artifacts at the Cline Mesa Sites, *Glen E. Rice*
15. Burial Practices at the Cline Mesa Sites, *Chris Loendorf*
16. Physical Anthropology of the Cline Mesa Sites, *Marcia H. Regan and Christy G. Turner II*
17. Pollen Results from the Cline Mesa Sites, *Suzanne K. Fish*
18. Plant Remains from the Cline Mesa Sites, *J. Phil Dering*
19. Faunal Remains from the Cline Mesa Sites, *Judi L. Cameron*
20. Historic Artifacts at U:3:131/761 and U:3:132/762, *Mark R. Hackbarth*
21. Changing Patterns of Settlement, Subsistence, and Society on Tonto Creek, *Theodore J. Oliver and David F. Jacobs*

Roosevelt Monograph Series **10**, *Anthropological Field Studies* **39**

Spielmann, Katherine (Editor)
   1996   Environment and Subsistence in the Classic Period Tonto Basin: Roosevelt Platform Mound Study (1996 Draft). *Roosevelt Monograph Series* 10, *Anthropological Field Studies* 39. Tempe: Office of Cultural Resource Management, Arizona State University.

Preface, *Katherine A. Spielmann*
1. Modern Vegetation of the Tonto Basin, *Marc Baker*
2. Geoarchaeological Investigations in the Tonto Basin, *Michael R. Waters*
3. Pollen Summary of the Roosevelt Platform Mound Study, *Suzanne K. Fish*
4. Macrobotanical Remains from Classic Period Farming Villages in the Tonto Basin, *J. Phil Dering*
5. Faunal Resource Use in the Prehistoric Tonto Basin, *Judi L. Cameron*
6. Diet and Subsistence in the Classic Period Tonto Basin, *Katherine A. Spielmann*

Roosevelt Monograph Series **11**, *Anthropological Field Studies* **40**

Simon, Arleyn W.
   1997   Salado Ceramics and Social Organization: Prehistoric Interaction in the Tonto Basin, Roosevelt Platform Mound Study (1997 Draft). *Roosevelt Monograph Series* 11, *Anthropological Field Studies* 40. Tempe: Office of Cultural Resource Management, Arizona State University.

Preface, *Arleyn W. Simon*
1. Salado Polychrome, Social Relationships, and Prehistoric Community, *Arleyn W. Simon*
2. Polychrome Systematics: Roosevelt Red Ware or Salado Polychromes, *Owen Lindauer*
3. Traditional and Nontraditional Pinto and Gila Polychrome, *Owen Lindauer*
4. Salado Decorated Ceramics: Paint, Pigment, and Style, *Arleyn W. Simon*
5. Ceramic Production and Exchange in the Tonto Basin: The Mineralogical Evidence
      Arleyn W. Simon, James H. Burton, and Jean-Christophe Komorowski
6. Ceramic Production and Exchange in the Tonto Basin: The Chemical Characterization Evidence, *Arleyn W. Simon*
7. Ceramic Burial Assemblages: Gender, Status, and Social Networks, *Arleyn W. Simon*

Roosevelt Monograph Series **12**, *Anthropological Field Studies* **41**

Rice, Glen E., and Charles L. Redman (Editors)
   1998   Platform Mound Communities of the Tonto Basin: Roosevelt Platform Mound Study. *Roosevelt Monograph Series* 12, *Anthropological Field Studies* 41. Tempe: Office of Cultural Resource Management, Arizona State University.
         In preparation.

References

Publications and reports sponsored by the Bureau of Reclamation in connection with the Roosevelt Lake Project are preceded by an asterisk (see also the Appendix). These References include citations in the text and and a few additional related sources from which information was summarized for the archaeological overview in Chapter 4.

Abbott, David R.

1994a   Synthesis and Conclusions. In "The Pueblo Grande Project, Vol. 3: Ceramics and the Production and Exchange of Pottery in the Central Phoenix Basin," edited by David R. Abbott, pp. 407–432. *Publications in Archaeology* 20. Phoenix: Soil Systems.

1994b   *Hohokam Social Structure and Irrigation Management: The Ceramic Evidence from the Central Phoenix Basin.* Doctoral dissertation, Arizona State University, Tempe. Ann Arbor: University Microfilms.

Abrams, Elliot M.

1989   Architecture and Energy: An Evolutionary Perspective. In *Archaeological Method and Theory*, Vol. 1, edited by Michael B. Schiffer, pp. 47–87. Tucson: University of Arizona Press.

1994   *How the Maya Built Their World: Energetics and Ancient Architecture.* Austin: University of Texas Press.

Adams, E. Charles

*1996   Salado: The View from the Colorado Plateau. Paper prepared for the advanced seminar "Prehistoric Salado Culture of the American Southwest," Amerind Foundation, Dragoon, Arizona. Revised for publication.

Adams, Robert McC.

1966   *The Evolution of Urban Society: Early Mesopotamia and Prehispanic Mexico.* Chicago: Aldine.

Adler, Michael A.

1989   Ritual Facilities and Social Integration in Nonranked Societies. In "The Architecture of Social Integration in Prehistoric Pueblos," edited by William D. Lipe and Michelle Hegmon, pp. 35–52. *Occasional Papers of the Crow Canyon Archaeological Center* 1. Cortez: Crow Canyon Archaeological Center.

1996   Land Tenure, Archaeology, and the Ancestral Pueblo Social Landscape. *Journal of Anthropological Archaeology* 15(4): 337–370.

Adler, Michael A., and Richard H. Wilshusen

1990   Large–Scale Integrative Facilities in Tribal Societies: Cross–Cultural and Southwestern U.S. Examples. *World Archaeology* 22(2): 133–146.

Ahlstrum, Richard V. N., Mark L. Chenault, and Kirk C. Anderson

1991   The Roosevelt Bajada Survey, Tonto Basin, Gila County, Arizona. *Archaeological Report* 91–24. Tucson: SWCA Environmental Consultants.

Akins, Nancy J.

1986   A Biocultural Approach to Human Burials from Chaco Canyon, New Mexico. *Reports of the Chaco Center* 9. Santa Fe: National Park Service.

Altschul, Jeffrey H., and Carla R. Van West

1992   Agricultural Productivity Estimates for the Tonto Basin, A.D. 740–1370. In "Proceedings of the Second Salado Conference, Globe, AZ 1992," edited by Richard C. Lange and Stephen Germick, pp. 172–182. *Arizona Archaeological Society Occasional Paper.* Phoenix: Arizona Archaeological Society.

Anderson, David G.

1994   *The Savannah River Chiefdoms: Political Change in the Late Prehistoric Southeast.* Tuscaloosa: University of Alabama Press.

1996   Fluctuations between Simple and Complex Chiefdoms: Cycling in the Late Prehistoric Southeast. In *Political Structure and Change in the Prehistoric Southeastern United States*, edited by John F. Scarry, pp. 231–252. Gainesville: University Press of Florida.

Bandelier, Adolph F.

1892   Final Report of Investigations Among the Indians of the Southwestern United States, Carried on Mainly in the Years From 1880 to 1885. Part II. *Papers of the Archaeological Institute of America,*

Bandelier, Adolph F. (*continued*)
   American Series 4. Cambridge: Cambridge University Press.

Bayman, James M.
   1992   Hohokam Craft Production and Platform Mound Community Organization in the Tucson Basin. Paper presented at the 3rd Annual Southwest Symposium, Tucson.
   1994   *Craft Production and Political Economy at the Marana Platform Mound Community*. Doctoral dissertation, Arizona State University, Tempe. Ann Arbor: University Microfilms.

Bennett, Wendell C.
   1949   Habitations. In "Handbook of South American Indians," Vol. 5, edited by Julian H. Steward, pp. 1–20. *Bureau of American Ethnology Bulletin* 143. Washington: Smithsonian Institution.

Blanton, Richard E., Gary M. Feinman, Stephen A. Kowalewski, and Peter N. Peregrine
   1996   A Dual-Processual Theory for the Evolution of Mesoamerican Civilization. *Current Anthropology* 37(1): 1–14.

Blanton, Richard E., Stephen A. Kowalewski, Gary Feinman, and Jill Appel
   1981   *Ancient Mesoamerica: A Comparison of Change in Three Regions*. Cambridge: Cambridge University Press.

Blitz, John H.
   1993   *Ancient Chiefdoms of the Tombigbee*. Tuscaloosa: University of Alabama Press.

Bostwick, Todd W., and Christian E. Downum (Editors)
   1994   Archaeology of the Pueblo Grande Platform Mound and Surrounding Features, Vol. 2: Features in the Central Precinct of the Pueblo Grande Community. *Anthropological Papers* 1. Phoenix: Pueblo Grande Museum.

Bourke, John G.
   1891   *On the Border with Crook*. New York: Charles Scribner.

Brandt, Elizabeth A.
   1994   Egalitarianism, Hierarchy, and Centralization in the Pueblos. In *The Ancient Southwestern Community*, edited by W. H. Wills and Robert D. Leonard, pp. 9–23. Albuquerque: University of New Mexico Press.

Brown, David E. (Editor)
   1982   Biotic Communities of the American Southwest–United States and Mexico. *Desert Plants* 4(1–4).

Brumfiel, Elizabeth M.
   1992   Distinguished Lecture in Archeology: Breaking and Entering the Ecosystem—Gender, Class, and Faction Steal the Show. *American Anthropologist* 94(3): 551–567.

Buck, Peter H.
   1930   Samoan Material Culture. *Bernice P. Bishop Museum Bulletin* 75. Honolulu: Bernice P. Bishop Museum.

Burrows, Edwin G., and Melford E. Spiro
   1953   An Atoll Culture, Ethnography of Ifaluk in the Central Carolines. *Behavior Science Monographs*. New Haven: Human Relations Area Files.

Cameron, Catherine M.
   1990   The Effect of Varying Estimates of Pit Structure Use-life on Prehistoric Population Estimates in the American Southwest. *Kiva* 55(2): 155–166.
   1995   (Editor) Migration and the Movement of Southwestern Peoples. *Journal of Anthropological Archaeology* 14(2).

Castetter, Edward F., and Willis H. Bell
   1942   *Pima and Papago Indian Agriculture*. Albuquerque: University of New Mexico Press.

Chisholm, Michael
   1979   *Rural Settlement and Land Use: An Essay on Location*. 3rd ed. New York: John Wiley and Sons.

Christenson, Andrew L.
   *1995   Non–Buffware Decorated Ceramics and Mean Ceramic Dating. In "The Roosevelt Community Development Study, Vol. 2: Ceramic Chronology, Technology, and Economics," edited by James M. Heidke and Miriam T. Stark, pp. 85–132. *Anthropological Papers* 14. Tucson: Center for Desert Archaeology.

Chronic, Halka
   1983   *Roadside Geology of Arizona*. Missoula, Montana: Mountain Press Publishing.

Ciolek-Torrello, Richard S.
   1987   Archaeology of the Mazatzal Piedmont, Central Arizona, 2 vols. *Research Paper* 33. Flagstaff: Museum of Northern Arizona.
   1988   Conclusions. In "Hohokam Settlement along the Slopes of the Picacho Mountains, Tucson Aqueduct Project, Vol. 6: Synthesis and Conclusions," edited by Richard S. Ciolek-Torrello and David R. Wilcox, pp. 300–314. *Research Paper* 35. Flagstaff: Museum of Northern Arizona.
   1997   Prehistoric Settlement and Demography in the Lower Verde Region. In *Vanishing River: Landscapes and Lives of the Lower Verde Valley: The Lower Verde Archaeological Project*, edited by Stephanie M. Whittlesey, Richard S. Ciolek-Torrello, and Jeffrey H. Altschul, pp. 531–595. Tucson: SRI Press.

Ciolek-Torrello, Richard S., and Stephanie M. Whittlesey
   *1994   Summary and Conclusions. In "The Roosevelt Rural Sites Study, Vol. 3: Changing Land Use in the Tonto Basin," edited by Richard S. Ciolek-Torrello and John R. Welch, pp. 473–492. *Technical Series* 28. Tucson: Statistical Research.

Ciolek-Torrello, Richard S., and David R. Wilcox (Editors)

1988 Hohokam Settlement along the Slopes of the Picacho Mountains, Tucson Aqueduct Project, Vol. 6: Synthesis and Conclusions. *Research Paper* 35. Flagstaff: Museum of Northern Arizona.

Ciolek-Torrello, Richard S., Martha M. Callahan, and David H. Greenwald (Editors)

1988 Hohokam Settlement along the Slopes of the Picacho Mountains, Tucson Aqueduct Project, Vol. 2: The Brady Wash Sites. *Research Paper* 35. Flagstaff: Museum of Northern Arizona.

Ciolek-Torrello, Richard S., Stephanie M. Whittlesey, and John R. Welch

*1994 A Synthetic Model of Prehistoric Land Use. In "The Roosevelt Rural Sites Study, Vol. 3: Changing Land Use in the Tonto Basin," edited by Richard S. Ciolek-Torrello and John R. Welch, pp. 437–472. *Technical Series* 28. Tucson: Statistical Research.

Clark, Jeffery J.

*1995a Domestic Architecture in the Early Classic Period. In "The Roosevelt Community Development Study: New Perspectives on Tonto Basin Prehistory," edited by Mark D. Elson, Miriam T. Stark, and David A. Gregory, pp. 251–305. *Anthropological Papers* 15. Tucson: Center for Desert Archaeology.

*1995b The Role of Migration in Social Change. In "The Roosevelt Community Development Study: New Perspectives on Tonto Basin Prehistory," edited by Mark D. Elson, Miriam T. Stark, and David A. Gregory, pp. 369–384. *Anthropological Papers* 15. Tucson: Center for Desert Archaeology.

*1997 *Migration and Integration: The Classic Period Salado in the Tonto Basin*. Doctoral dissertation, University of Arizona, Tucson. Ann Arbor: University Microfilms.

Clark, John E., and Michael Blake

1994 The Power of Prestige: Competitive Generosity and the Emergence of Rank Societies in Lowland Mesoamerica. In *Factional Competition and Political Development in the New World*, edited by Elizabeth M. Brumfiel and John W. Fox, pp. 17–30. Cambridge: Cambridge University Press.

Connelly, John C.

1979 Hopi Social Organization. In *Handbook of North American Indians*, Vol. 9: *Southwest*, edited by Alfonso Ortiz, pp. 539–553. W. C. Sturtevant, general editor. Washington: Smithsonian Institution.

Cordell, Linda S., Steadman Upham, and Sharon L. Brock

1987 Obscuring Cultural Patterns in the Archaeological Record: A Discussion from Southwestern Archaeology. *American Antiquity* 52(3): 565–577.

Craig, Douglas B.

1992 Rye Creek Ruin. In "The Rye Creek Project: Archaeology in the Upper Tonto Basin, Vol. 3: Synthesis and Conclusions," by Mark D. Elson and Douglas B. Craig, pp. 107–117. *Anthropological Papers* 11. Tucson: Center For Desert Archaeology.

*1995 The Social Consequences of Irrigation Agriculture: A Perspective from Meddler Point. In "The Roosevelt Community Development Study: New Perspectives on Tonto Basin Prehistory," edited by Mark D. Elson, Miriam T. Stark, and David A. Gregory, pp. 227–249. *Anthropological Papers* 15. Tucson: Center for Desert Archaeology.

Craig, Douglas B., and Jeffery J. Clark

*1994 The Meddler Point Site, AZ V:5:4/26 (ASM/ TNF). In "The Roosevelt Community Development Study, Vol. 2: Meddler Point, Pyramid Point, and Griffin Wash Sites," by Mark D. Elson, Deborah L. Swartz, Douglas B. Craig, and Jeffery J. Clark, pp. 1–198. *Anthropological Papers* 13. Tucson: Center for Desert Archaeology.

Craig, Douglas B., Mark D. Elson, and J. Scott Wood

*1992 The Growth and Development of a Platform Mound Community in the Eastern Tonto Basin. In "Proceedings of the Second Salado Conference, Globe, AZ 1992," edited by Richard C. Lange and Stephen Germick, pp. 22–30. *Arizona Archaeological Society Occasional Paper*. Phoenix: Arizona Archaeological Society.

Crary, Joseph S., Stephen Germick, and Michael Golio

1992 Las Sierras and Los Alamos: A Comparative Study of Classic Period Upland and Riverine Community Patterns in the Tonto-Globe Region of Central Arizona. In "Proceedings of the Second Salado Conference, Globe, AZ 1992," edited by Richard C. Lange and Stephen Germick, pp. 149–160. *Arizona Archaeological Society Occasional Paper*. Phoenix: Arizona Archaeological Society.

Crown, Patricia L.

1987 Classic Period Hohokam Settlement and Land Use in the Casa Grande Ruins Area, Arizona. *Journal of Field Archaeology* 14(2): 147–162.

1994 *Ceramics and Ideology: Salado Polychrome Pottery*. Albuquerque: University of New Mexico Press.

Cushing, Frank Hamilton

1892 The Hemenway Southwestern Archaeological Expedition. MS on file, Peabody Museum, Harvard University, Cambridge.

Dean, Jeffrey S.

1988 A Model of Anasazi Behavioral Adaptation. In *The Anasazi in a Changing Environment*, edited by George J. Gumerman, pp. 25–44. Cambridge: Cambridge University Press.

Dean, Jeffrey S. (*continued*)

1996   Demography, Environment, and Subsistence Stress. In *Evolving Complexity and Environmental Risk in the Prehistoric Southwest*, edited by J. A. Tainter and B. B. Tainter, pp. 25–56. Reading, Massachusetts: Addison–Wesley.

*1998   (Editor) Prehistoric Salado Culture of the American Southwest. *Amerind Foundation New World Studies Series*. Albuquerque: University of New Mexico Press. In preparation.

Dean, Jeffrey S., and Gary S. Funkhouser

1995   Dendroclimatic Reconstructions for the Southern Colorado Plateau. In *Climate Change in the Four Corners and Adjacent Regions: Implications for Environmental Restoration and Land–Use Planning*, edited by W. J. Waugh, pp. 85–104. Grand Junction, Colorado: U.S. Department of Energy, Grand Junction Projects Office.

Dean, Jeffrey S., William H. Doelle, and Janet D. Orcutt

1994   Adaptive Stress, Environment, and Demography. In *Themes in Southwest Prehistory*, edited by George J. Gumerman, pp. 53–86. Santa Fe: School of American Research Press.

Dean, Jeffrey S., Robert C. Euler, George J. Gumerman, Fred Plog, Richard H. Hevly, and Thor N. V. Karlstrom

1985   Human Behavior, Demography, and Paleoenvironment on the Colorado Plateaus. *American Antiquity* 50(3): 537–554.

Debo, Angie

1934   *The Rise and Fall of the Choctaw Republic.* Norman: University of Oklahoma Press.

DePratter, Chester B.

1994   The Chiefdom of Cofitachequi. In *The Forgotten Centuries, Indians and Europeans in the American South, 1521–1704*, edited by Charles Hudson and Carmen C. Tesser, pp. 197–227. Athens: University of Georgia Press.

Dillehay, Tom D.

1990   Mapuche Ceremonial Landscape, Social Recruitment and Resource Rights. *World Archaeology* 22(2): 223–241.

1992   Keeping Outsiders Out: Public Ceremony, Resource Rights, and Hierarchy in Contemporary Mapuche Society. In *Wealth and Hierarchy in the Intermediate Area*, edited by Frederick W. Lange, pp. 379–422. Washington: Dumbarton Oaks.

Doelle, William H.

1985   Excavations at the Valencia Site, a Preclassic Hohokam Village in the Southern Tucson Basin. *Anthropological Papers* 3. Tucson: Institute for American Research.

*1995a   Regional Platform Mound Systems: Background and Inventory. Appendix F in "The Roosevelt Community Development Study: New Perspectives on Tonto Basin Prehistory," edited by Mark

D. Elson, Miriam T. Stark, and David A. Gregory, pp. 555–560. *Anthropological Papers* 15. Tucson: Center for Desert Archaeology.

*1995b   Tonto Basin Demography in a Regional Perspective. In "The Roosevelt Community Development Study: New Perspectives on Tonto Basin Prehistory," edited by Mark D. Elson, Miriam T. Stark, and David A. Gregory, pp. 201–226. *Anthropological Papers* 15. Tucson: Center for Desert Archaeology.

Doelle, William H., and Henry D. Wallace

1986   Hohokam Settlement Patterns in the San Xavier Project Area, Southern Tucson Basin. *Technical Report* 84-6. Tucson: Institute for American Research.

1991   The Changing Role of the Tucson Basin in the Hohokam Regional System. In "Exploring the Hohokam: Prehistoric Desert Peoples of the American Southwest," edited by George J. Gumerman, pp. 279–345. *Amerind Foundation New World Studies Series* 1. Albuquerque: University of New Mexico Press.

1997   A Classic Period Platform Mound System on the Lower San Pedro River, Southern Arizona. In "Prehistory of the Borderlands, Recent Research in the Archaeology of Northern Mexico and the Southern Southwest," edited by John Carpenter and Guadalupe Sanchez, pp. 71–84. *Arizona State Museum Archaeological Series* 186. Tucson: Arizona State Museum, University of Arizona.

Doelle, William H., David A. Gregory, and Henry D. Wallace

*1995   Classic Period Platform Mound Systems in Southern Arizona. In "The Roosevelt Community Development Study: New Perspectives on Tonto Basin Prehistory," edited by Mark D. Elson, Miriam T. Stark, and David A. Gregory, pp. 385–440. *Anthropological Papers* 15. Tucson: Center for Desert Archaeology.

Downum, Christian E.

1986   The Occupational Use of Hill Space in the Tucson Basin: Evidence from Linda Vista Hill. *The Kiva* 51(4): 219–232.

1993   Between Desert and River: Hohokam Settlement and Land Use in the Los Robles Community. *Anthropological Papers of the University of Arizona* 57. Tucson: University of Arizona Press.

Downum, Christian E., and Todd W. Bostwick

1993   Archaeology of the Pueblo Grande Platform Mound and Surrounding Features, Vol. 1: Introduction to the Archival Project and History of Archaeological Research. *Anthropological Papers* 1. Phoenix: Pueblo Grande Museum.

Doyel, David E.

1974   Excavations in the Escalante Ruin Group, Southern Arizona. *Arizona State Museum Archaeological Series* 37. Tucson: Arizona State Museum, University of Arizona.

1976 Salado Cultural Development in the Tonto Basin and Globe–Miami Areas, Central Arizona. *The Kiva* 42(1): 5–16.

1978 The Miami Wash Project: Hohokam and Salado in the Globe–Miami Area, Central Arizona. *Contribution to Highway Salvage Archaeology in Arizona* 52. Tucson: Arizona State Museum, University of Arizona.

1979 The Prehistoric Hohokam of the Arizona Desert. *American Scientist* 67(5): 544–554.

1980 Hohokam Social Organization and the Sedentary to Classic Transition. In "Current Issues in Hohokam Prehistory: Proceedings of a Symposium," edited by David E. Doyel and Fred Plog, pp. 23–40. *Anthropological Research Papers* 23. Tempe: Arizona State University.

1981 Late Hohokam Prehistory in Southern Arizona. *Contributions to Archaeology* 2. Scottsdale: Gila Press.

Doyel, David E., and Mark D. Elson (Editors)
1985 Hohokam Settlement and Economic Systems in the Central New River Drainage, Arizona. *Publications in Archaeology* 4. Phoenix: Soil Systems.

Dozier, Edward P.
1966 *Hano: A Tewa Indian Community in Arizona*. New York: Holt, Rinehart, and Winston.

Drennan, Robert D., and Carlos A. Uribe (Editors)
1987 *Chiefdoms in the Americas*. Lanham, Maryland: University Press of America.

Eighmy, Jeffrey L., and David E. Doyel
1987 A Reanalysis of First Reported Archaeomagnetic Dates from the Hohokam Area, Southern Arizona. *Journal of Field Archaeology* 14: 331–342.

Elson, Mark D.
1986 Archaeological Investigations at the Tanque Verde Wash Site, a Middle Rincon Settlement in the Eastern Tucson Basin. *Anthropological Papers* 7. Tucson: Institute for American Research.

1992a Settlement, Subsistence, and Cultural Affiliation within the Upper Tonto Basin. In "The Rye Creek Project: Archaeology in the Upper Tonto Basin, Vol. 3: Synthesis and Conclusions," by Mark D. Elson and Douglas B. Craig, pp. 119–153. *Anthropological Papers* 11. Tucson: Center for Desert Archaeology.

1992b Temporal Issues in Tonto Basin Prehistory: The Rye Creek Chronology. In "The Rye Creek Project: Archaeology in the Upper Tonto Basin, Vol. 3: Synthesis and Conclusions," by Mark D. Elson and Douglas B. Craig, pp. 55–77. *Anthropological Papers* 11. Tucson: Center for Desert Archaeology.

*1994 The Pyramid Point Site, AZ V:5:1/25 (ASM/TNF). In "The Roosevelt Community Development Study, Vol. 2: Meddler Point, Pyramid Point, and Griffin Wash Sites," by Mark D. Elson, Deborah L. Swartz, Douglas B. Craig, and Jeffery J. Clark, pp. 199–295. *Anthropological Papers* 13. Tucson: Center for Desert Archaeology.

*1995 Assessment of Chronometric Methods and Dates. In "The Roosevelt Community Development Study: New Perspectives on Tonto Basin Prehistory," edited by Mark D. Elson, Miriam T. Stark, and David A. Gregory, pp. 39–60. *Anthropological Papers* 15. Tucson: Center for Desert Archaeology.

*1996a *An Ethnographic Perspective on Prehistoric Platform Mounds of the Tonto Basin, Central Arizona*. Doctoral dissertation, University of Arizona, Tucson. Ann Arbor: University Microfilms.

*1996b A Revised Chronology and Phase Sequence for the Lower Tonto Basin of Central Arizona. *Kiva* 62(2): 117–147.

Elson, Mark D., and Jeffery J. Clark (Editors)
*1995a The Roosevelt Community Development Study, Vol 1: Stone and Shell Artifacts. *Anthropological Papers* 14. Tucson: Center for Desert Archaeology.

*1995b The Roosevelt Community Development Study, Vol. 3: Paleobotanical and Osteological Analyses. *Anthropological Papers* 14. Tucson: Center for Desert Archaeology.

Elson, Mark D., and Douglas B. Craig
1992 The Rye Creek Project: Archaeology in the Upper Tonto Basin, 3 vols. *Anthropological Papers* 11. Tucson: Center for Desert Archaeology.

*1994 Project Methods. In "The Roosevelt Community Development Study, Vol. 1: Introduction and Small Sites," by Mark D. Elson and Deborah L. Swartz, pp. 13–21. *Anthropological Papers* 13. Tucson: Center for Desert Archaeology.

Elson, Mark D., and Michael Lindeman
*1994 The Eagle Ridge Site, AZ V:5:104/1045 (ASM/TNF). In "The Roosevelt Community Development Study, Vol. 1: Introduction and Small Sites," by Mark D. Elson and Deborah L. Swartz, pp. 23–116. *Anthropological Papers* 13. Tucson: Center for Desert Archaeology.

Elson, Mark D., and Alan P. Sullivan III
1981 Archaeology on the Eastern Mazatzal Piedmont. A Research Design for the Investigation of 25 Archaeological Sites Associated with Arizona Department of Transportation Project F–053–1–511 (SR 87 from Ord Mine Road to SR 188), Tonto National Forest, Gila County, Arizona. MS on file, Arizona State Museum, University of Arizona, Tucson.

Elson, Mark D., and Deborah L. Swartz
*1994   The Roosevelt Community Development Study, Vol. 1: Introduction and Small Sites. *Anthropological Papers* 13. Tucson: Center for Desert Archaeology.

Elson, Mark D., David A. Gregory, and Miriam T. Stark
*1995   New Perspectives on Tonto Basin Prehistory. In "The Roosevelt Community Development Study: New Perspectives on Tonto Basin Prehistory," edited by Mark D. Elson, Miriam T. Stark, and David A. Gregory, pp. 441–479. *Anthropological Papers* 15. Tucson: Center for Desert Archaeology.

Elson, Mark D., Miriam T. Stark, and David A. Gregory
*1995   (Editors) The Roosevelt Community Development Study: New Perspectives on Tonto Basin Prehistory. *Anthropological Papers* 15. Tucson: Center for Desert Archaeology.
*1996   Tonto Basin Local Systems: Implications for Cultural Affiliation and Migration. Paper prepared for the advanced seminar "Prehistoric Salado Culture of the American Southwest," Amerind Foundation, Dragoon, Arizona. Revised for publication.

Elson, Mark D., Miriam T. Stark, and James M. Heidke
*1992   Prelude to Salado: Preclassic Period Settlement in the Upper Tonto Basin. In "Proceedings of the Second Salado Conference, Globe, AZ 1992," edited by Richard C. Lange and Stephen Germick, pp. 274–285. *Arizona Archaeological Society Occasional Paper*. Phoenix: Arizona Archaeological Society.

Elson, Mark D., Deborah L. Swartz, Douglas B. Craig, and Jeffery J. Clark
*1994   The Roosevelt Community Development Study, Vol. 2: Meddler Point, Pyramid Point, and Griffin Wash Sites. *Anthropological Papers* 13. Tucson: Center for Desert Archaeology.

Erasmus, Charles J.
1965   Monument Building: Some Field Experiments. *Southwestern Journal of Anthropology* 21(4): 277–301.

Euler, Robert C., George J. Gumerman, Thor N. V. Karlstrom, Jeffrey S. Dean, and Richard H. Hevly
1979   The Colorado Plateaus: Cultural Dynamics and Paleoenvironment. *Science* 205: 1089–1101.

Faron, Louis C.
1986   *The Mapuche Indians of Chile*. Prospect Heights, Illinois: Waveland Press.

Feinman, Gary M.
1992   An Outside Perspective on Chaco Canyon. In "Anasazi Regional Organization and the Chaco System," edited by David E. Doyel, pp. 177–182. *Anthropological Papers* 5. Albuquerque: Maxwell Museum of Anthropology.
1994   Boundaries and Social Organization: An Outside View on Debate in the Ancient American Southwest. In *The Ancient Southwestern Community*, edited by W. H. Wills and Robert D. Leonard, pp. 241–247. Albuquerque: University of New Mexico Press.
1995   The Emergence of Inequality. In *Foundations of Social Inequality*, edited by T. Douglas Price and Gary M. Feinman, pp. 255–279. New York: Plenum Press.

Feinman, Gary M., and Jill Neitzel
1984   Too Many Types: An Overview of Sedentary Prestate Societies in the Americas. In *Advances in Archaeological Method and Theory*, Vol. 7, edited by Michael B. Schiffer, pp. 39–102. New York: Academic Press.

Ferdon, Edwin N., Jr.
1987   *Early Tonga, as the Explorers Saw It, 1616–1810*. Tucson: University of Arizona Press.
1993   *Early Observations of Marquesan Culture, 1595–1813*. Tucson: University of Arizona Press.

Fewkes, Jesse Walter
1907   Excavations at Casa Grande, Arizona, in 1906–1907. *Smithsonian Miscellaneous Collections* 50(3): 289–329. Washington.
1912   Casa Grande, Arizona. *Twenty-eighth Annual Report of the Bureau of American Ethnology for the Years 1906–1907*, pp. 25–179. Washington.

Firth, Raymond
1957   *We, the Tikopia* (2nd edition). Boston: Beacon Press.

Fish, Paul R.
1989   The Hohokam: 1000 Years of Prehistory in the Sonoran Desert. In *Dynamics of Southwestern Prehistory*, edited by Linda S. Cordell and George J. Gumerman, pp. 19–63. Washington: Smithsonian Institution Press.

Fish, Paul R., Suzanne K. Fish, Curtiss Brennan, Douglas Gann, and James M. Bayman
1992   Marana: Configuration of an Early Classic Period Hohokam Platform Mound Site. In "Proceedings of the Second Salado Conference, Globe, AZ 1992," edited by Richard C. Lange and Stephen Germick, pp. 62–68. *Arizona Archaeological Society Occasional Paper*. Phoenix: Arizona Archaeological Society.

Fish, Suzanne K., and Paul R. Fish
1992   The Marana Community in Comparative Context. In "The Marana Community in the Hohokam World," edited by Suzanne K. Fish, Paul R. Fish, and John H. Madsen, pp. 97–105. *Anthropological Papers of the University of Arizona* 56. Tucson: University of Arizona Press.

Fish, Suzanne K., Paul R. Fish,
and John H. Madsen

1985   A Preliminary Analysis of Hohokam Settlement and Agriculture in the Northern Tucson Basin. In "Proceedings of the 1983 Hohokam Symposium," edited by Alfred E. Dittert, Jr., and Donald E. Dove, pp. 75–100. *Arizona Archaeological Society Occasional Paper* 2. Phoenix: Arizona Archaeological Society.

1989   Classic Period Hohokam Community Integration in the Tucson Basin. In *The Sociopolitical Structure of Prehistoric Southwestern Societies*," edited by Steadman Upham, Kent G. Lightfoot, and Roberta A. Jewett, pp. 237–268. Boulder: Westview Press.

1992   (Editors) The Marana Community in the Hohokam World. *Anthropological Papers of the University of Arizona* 56. Tucson: University of Arizona Press.

Flanagan, James G.

1989   Hierarchy in Simple "Egalitarian" Societies. *Annual Review of Anthropology* 18: 245–266.

Flannery, Kent V.

1972   The Cultural Evolution of Civilizations. *Annual Review of Ecology and Systematics* 3: 339–426.

Friedman, Jonathan, and M. J. Rowlands

1977   Notes toward an Epigenetic Model of the Evolution of "Civilization." In *The Evolution of Social Systems*, edited by Jonathan Friedman and M. J. Rowlands, pp. 201–276. London: Duckworth.

Fuller, Steven L., A. E. Rogge,
and Linda M. Gregonis

1976   The Archaeological Resources of Roosevelt Lake and Horseshoe Reservoir, 2 vols. *Arizona State Museum Archaeological Series* 98. Tucson: Arizona State Museum, University of Arizona.

Furness, William H.

1910   *The Island of Stone Money: Yap of the Carolines.* Philadelphia: J. B. Lippincott.

Gabel, Norman E.

1931   Martinez Hill Ruins: An Example of Prehistoric Culture of the Middle Gila. Master's thesis, Department of Anthropology, University of Arizona, Tucson.

Galloway, Patricia

1995   *Choctaw Genesis, 1500–1700.* Lincoln: University of Nebraska Press.

Gasser, Robert E.

1987   Vegetation. In "Archaeology of the Mazatzal Piedmont, Central Arizona," edited by Richard S. Ciolek-Torrello, pp. 18–26. *Research Paper* 33(1). Flagstaff: Museum of Northern Arizona.

Gasser, Robert E., and Richard S. Ciolek-Torrello

1988   Locus S. In "Hohokam Settlement along the Slopes of the Picacho Mountains, Vol. 2: The Brady Wash Sites, Tucson Aqueduct Project," edited by Richard S. Ciolek-Torrello, Martha M. Callahan, and David H. Greenwald, pp. 496–579. *Research Paper* 35. Flagstaff: Museum of Northern Arizona.

Germick, Stephen, and Joseph S. Crary

1989   Prehistoric Adaptations in the Bajada–Upland Areas of Tonto Basin: Examples from the A–Cross and Henderson Mesa Surveys. Paper presented at the 62nd Pecos Conference, Bandelier National Monument, New Mexico.

1992   From Shadow to Substance: An Alternative Perspective on the Roosevelt Phase. In "Proceedings of the Second Salado Conference, Globe, AZ 1992," edited by Richard C. Lange and Stephen Germick, pp. 286–303. *Arizona Archaeological Society Occasional Paper.* Phoenix: Arizona Archaeological Society.

Gifford, Edward W., and Delila S. Gifford

1959   Archaeological Excavations in Yap. *Anthropological Records* 18(2). Berkeley: University of California Press.

Gladwin, Harold S.

1957   *A History of the Ancient Southwest.* Portland, Maine: Bond–Wheelwright.

Gladwin, Winifred, and Harold S. Gladwin

1935   The Eastern Range of the Red-on-Buff Culture. *Medallion Papers* 16. Globe, Arizona: Gila Pueblo.

Goldman, Irving

1955   Status Rivalry and Cultural Evolution in Polynesia. *American Anthropologist* 57(4): 680–697.

Grattan, F. J. H.

1948   *An Introduction to Samoan Custom.* Apia, Western Samoa: Samoa Printing and Publishing.

Graves, Michael W., and Thegn N. Ladefoged

1995   The Evolutionary Significance of Ceremonial Architecture in Polynesia. In *Evolutionary Archaeology, Methodological Issues*, edited by Patrice A. Teltser, pp. 149–174. Tucson: University of Arizona Press.

Graves, Michael W., and Maria Sweeney

1993   Ritual Behavior and Ceremonial Structures in Eastern Polynesia: Changing Perspectives on Archaeological Variability. In "The Evolution and Organisation of Prehistoric Society in Polynesia," edited by Michael W. Graves and Roger C. Green, pp. 106–125. *New Zealand Archaeological Association Monograph* 19. Auckland: New Zealand Archaeological Association.

Gregory, David A.

1980   Research Design for Data Recovery at Fifteen Archaeological Sites, Arizona Department of Transportation Project S–456–201, Ash Creek to Roosevelt Dam Section, State Route 188, Roose-

Gregory, David A. (*continued*)
velt–Payson Highway, Tonto National Forest, Gila County, Arizona. MS on file, Arizona State Museum, University of Arizona, Tucson.

1987   The Morphology of Platform Mounds and the Structure of Classic Period Hohokam Sites. In *The Hohokam Village: Site Structure and Organization*, edited by David E. Doyel, pp. 183-210. Glenwood Springs, Colorado: American Association for the Advancement of Science, Southwestern and Rocky Mountain Division.

1988a   (Editor) The 1982–1984 Excavations at Las Colinas, Vol. 3: The Mound 8 Precinct. *Arizona State Museum Archaeological Series* 162. Tucson: Arizona State Museum, University of Arizona.

1988b   The Changing Spatial Structure of the Mound 8 Precinct. In "The 1982–1984 Excavations at Las Colinas, Vol. 3: The Mound 8 Precinct," edited by David A. Gregory, pp. 25–49. *Arizona State Museum Archaeological Series* 162. Tucson: Arizona State Museum, University of Arizona.

1991   Form and Variation in Hohokam Settlement Patterns. In *Chaco and Hohokam: Prehistoric Regional Systems in the American Southwest*, edited by Patricia L. Crown and W. James Judge, pp. 159–193. Santa Fe: School of American Research Press.

*1995   Prehistoric Settlement Patterns in the Eastern Tonto Basin. In "The Roosevelt Community Development Study: New Perspectives on Tonto Basin Prehistory," edited by Mark D. Elson, Miriam T. Stark, and David A. Gregory, pp. 127–184. *Anthropological Papers* 15. Tucson: Center for Desert Archaeology.

1996   A Cultural Resources Overview of the Rye Creek Geographic Study Area, Payson and Tonto Basin Ranger Districts, Tonto National Forest, Gila County, Arizona. *Technical Report* 95–10. Tucson: Center for Desert Archaeology.

Gregory, David A., and David R. Abbott
1988   Stages of Mound Construction and Architectural Details. In "The 1982–1984 Excavations at Las Colinas, Vol. 3: The Mound 8 Precinct," edited by David A. Gregory, pp. 9–24. *Arizona State Museum Archaeological Series* 162. Tucson: Arizona State Museum, University of Arizona.

Gregory, David A., and Gary Huckleberry
1994   An Archaeological Survey in the Blackwater Area, Vol. 1: The History of Human Settlement in the Blackwater Area. *Cultural Resources Report* 86. Tempe: Archaeological Consulting Services.

Gregory, David A., and Fred L. Nials
1985   Observations Concerning the Distribution of Classic Period Hohokam Platform Mounds. In "Proceedings of the 1983 Hohokam Symposium,"
edited by Alfred E. Dittert, Jr., and Donald E. Dove, pp. 373–388. *Arizona Archaeological Society Occasional Paper* 2. Phoenix: Arizona Archaeological Society.

Gregory, David A., Fred L. Nials, Patricia L. Crown, Lynn S. Teague, and David A. Phillips, Jr.
1985   The 1982–1984 Excavations at Las Colinas, Vol. 1: Research Design. *Arizona State Museum Archaeological Series* 162. Tucson: Arizona State Museum, University of Arizona.

Gumerman, George J.
1991   Understanding the Hohokam. In "Exploring the Hohokam: Prehistoric Desert Peoples of the American Southwest," edited by George J. Gumerman, pp. 1–27. *Amerind Foundation New World Studies Series* 1. Albuquerque: University of New Mexico Press.

Haas, Jonathan
1971   The Ushklish Ruin (Draft Final Report). MS on file, Arizona State Museum, University of Arizona, Tucson.

Hally, David J.
1994   The Chiefdom of Coosa. In *The Forgotten Centuries, Indians and Europeans in the American South, 1521–1704*, edited by Charles Hudson and Carmen C. Tesser, pp. 227–253. Athens: University of Georgia Press.

1996a   The Settlement Pattern of Mississippian Chiefdoms in Northern Georgia (Draft). Paper presented at the 61st Annual Meeting of the Society for American Archaeology, New Orleans.

1996b   Platform-Mound Construction and the Instability of Mississippian Chiefdoms. In *Political Structure and Change in the Prehistoric Southeastern United States*, edited by John F. Scarry, pp. 92–127. Gainesville: University Press of Florida.

Hammack, Laurens C.
1969   Highway Salvage Excavations in the Upper Tonto Basin, Arizona. *The Kiva* 34(2–3): 132–175.

Hammack, Laurens C., and Alan P. Sullivan (Editors)
1981   The 1968 Excavations at Mound 8, Las Colinas Ruins Group, Phoenix, Arizona. *Arizona State Museum Archaeological Series* 154. Tucson: Arizona State Museum, University of Arizona.

Handy, E. S. Craighill
1923   The Native Culture in the Marquesas. *Bernice P. Bishop Museum Bulletin* 9. Honolulu: Bernice P. Bishop Museum.

Hastorf, Christine A.
1990   One Path to the Heights: Negotiating Political Inequality in the Sausa of Peru. In *The Evolution of Political Systems: Sociopolitics in Small-Scale Sedentary Societies*, edited by Steadman Upham, pp. 146–176. Cambridge: Cambridge University Press.

Haury, Emil W.
1930   A Report on Excavations at the Rye Creek Ruin. MS on file, Tonto National Forest, Arizona.
1932   Roosevelt 9:6: A Hohokam Site of the Colonial Period. *Medallion Papers* 1. Globe, Arizona: Gila Pueblo.
1945   The Excavation of Los Muertos and Neighboring Ruins in the Salt River Valley, Southern Arizona. *Papers of the Peabody Museum of American Archaeology and Ethnology* 24(1). Cambridge: Harvard University.
1976   *The Hohokam: Desert Farmers and Craftsmen. Excavations at Snaketown, 1964-1965.* Tucson: University of Arizona Press.

Haury, Emil W., and E. B. Sayles
1947   An Early Pit House Village of the Mogollon Culture, Forestdale Valley, Arizona. *University of Arizona Bulletin* 18(4), *Social Science Bulletin* 16. Tucson: University of Arizona.

Hayden, Brian
1995   Pathways to Power: Principles for Creating Socioeconomic Inequalities. In *Foundations of Social Inequality*, edited by T. Douglas Price and Gary M. Feinman, pp. 15–86. New York: Plenum Press.

Hayden, Julian D.
1957   Excavations, 1940, at University Indian Ruin. *Southwestern Monuments Association Technical Series* 5. Globe, Arizona: Southwestern Monuments Association.

Heidke, James M.
*1995   Overview of the Ceramic Collection. In "The Roosevelt Community Development Study, Vol. 2: Ceramic Chronology, Technology, and Economics," edited by James M. Heidke and Miriam T. Stark, pp. 7–18. *Anthropological Papers* 14. Tucson: Center for Desert Archaeology.

Heidke, James M., and Miriam T. Stark (Editors)
*1995   The Roosevelt Community Development Study, Vol. 2: Ceramic Chronology, Technology, and Economics. *Anthropological Papers* 14. Tucson: Center for Desert Archaeology.

Henderson, T. Kathleen
1993   Perspectives on the Classic Period Occupation of the Santa Cruz Flats. In *Classic Period Occupation on the Santa Cruz Flats: The Santa Cruz Flats Archaeological Project*, edited by T. Kathleen Henderson and Richard J. Martynec, pp. 579–596. Flagstaff: Northland Research.

Herdrich, David J., and Jeffrey T. Clark
1993   Samoan *tia 'ave* and Social Structure: Methodological and Theoretical Considerations. In "The Evolution and Organisation of Prehistoric Society in Polynesia," edited by Michael W. Graves and Roger C. Green, pp. 52–63. *New Zealand Archaeological Association Monograph* 19. Auckland: New Zealand Archaeological Association.

Hill, James N.
1970   Broken K Pueblo: Prehistoric Social Organization in the American Southwest. *Anthropological Papers of the University of Arizona* 18. Tucson: University of Arizona Press.

Hodder, Ian
1985   Postprocessual Archaeology. In *Advances in Archaeological Method and Theory*, Vol. 8, edited by Michael B. Schiffer, pp. 1-28. New York: Academic Press.

Hodge, Frederick W. (Editor)
1990   The Narrative of Alvar Nuñez Cabeza de Vaca. In *Spanish Explorers in the Southern United States, 1528–1543*, edited by Frederick W. Hodge and Theodore H. Lewis, pp. 1–126. Austin: Texas State Historical Association.

Hoffman, Paul E.
1994   Narváez and Cabeza de Vaca in Florida. In *The Forgotten Centuries, Indians and Europeans in the American South, 1521–1704*, edited by Charles Hudson and Carmen C. Tesser, pp. 50–73. Athens: University of Georgia Press.

Hohmann, John W.
1992   An Overview of Salado Heartland Archaeology. In "Proceedings of the Second Salado Conference, Globe, AZ 1992," edited by Richard C. Lange and Stephen Germick, pp. 1–16. *Arizona Archaeological Society Occasional Paper*. Phoenix: Arizona Archaeological Society.

Hohmann, John W., and Linda B. Kelley
1988   Erich F. Schmidt's Investigations of Salado Sites in Central Arizona: The Mrs. W. B. Thompson Archaeological Expedition of the American Museum of Natural History. *Museum of Northern Arizona Bulletin* 56. Flagstaff: Museum of Northern Arizona.

Holmes, Lowell D.
1987   *Quest for the Real Samoa: The Mead/Freeman Controversy and Beyond.* South Hadley, Massachusetts: Bergin and Garvey.

Howard, Jerry B.
1992   Architecture and Ideology: An Approach to the Functional Analysis of Platform Mounds. In "Proceedings of the Second Salado Conference, Globe, AZ 1992," edited by Richard C. Lange and Stephen Germick, pp. 69–77. *Arizona Archaeological Society Occasional Papers*. Phoenix: Arizona Archaeological Society.
1993   A Paleohydraulic Approach to Examining Agricultural Intensification in Hohokam Irrigation Systems. *Research in Economic Anthropology, Supplement* 7: 263–324.

Howard, Jerry B., and Gary Huckleberry
1991   *Maricopa County, Arizona, Central Phoenix Basin, Archaeology Map.* Computer Cartography by Geo-Map, Tucson. Phoenix: Soil Systems.

Howell, Todd L.
1996   Identifying Leaders at Hawikku. *Kiva* 62(1): 61–82.

Howell, Todd L., and Keith W. Kintigh
1996   Archaeological Identification of Kin Groups Using Mortuary and Biological Data: An Example from the American Southwest. *American Antiquity* 61(3): 537–554.

Huckell, Bruce B.
1977   Arizona U:3:28, The Slate Creek Ruin. MS on file, Arizona State Museum, University of Arizona, Tucson.
1978   The Oxbow Hill–Payson Project. *Contribution to Highway Salvage Archaeology in Arizona* 48. Tucson: Arizona State Museum, University of Arizona.

Hudson, Charles M.
1976   *The Southeastern Indians.* Knoxville: University of Tennessee Press.
1990   *The Juan Pardo Expeditions, Exploration of the Carolinas and Tennessee, 1566–1568.* Washington: Smithsonian Institution Press.
1994   The Hernando de Soto Expedition, 1539–1543. In *The Forgotten Centuries, Indians and Europeans in the American South, 1521–1704*, edited by Charles Hudson and Carmen C. Tesser, pp. 74–103. Athens: University of Georgia Press.

Hudson, Charles, and Carmen C. Tesser (Editors)
1994   *The Forgotten Centuries, Indians and Europeans in the American South, 1521–1704.* Athens: University of Georgia Press.

Hunt, Nicola M., and Michael W. Diehl
1992   Archaeological Attributes of Institutionalized Feasting. Paper presented at the 32nd Annual Meeting of the Northeastern Anthropological Association, Bridgewater, Massachusetts.

Intoh, Michiko, and Foss Leach
1985   Archaeological Investigations in the Yap Islands, Micronesia: First Millennium B.C. to the Present Day. *BAR International Series* 277. Oxford.

Jacobs, David F.
*1994a   Archaeology of the Salado in the Livingston Area of Tonto Basin: Roosevelt Platform Mound Study, Report on the Livingston Management Group, Pinto Creek Complex. *Roosevelt Monograph Series* 3, *Anthropological Field Studies* 32. Tempe: Office of Cultural Resource Management, Arizona State University.
*1994b   The Architecture and Chronology of V:5:76/700. In "Archaeology of the Salado in the Livingston Area of Tonto Basin: Roosevelt Platform Mound Study, Report on the Livingston Management Group, Pinto Creek Complex" by David F. Jacobs, pp. 119–132. *Roosevelt Monograph Series* 3, *Anthropological Field Studies* 32. Tempe: Office of Cultural Resource Management, Arizona State University.
*1994c   The Architecture and Chronology of V:5:66/15a. In "Archaeology of the Salado in the Livingston Area of Tonto Basin: Roosevelt Platform Mound Study, Report on the Livingston Management Group, Pinto Creek Complex," by David F. Jacobs, pp. 249–266. *Roosevelt Monograph Series* 3, *Anthropological Field Studies* 32. Tempe: Office of Cultural Resource Management, Arizona State University.
*1994d   The Excavation and Description of V:5:66/15a. In "Archaeology of the Salado in the Livingston Area of Tonto Basin: Roosevelt Platform Mound Study, Report on the Livingston Management Group, Pinto Creek Complex," by David F. Jacobs, pp. 133–248. *Roosevelt Monograph Series* 3, *Anthropological Field Studies* 32. Tempe: Office of Cultural Resource Management, Arizona State University.
*1994e   The Excavation and Description of V:5:76/700. In "Archaeology of the Salado in the Livingston Area of Tonto Basin: Roosevelt Platform Mound Study, Report on the Livingston Management Group, Pinto Creek Complex," by David F. Jacobs, pp. 75–118. *Roosevelt Monograph Series* 3, *Anthropological Field Studies* 32. Tempe: Office of Cultural Resource Management, Arizona State University.
*1997   A Salado Platform Mound on Tonto Creek: Roosevelt Platform Mound Study, Report on the Cline Terrace Mound, Cline Terrace Complex. *Roosevelt Monograph Series* 7, *Anthropological Field Studies* 36. Tempe: Office of Cultural Resource Management, Arizona State University.

Jacobs, David F., and Glen E. Rice
*1994   Summary. In "Archaeology of the Salado in the Livingston Area of Tonto Basin: Roosevelt Platform Mound Study, Report on the Livingston Management Group, Pinto Creek Complex," by David F. Jacobs, pp. 923–926. *Roosevelt Monograph Series* 3, *Anthropological Field Studies* 32. Tempe: Office of Cultural Resource Management, Arizona State University.
*1997   The Function of U:4:33/132, The Cline Terrace Mound. In "A Salado Platform Mound on Tonto Creek: Roosevelt Platform Mound Study, Report on the Cline Terrace Mound, Cline Terrace Complex," by David F. Jacobs, pp. 577–585. *Roosevelt Monograph Series* 7, *Anthropological Field Studies* 36. Tempe: Office of Cultural

Resource Management, Arizona State University.

James, Steven R.
*1995 Hunting and Fishing Patterns at Prehistoric Sites along the Salt River: The Archaeofaunal Analysis. In "The Roosevelt Community Development Study, Vol. 3: Paleobotanical and Osteological Analyses," edited by Mark D. Elson and Jeffery J. Clark, pp. 85–168. *Anthropological Papers* 14. Tucson: Center for Desert Archaeology.

Jennings, Jesse D., and Richard N. Holmer
1980 Archaeological Excavations in Western Samoa. *Pacific Anthropological Records* 32. Honolulu: Department of Anthropology, Bernice P. Bishop Museum.

Jeter, Marvin D.
1978 The Reno–Park Creek Project: Archaeological Investigations in Tonto Basin, Arizona. *Contribution to Highway Salvage Archaeology in Arizona* 49. Tucson: Arizona State Museum, University of Arizona.

Johnson, Gregory A.
1982 Organizational Structure and Scalar Stress. In *Theory and Explanation in Archaeology: The Southampton Conference*, edited by Colin Renfrew, M. J. Rowlands, and Barbara A. Segraves, pp. 389–418. New York: Academic Press.
1983 Decision–Making Organization and Pastoral Nomad Camp Size. *Human Ecology* 11(2): 175–199.
1989 Dynamics of Southwestern Prehistory: Far Outside–Looking In. In *Dynamics of Southwestern Prehistory*, edited by Linda S. Cordell and George J. Gumerman, pp. 371–389. Washington: Smithsonian Institution Press.

Joyce, Arthur A., and Marcus Winter
1996 Ideology, Power, and Urban Society in Pre-Hispanic Oaxaca. *Current Anthropology* 37(1): 33-46.

Keesing, Roger M.
1975 *Kin Groups and Social Structure*. New York: Harcourt Brace Jovanovich College Publishers.

Kent, Susan (Editor)
1990 *Domestic Architecture and the Use of Space: An Interdisciplinary Cross-Cultural Study*. Cambridge: Cambridge University Press.

Kirch, Patrick V.
1990 Monumental Architecture and Power in Polynesian Chiefdoms: A Comparison of Tonga and Hawaii. *World Archaeology* 22(2): 206–222.

Kirch, Patrick V., and Marshall Sahlins
1992 *Anahulu, The Anthropology of History in the Kingdom of Hawaii*. Chicago: University of Chicago Press.

Kolb, Michael J.
1994 Monumentality and the Rise of Religious Author-

ity in Precontact Hawai'i. *Current Anthropology* 34(5): 521–547.

Labby, David
1976 *The Demystification of Yap: Dialectics of Culture on a Micronesian Island*. Chicago: University of Chicago Press.

Lekson, Stephen H.
1991 Settlement Pattern and the Chaco Region. In *Chaco and Hohokam: Prehistoric Regional Systems in the American Southwest*, edited by Patricia L. Crown and W. James Judge, pp. 31–55. Santa Fe: School of American Research Press.

Lekson, Stephen H., Mark D. Elson, and Douglas B. Craig
*1992 Previous Research and Culture History. In "Research Design for the Roosevelt Community Development Study," by William H. Doelle, Henry D. Wallace, Mark D. Elson, and Douglas B. Craig, pp. 19–33. *Anthropological Papers* 12. Tucson: Center for Desert Archaeology.

Levy, Jerrold E.
1992 *Orayvi Revisited: Social Stratification in an "Egalitarian" Society*. Santa Fe: School of American Research Press.

Lewis, Theodore H. (Editor)
1990 The Narrative of the Expedition of Hernando de Soto by the Gentleman of Elvas. In *Spanish Explorers in the Southern United States, 1528–1543*, edited by Frederick W. Hodge and Theodore H. Lewis, pp. 127–272. Austin: Texas State Historical Association.

Lightfoot, Kent G., and Steadman Upham
1989 Complex Societies in the Prehistoric Southwest: A Consideration of the Controversy. In *The Sociopolitical Structure of Prehistoric Southwestern Societies*, edited by Steadman Upham, Kent G. Lightfoot, and Roberta A. Jewett, pp. 3–32. Boulder, Colorado: Westview Press.

Lincoln, Thomas R.
1998 Off the Back Roads and onto the Superhighway: Reclamation Reports. Paper presented at the 63rd Annual Meeting of the Society for American Archaeology, Seattle.

Lindauer, Owen
*1989 Field Strategies for the Roosevelt Platform Mound Study. Paper presented at the Fall Meeting of the Arizona Archaeological Council, Phoenix, Arizona.
*1992 A Consideration of Mounds and Mound Communities in the Tonto Basin as Evidence of Sociopolitical Development. Paper presented at the 57th Annual Meeting of the Society for American Archaeology, Pittsburgh.
*1994a Site V:5:128/1011, Saguaro Muerto. In "Archae-

Lindauer, Owen (*continued*)

ology of the Salado in the Livingston Area of Tonto Basin: Roosevelt Platform Mound Study, Report on the Livingston Management Group, Pinto Creek Complex," by David F. Jacobs, pp. 399–462. *Roosevelt Monograph Series 3, Anthropological Field Studies* 32. Tempe: Office of Cultural Resource Management, Arizona State University.

*1994b Systematics of Decorated Wares. In "Archaeology of the Salado in the Livingston Area of Tonto Basin: Roosevelt Platform Mound Study, Report on the Livingston Management Group, Pinto Creek Complex," by David F. Jacobs, pp. 605–633. *Roosevelt Monograph Series 3, Anthropological Field Studies* 32. Tempe: Office of Cultural Resource Management, Arizona State University.

*1995 Where the Rivers Converge: Roosevelt Platform Mound Study, Report on the Rock Island Complex. *Roosevelt Monograph Series 4, Anthropological Field Studies* 33. Tempe: Office of Cultural Resource Management, Arizona State University.

*1996a The Place of the Storehouses: Roosevelt Platform Mound Study, Report on the Schoolhouse Point Mound, Pinto Creek Complex. *Roosevelt Monograph Series* 6, *Anthropological Field Studies* 35. Tempe: Office of Cultural Resource Management, Arizona State University.

*1996b Understanding the Salado through Work at the Schoolhouse Point Mound, U:8:24/13a. In "The Place of the Storehouses: Roosevelt Platform Mound Study, Report on the Schoolhouse Point Mound, Pinto Creek Complex," by Owen Lindauer, pp. 841–858. *Roosevelt Monograph Series* 6, *Anthropological Field Studies* 35. Tempe: Office of Cultural Resource Management, Arizona State University.

*1997a The Archaeology of Schoolhouse Point Mesa: Roosevelt Platform Mound Study, Report on the Schoolhouse Point Mesa Sites, Schoolhouse Management Group, Pinto Creek Complex. *Roosevelt Monograph Series* 8, *Anthropological Field Studies* 37. Tempe: Office of Cultural Resource Management, Arizona State University.

*1997b Understanding the Salado through Work at Schoolhouse Point Mesa. In "The Archaeology of Schoolhouse Point Mesa: Roosevelt Platform Mound Study, Report on the Schoolhouse Point Mesa Sites, Schoolhouse Management Group, Pinto Creek Complex," by Owen Lindauer, pp. 669–685. *Roosevelt Monograph Series* 8, *Anthropological Field Studies* 37. Tempe: Office of

Cultural Resource Management, Arizona State University.

Lindauer, Owen, and John H. Blitz

1997 Higher Ground: The Archaeology of North American Platform Mounds. *Journal of Archaeological Research* 5(2): 169–207.

Lingenfelter, Sherwood G.

1975 *Yap: Political Leadership and Culture Change in an Island Society.* Honolulu: University Press of Hawaii.

Linton, Ralph

1923 The Material Culture of the Marquesas Islands. *Bernice P. Bishop Museum Memoir* 8(5). Honolulu: Bernice P. Bishop Museum Press.

1939 Marquesan Culture. In *The Individual and His Society*, by Abram Kardiner, pp. 137–196. New York: Columbia University Press.

Lipe, William D., and Michelle Hegmon (Editors)

1989 The Architecture of Social Integration in Prehistoric Pueblos. *Occasional Papers of the Crow Canyon Archaeological Center* 1. Cortez, Colorado: Crow Canyon Archaeological Center.

Longacre, William A.

1970 Archaeology as Anthropology: A Case Study. *Anthropological Papers of the University of Arizona* 17. Tucson: University of Arizona Press.

Lowe, Charles H.

1964 *Arizona's Natural Environment, Landscapes and Habitat.* Tucson: University of Arizona Press.

McCartney, Peter H., and Owen Lindauer

*1996 The Developmental Sequence and Site Chronology of Schoolhouse Point Mound, U:8:24/13a. In "The Place of the Storehouses: Roosevelt Platform Mound Study, Report on the Schoolhouse Point Mound, Pinto Creek Complex," by Owen Lindauer, pp. 383–417. *Roosevelt Monograph Series* 6, *Anthropological Field Studies* 35. Tempe: Office of Cultural Resource Management, Arizona State University.

McCartney, Peter H., Owen Lindauer,
Glen E. Rice, and John C. Ravesloot

*1994 Chronological Methods. In "Archaeology of the Salado in the Livingston Area of the Tonto Basin: Roosevelt Platform Mound Study, Report on the Livingston Management Group, Pinto Creek Complex," by David F. Jacobs, pp. 21–50. *Roosevelt Monograph Series* 3, *Anthropological Field Studies* 32. Tempe: Office of Cultural Resource Management, Arizona State University.

McGregor, John C.

1940 Burial of an Early Magician. *Proceedings of the American Philosophical Society* 86(2): 270–298.

McGuire, Randall H.

1983 Breaking Down Cultural Complexity: Inequality and Heterogeneity. In *Advances in Archaeological*

Method and Theory, Vol. 6, edited by Michael B. Schiffer, pp. 91–142. New York: Academic Press.

McGuire, Randall H., and Dean J. Saitta
1996 Although They Have Petty Captains, They Obey Them Badly: The Dialectics of Prehispanic Western Pueblo Social Organization. *American Antiquity* 61(2): 197–216.

Masse, W. Bruce
1991 The Quest for Subsistence Sufficiency and Civilization in the Sonoran Desert. In *Chaco and Hohokam: Prehistoric Regional Systems in the American Southwest*, edited by Patricia L. Crown and W. James Judge, pp. 195–223. Santa Fe: School of American Research Press.

Mead, Margaret
1930 Social Organization of Manua. *Bernice P. Bishop Museum Bulletin* 76. Honolulu: Bernice P. Bishop Museum.
1968 The Samoans. In *Peoples and Cultures of the Pacific*, edited by Andrew P. Vayda, pp. 244–273. New York: The Natural History Press.
1973 *Coming of Age in Samoa*. American Museum of Natural History Special Members Edition. Garden City: American Museum of Natural History.

Miksa, Elizabeth, and James M. Heidke
*1995 Drawing a Line in the Sands: Models of Ceramic Temper Provenance. In "The Roosevelt Community Development Study, Vol. 2: Ceramic Chronology, Technology, and Economics," edited by James M. Heidke and Miriam T. Stark, pp. 133–205. *Anthropological Papers* 14. Tucson: Center for Desert Archaeology.

Miksicek, Charles H.
*1995 Temporal Trends in the Eastern Tonto Basin: An Archaeobotanical Perspective. In "The Roosevelt Community Development Study, Vol. 3: Paleobotanical and Osteological Analyses," edited by Mark D. Elson and Jeffery J. Clark, pp. 43–83. *Anthropological Papers* 14. Tucson: Center for Desert Archaeology.

Milanich, Jerald T., and Charles M. Hudson
1993 *Hernando de Soto and the Indians of Florida*. Gainesville: University Press of Florida.

Mindeleff, Cosmos
1896 Casa Grande Ruin. *Thirteenth Annual Report of the Bureau of American Ethnology for the Years 1891–1892*, pp. 289–319. Washington.
1897 The Repair of Casa Grande Ruin. *Fifteenth Annual Report of the Bureau of American Ethnology*. Washington.

Morgan, William N.
1988 *Prehistoric Architecture in Micronesia*. Austin: University of Texas Press.

Morris, Donald H.
1970 Walnut Creek Village: A Ninth-Century Hoho-kam–Anasazi Settlement in the Mountains of Central Arizona. *American Antiquity* 35(1): 49–61.

Müller, Wilhelm
1917 *Yap*. Hamburg: L. Friederichsen.

Murdock, George P., Clellan S. Ford, Alfred E. Hudson, Raymond Kennedy, Leo W. Simmons, and John W. M. Whiting
1971 *Outline of Cultural Materials*. New Haven: Human Relations Area Files. Fifth printing with modifications.

Nabakov, Peter, and Robert Easton
1989 *Native American Architecture*. Oxford: Oxford University Press.

Neitzel, Robert S.
1965 Archaeology of the Fatherland Site: The Grand Village of the Natchez. *Anthropological Papers of the American Museum of Natural History* 51(1). New York: American Museum of Natural History.

Nelson, Ben A.
1995 Complexity, Hierarchy, and Scale: A Controlled Comparison between Chaco Canyon, New Mexico, and La Quemada, Zacatecas. *American Antiquity* 60(4): 597–618.

Oliver, Theodore J.
*1994 Classic Period Settlement in the Uplands of the Tonto Basin, Report on the Uplands Complex, Roosevelt Platform Mound Study (1994 Draft). *Roosevelt Monograph Series* 5, *Anthropological Field Studies* 34. Tempe: Office of Cultural Resource Management, Arizona State University.

Parsons, Elsie Clews
1939 *Pueblo Indian Religion*. Chicago: University of Chicago Press.

Pedrick, Kathryn E.
*1992 Introduction. In "Developing Perspectives on Tonto Basin Prehistory," edited by Charles L. Redman, Glen E. Rice, and Kathryn E. Pedrick, pp. 1–4. *Roosevelt Monograph Series* 2, *Anthropological Field Studies* 26. Tempe: Office of Cultural Resource Management, Arizona State University.

Peebles, Christopher S., and Susan M. Kus
1977 Some Archaeological Correlates of Ranked Societies. *American Antiquity* 42(3): 421–448.

Pilles, Peter J., Jr.
1976 Sinagua and Salado Similarities as Seen from the Verde Valley. *The Kiva* 42(1): 113–124.

Plog, Stephen
1995 Equality and Hierarchy: Holistic Approaches to Understanding Social Dynamics in the Pueblo Southwest. In *Foundations of Social Inequality*, edited by T. Douglas Price and Gary M. Feinman, pp. 189–206. New York: Plenum Press.

Price, T. Douglas, and Gary M. Feinman
  1995   Foundations of Prehistoric Social Inequality. In *Foundations of Social Inequality*, edited by T. Douglas Price and Gary M. Feinman, pp. 3–11. New York: Plenum Press.
Ravesloot, John C., and Marcia H. Regan
  *1995   Demographic, Health, Genetic and Mortuary Characteristics of Late Prehistoric Central Arizona Populations. Paper prepared for the advanced seminar "Prehistoric Salado Culture of the American Southwest," Amerind Foundation, Dragoon, Arizona.
Redman, Charles L.
  *1992   Pursuing Southwestern Social Complexity in the 1990s. In "Developing Perspectives on Tonto Basin Prehistory," edited by Charles L. Redman, Glen E. Rice, and Kathryn E. Pedrick, pp. 5–10. *Roosevelt Monograph Series* 2, *Anthropological Field Studies* 26. Tempe: Office of Cultural Resource Management, Arizona State University.
Reid, J. Jefferson
  1989   A Grasshopper Perspective on the Mogollon of the Arizona Mountains. In *Dynamics of Southwest Prehistory*, edited by Linda S. Cordell and George J. Gumerman, pp. 65–97. Washington: Smithsonian Institution Press.
Reid, J. Jefferson, and Stephanie M. Whittlesey
  1990   The Complicated and the Complex: Observations on the Archaeological Record of Large Pueblos. In *Perspectives on Southwestern Prehistory*, edited by Paul E. Minnis and Charles L. Redman, pp. 184–195. Boulder: Westview Press.
Reid, J. Jefferson, Michael B. Schiffer,
Stephanie M. Whittlesey, Madeleine J. Hinkes,
Alan P. Sullivan III, Christian E. Downum,
William A. Longacre, and H. David Tuggle
  1989   Perception and Interpretation in Contemporary Southwestern Archaeology: Comments on Cordell, Upham, and Brock. *American Antiquity* 54(4): 802–814.
Renfrew, Colin, and John F. Cherry (Editors)
  1986   *Peer Polity Interaction and Sociopolitical Change*. Cambridge: Cambridge University Press.
Rice, Glen E.
  1985   (Editor) Studies in the Hohokam and Salado of the Tonto Basin. *OCRM Report* 63. Tempe: Office of Cultural Resource Management, Arizona State University.
  1987a   (Editor) Studies in the Hohokam Community of Marana. *Anthropological Field Studies* 15. Tempe: Office of Cultural Resource Management, Arizona State University.
  1987b   The Marana Community Complex: A Twelfth Century Hohokam Chiefdom. In "Studies in the Hohokam Community of Marana," edited by Glen E. Rice, pp. 249–253. *Anthropological Field Studies* 15. Tempe: Office of Cultural Resource Management, Arizona State University.
  *1990a Toward a Study of the Salado of the Tonto Basin. In "A Design for Salado Research," edited by Glen E. Rice, pp. 1–19. *Roosevelt Monograph Series* 1, *Anthropological Field Studies* 22. Tempe: Office of Cultural Resource Management, Arizona State University.
  *1990b Variability in the Development of Classic Period Elites. In "A Design for Salado Research," edited by Glen E. Rice, pp. 31–40. *Roosevelt Monograph Series* 1, *Anthropological Field Studies* 22. Tempe: Office of Cultural Resource Management, Arizona State University.
  *1992   Modeling the Development of Complexity in the Sonoran Desert of Arizona. In "Developing Perspectives on Tonto Basin Prehistory," edited by Charles L. Redman, Glen E. Rice, and Kathryn E. Pedrick, pp. 11–26. *Roosevelt Monograph Series* 2, *Anthropological Field Studies* 26. Tempe: Office of Cultural Resource Management, Arizona State University.
  *1994   The Distribution of Special Artifacts. In "Archaeology of the Salado in the Livingston Area of Tonto Basin: Roosevelt Platform Mound Study, Report on the Livingston Management Group, Pinto Creek Complex," by David F. Jacobs, pp. 809–817. *Roosevelt Monograph Series* 3, *Anthropological Field Studies* 32. Tempe: Office of Cultural Resource Management, Arizona State University.
Rice, Glen E., and Todd W. Bostwick (Editors)
  1986   *Studies in the Prehistory of Central Arizona; The Central Arizona Water Control Study*, Vol. 2 (Draft Report). Tempe: Office of Cultural Resource Management, Arizona State University.
Rice, Glen E., and Owen Lindauer
  *1994   Phase Chronology. In "Archaeology of the Salado in the Livingston Area of Tonto Basin: Roosevelt Platform Mound Study, Report on the Livingston Management Group, Pinto Creek Complex," by David F. Jacobs, pp. 51–67. *Roosevelt Monograph Series* 3, *Anthropological Field Studies* 32. Tempe: Office of Cultural Resource Management, Arizona State University.
Rice, Glen E., and Charles L. Redman
  *1993   Platform Mounds of the Arizona Desert. *Expedition* 35: 53–63.
  *1996   Compounds, Villages and Mounds: The Salado Alternative. Paper presented at the Annual Meeting of the Southwestern and Rocky Mountain Division of the American Association for the Advancement of Science, Flagstaff, Arizona.

Royse, Chester, Michael Sheridan,
and H. Wesley Pierce
    1971   Geologic Guidebook 4: Highways of Arizona. Arizona Highways 87, 88 and 188. *Arizona Bureau of Mines Bulletin* 184. Tucson: University of Arizona.

Russell, Frank
    1908   The Pima Indians. *Twenty-Sixth Annual Report of the Bureau of American Ethnology for the Years 1904-1905*, pp. 3-389. Washington.

Sahlins, Marshall D.
    1958   *Social Stratification in Polynesia*. Seattle: University of Washington Press.

Salesius, Von P.
    1907   *The Carolines Island Yap*. Berlin: W. Susserott.

Sand, Christophe
    1993   A Preliminary Study of the Impact of the Tongan Maritime Chiefdom on the Late Prehistoric Society of 'Uvea, Western Polynesia. In "The Evolution and Organisation of Prehistoric Society in Polynesia," edited by Michael W. Graves and Roger C. Green, pp. 43-51. *New Zealand Archaeological Association Monograph* 19. Auckland: New Zealand Archaeological Association.

Saunders, Joe W., and Thurman Allen
    1994   Hedgepeth Mounds, An Archaic Mound Complex in North-Central Louisiana. *American Antiquity* 59(3): 471-489.

Saunders, Joe W., Rolfe D. Mandel, Roger T.
Saucier, E. Thurman Allen, C. T. Hallmark,
Jay K. Johnson, Edwin H. Jackson, Charles M.
Allen, Gary L. Stringer, Douglas S. Frink,
James K. Feathers, Stephen Williams,
Kristen J. Gremillion, Malcolm F. Vidrine,
and Reca Jones
    1997   A Mound Complex in Louisiana at 5400-5000 Years Before the Present. *Science* 277: 1796-1799.

Scantling, Frederick H.
    1940   Excavations at the Jackrabbit Ruin, Papago Indian Reservation, Arizona. Master's thesis, Department of Anthropology, University of Arizona, Tucson.

Scarry, John F.
    1994   The Late Prehistoric Southeast. In *The Forgotten Centuries, Indians and Europeans in the American South, 1521-1704*, edited by Charles Hudson and Carmen C. Tesser, pp. 17-35. Athens: University of Georgia Press.
    1996   Stability and Change in the Apalachee Chiefdom. In *Political Structure and Change in the Prehistoric Southeastern United States*, edited by John F. Scarry, pp. 192-228. Gainesville: University Press of Florida.

Schlegel, Alice
    1992   African Political Models in the American Southwest: Hopi as an Internal Frontier Society. *American Anthropologist* 94(2): 376-397.

Schmidt, Erich F.
    1928   Time-relations of Prehistoric Pottery Types in Southern Arizona. *Anthropological Papers of the American Museum of Natural History* 30(5): 247-302.

Sellers, William D., and Richard H. Hill (Editors)
    1974   *Arizona Climate, 1931-1972*. 2nd ed. Tucson: University of Arizona Press.

Shelley, Steven D., and Richard S. Ciolek-Torrello
    *1994   Grapevine Recreation and Stockpile Areas. In "The Roosevelt Rural Sites Study, Vol. 2: Prehistoric Rural Settlements in the Tonto Basin," edited by Richard S. Ciolek-Torrello, Steven D. Shelley, and Su Benaron, pp. 223-344. *Technical Series* 28. Tucson: Statistical Research.

Shennan, Stephen J. (Editor)
    1989   *Archaeological Approaches to Cultural Identity*. London: Unwin Hyman.

Spielmann, Katherine A.
    *1994   Subsistence Patterns at the Livingston Sites. In "Archaeology of the Salado in the Livingston Area of Tonto Basin: Roosevelt Platform Mound Study, Report on the Livingston Management Group, Pinto Creek Complex," by David F. Jacobs, pp. 915-921. *Roosevelt Monograph Series* 3, *Anthropological Field Studies* 32. Tempe: Office of Cultural Resource Management, Arizona State University.
    *1996   (Editor) Environment and Subsistence in the Classic Period Tonto Basin: Roosevelt Platform Mound Study (1996 Draft). *Roosevelt Monograph Series* 10, *Anthropological Field Studies* 39. Tempe: Office of Cultural Resource Management, Arizona State University.

Stair, John B.
    1897   *Old Samoa: Or, Flotsam and Jetsam from the Pacific Ocean*. London: The Religious Tract Society.

Stark, Miriam T.
    *1995   Commodities and Interaction in the Prehistoric Tonto Basin. In "The Roosevelt Community Development Study: New Perspectives on Tonto Basin Prehistory," edited by Mark D. Elson, Miriam T. Stark, and David A. Gregory, pp. 307-342. *Anthropological Papers* 15. Tucson: Center for Desert Archaeology.
    1998   (Editor) *The Archaeology of Social Boundaries*. Washington: Smithsonian Institution Press.

Stark, Miriam T., and Mark D. Elson
    *1995   Introduction. In "The Roosevelt Community Development Study: New Perspectives on Tonto Basin Prehistory," edited by Mark D. Elson,

Stark, Miriam T., and Mark D. Elson (*continued*)
   Miriam T. Stark, and David A. Gregory, pp. 1–37. *Anthropological Papers* 15. Tucson: Center for Desert Archaeology.

Stark, Miriam T., and James M. Heidke
   *1995 Early Classic Period Variability in Utilitarian Ceramic Production and Distribution. In "The Roosevelt Community Development Study, Vol. 2: Ceramic Chronology, Technology, and Economics," edited by James M. Heidke and Miriam T. Stark, pp. 363–393. *Anthropological Papers* 14. Tucson: Center for Desert Archaeology.

Stark, Miriam T., Jeffery J. Clark, and Mark D. Elson
   *1995 Causes and Consequences of Migration in the 13th-Century Tonto Basin. *Journal of Anthropological Archaeology* 14(2): 212–246.

Stark, Miriam T., James M. Vint, and James M. Heidke
   *1995 Compositional Variability in Utilitarian Ceramics at a Colonial Period Site. In "The Roosevelt Community Development Study, Vol. 2: Ceramic Chronology, Technology, and Economics," edited by James M. Heidke and Miriam T. Stark, pp. 273–295. *Anthropological Papers* 14. Tucson: Center for Desert Archaeology.

Steadman, Sharon R.
   1996 Recent Research in the Archaeology of Architecture: Beyond the Foundations. *Journal of Archaeological Research* 4(1): 51–93.

Steponaitis, Vincas P.
   1978 Locational Theory and Complex Chiefdoms: A Mississippian Example. In *Mississippian Settlement Patterns*, edited by Bruce D. Smith, pp. 417–153. New York: Academic Press.
   1986 Prehistoric Archaeology in the Southeastern United States, 1970–1985. *Annual Review of Anthropology* 15: 363–404.

Stuchlik, Milan
   1976 *Life on a Half Share: Mechanisms of Social Recruitment among the Mapuche of Southern Chile*. London: C. Hurst.

Suggs, Robert C.
   1965 *The Hidden Worlds of Polynesia*. New York: Mentor Books.

Swanton, John R.
   1911 Indian Tribes of the Lower Mississippi Valley and Adjacent Coast of the Gulf of Mexico. *Bureau of American Ethnology Bulletin* 43. Washington: Smithsonian Institution.
   1922 Early History of the Creek Indians and Their Neighbors. *Bureau of American Ethnology Bulletin* 73. Washington: Smithsonian Institution.
   1946 The Indians of the Southeastern United States. *Bureau of American Ethnology Bulletin* 137. Washington: Smithsonian Institution.

Swartz, Deborah L., and Brenda G. Randolph
   *1994 The Griffin Wash Site, AZ V:5:90/96 (ASM/TNF). In "The Roosevelt Community Development Study, Vol. 2: Meddler Point, Pyramid Point, and Griffin Wash Sites," by Mark D. Elson, Deborah L. Swartz, Douglas B. Craig, and Jeffery J. Clark, pp. 297–415. *Anthropological Papers* 13. Tucson: Center for Desert Archaeology.

Szuter, Christine R.
   1992 Seasonality and Resource Use: Analysis of the Rye Creek Faunal Assemblages. In "The Rye Creek Project: Archaeology in the Upper Tonto Basin, Vol. 2: Artifact and Specific Analyses," by Mark D. Elson and Douglas B. Craig, pp. 409–427. *Anthropological Papers* 11. Tucson: Center for Desert Archaeology.

Thomas, Cyrus
   1894 Report on the Mound Explorations of the Bureau of Ethnology. *Twelfth Annual Report of the Bureau of Ethnology, 1890–1891*. Washington.

Thomas, William L., Jr.
   1968 The Pacific Basin: An Introduction. In *Peoples and Cultures of the Pacific*, edited by Andrew P. Vayda, pp. 3–26. New York: The Natural History Press.

Trigger, Bruce G.
   1990 Monumental Architecture: A Thermodynamic Explanation of Symbolic Behaviour. *World Archaeology* 22(2): 119–132.

Turner, George
   1884 *Samoa, a Hundred Years Ago and Long Before: Together with Notes on the Cults and Customs of Twenty-three other Islands in the Pacific*. London: Macmillan.

Upham, Steadman
   1982 *Polities and Power: An Economic and Political History of the Western Pueblos*. New York: Academic Press.
   1987 A Theoretical Consideration of Middle Range Societies. In *Chiefdoms in the Americas*, edited by Robert D. Drennan and Carlos A. Uribe, pp. 345–367. Lanham, Maryland: University Press of America.
   1990 (Editor) *The Evolution of Political Systems: Sociopolitics in Small-Scale, Sedentary Societies*. Cambridge: Cambridge University Press.

Van West, Carla R., and Jeffrey H. Altschul
   *1994 Agricultural Productivity and Carrying Capacity in the Tonto Basin. In "The Roosevelt Rural Sites Study, Vol. 3: Changing Land Use in the Tonto Basin," edited by Richard S. Ciolek–Torrello and John R. Welch, pp. 361–435. *Technical Series* 28. Tucson: Statistical Research.

Van West, Carla R., and
Richard S. Ciolek–Torrello
 *1995 Subsistence and Environmental Interaction. Paper prepared for the advanced seminar "Prehistoric Salado Culture of the American Southwest," Amerind Foundation, Dragoon, Arizona.

Wallace, Henry D.
 *1995a Ceramic Accumulation Rates and Prehistoric Tonto Basin Households. In "The Roosevelt Community Development Study: New Perspectives on Tonto Basin Prehistory," edited by Mark D. Elson, Miriam T. Stark, and David A. Gregory, pp. 79–126. *Anthropological Papers* 15. Tucson: Center for Desert Archaeology.
 1995b Archaeological Investigations at Los Morteros, a Prehistoric Settlement in the Northern Tucson Basin. *Anthropological Papers* 17. Tucson: Center for Desert Archaeology.
 1995c Summary and Concluding Remarks. In "Archaeological Investigations at Los Morteros, a Prehistoric Settlement in the Northern Tucson Basin," by Henry D. Wallace, pp. 801–835. *Anthropological Papers* 17. Tucson: Center for Desert Archaeology.

Wasley, William W.
 1960 A Hohokam Platform Mound at the Gatlin Site, Gila Bend, Arizona. *American Antiquity* 26(2): 244-262.

Waters, Michael R.
 *1996 Geoarchaeological Investigations in the Tonto Basin. In "Environment and Subsistence in the Classic Period Tonto Basin, Roosevelt Platform Mound Study (1996 Draft)," edited by Katherine A. Spielmann, pp. 2.1–2.39. *Roosevelt Monograph Series* 10, *Anthropological Field Studies* 39. Tempe: Office of Cultural Resource Management, Arizona State University.

Welch, John R.
 *1994 Environmental Influences on Tonto Basin Agricultural Productivity and Sustainability. In "The Roosevelt Rural Sites Study, Vol. 3: Changing Land Use in the Tonto Basin," edited by Richard S. Ciolek-Torrello and John R. Welch, pp. 19–39. *Technical Series* 28. Tucson: Statistical Research.

Whittlesey, Stephanie M.
 1978 *Status and Death at Grasshopper Pueblo: Experiments toward an Archaeological Theory of Correlates*. Doctoral dissertation, University of Arizona, Tucson. Ann Arbor: University Microfilms.

Whittlesey, Stephanie M., and Richard S. Ciolek–Torrello
 1992 A Revolt Against Rampant Elites: Toward an Alternative Paradigm. In "Proceedings of the Second Salado Conference, Globe, AZ 1992,"
edited by Richard C. Lange and Stephen Germick, pp. 312–324. *Arizona Archaeological Society Occasional Paper*. Phoenix: Arizona Archaeological Society.

Whittlesey, Stephanie M., and J. Jefferson Reid
 1982 Cholla Project Perspectives on Salado. In Cholla Project Archaeology, Vol. 1: Introduction and Special Studies," edited by J. Jefferson Reid, pp. 63–80. *Arizona State Museum Archaeological Series* 161. Tucson: Arizona State Museum, University of Arizona.

Whittlesey, Stephanie M., Richard Ciolek–Torrello, and J. Jefferson Reid
 *1995 Lessons from the Fourth World: Salado Social Organization and Settlement from a Regional Perspective. Paper prepared for the advanced seminar "Prehistoric Salado Culture of the American Southwest," Amerind Foundation, Dragoon, Arizona.

Wilcox, David R.
 1987 Frank Midvale's Investigation of the Site of La Ciudad. *Anthropological Field Studies* 19(4). Tempe: Office of Cultural Resource Management, Arizona State University.
 1988 Making a Living Near the Picachos. In "Hohokam Settlement along the Slopes of the Picacho Mountains, Vol. 6: Synthesis and Conclusions, Tucson Aqueduct Project," edited by Richard S. Ciolek-Torrello and David R. Wilcox, pp. 268–299. *Research Paper* 35. Flagstaff: Museum of Northern Arizona.
 1991 Hohokam Social Complexity. In *Chaco and Hohokam: Prehistoric Regional Systems in the American Southwest*, edited by Patricia L. Crown and W. James Judge, pp. 253–275. Santa Fe: School of American Research Press.
 1993 Pueblo Grande in the Nineteenth Century. In "Archaeology of the Pueblo Grande Platform Mound and Surrounding Features, Vol. 1: Introduction to the Archival Project and History of Archaeological Research," edited by Christian E. Downum and Todd W. Bostwick, pp. 43–72. *Anthropological Papers* 1. Phoenix: Pueblo Grande Museum.

Wilcox, David R., and Jonathan Haas
 1994 The Scream of the Butterfly: Competition and Conflict in the Prehistoric Southwest. In *Themes in Southwest Prehistory*, edited by George J. Gumerman, pp. 211–238. Santa Fe: School of American Research Press.

Wilcox, David R., and Lynette O. Shenk
 1977 The Architecture of the Casa Grande and Its Interpretation. *Arizona State Museum Archaeological Series* 115. Tucson: Arizona State Museum, University of Arizona.

Wood, J. Scott
  1985   The Northeastern Periphery. In "Proceedings of the 1983 Hohokam Symposium," edited by Alfred E. Dittert, Jr., and Donald E. Dove, pp. 239–262. *Arizona Archaeological Society Occasional Paper* 2. Phoenix: Arizona Archaeological Society.
  1989   Vale of Tiers, Too: Late Classic Period Salado Settlement Patterns and Organizational Models for Tonto Basin. *Cultural Resources Inventory Report* 89–12–280. Phoenix: Tonto National Forest.
  *1992   Toward a New Definition of Salado: Comments and Discussion on the Second Salado Conference. In "Proceedings of the Second Salado Conference, Globe, AZ 1992," edited by Richard C. Lange and Stephen Germick, pp. 337–344. *Arizona Archaeological Society Occasional Paper*. Phoenix: Arizona Archaeological Society.
  *1995   Vale of Tiers Palimpsest: Salado Settlement and Internal Relationships in the Tonto Basin Area. Paper prepared for the advanced seminar "Prehistoric Salado Culture of the American Southwest," Amerind Foundation, Dragoon, Arizona.

Wood, J. Scott, and John W. Hohmann
  1985   Foundation's Edge: The Northeastern Periphery and the Development of the Hohokam Classic Period. Paper presented at the 50th Annual Meeting of the Society for American Archaeology, Denver.

Wood, J. Scott, and Martin E. McAllister
  1980   Foundation and Empire: The Colonization of the Northeastern Hohokam Periphery. In "Current Issues in Hohokam Prehistory: Proceedings of a Symposium," edited by David E. Doyel and Fred T. Plog, pp. 180–199. *Anthropological Research Papers* 23. Tempe: Arizona State University.
  1982   The Salado Tradition: An Alternative View. In "Cholla Project Archaeology, Vol. 1: Introduction and Special Studies," edited by J. Jefferson Reid, pp. 81–94. *Arizona State Museum Archaeological Series* 161. Tucson: Arizona State Museum, University of Arizona.
  1984   Second Foundation: Settlement Patterns and Agriculture in the Northeastern Hohokam Periphery, Central Arizona. In "Prehistoric Agricultural Strategies in the Southwest," edited by Suzanne K. Fish and Paul R. Fish, pp. 271–289. *Anthropological Research Papers* 33. Tempe: Arizona State University.

Wood, J. Scott, Glen E. Rice,
and David F. Jacobs
  *1992   Factors Affecting Prehistoric Salado Irrigation in the Tonto Basin. In "Developing Perspectives on Tonto Basin Prehistory," edited by Charles L. Redman, Glen E. Rice, and Kathryn E. Pedrick, pp. 27–32. *Roosevelt Monograph Series* 2, *Anthropological Field Studies* 26. Tempe: Office of Cultural Resource Management, Arizona State University.

Yoffee, Norman, and Andrew Sherratt
  1993   *Archaeological Theory: Who Sets the Agenda?* Cambridge: Cambridge University Press.

Zedeño, María Nieves
  1997   Landscapes, Land Use, and the History of Territory Formation: An Example from the Puebloan Southwest. *Journal of Archaeological Method and Theory* 4(1): 67–103.

Index

Abstract

The function of prehistoric platform mounds in the Hohokam region of the American Southwest has been the subject of intense archaeological debate for more than a hundred years. Two basic theories have been proposed through past research: platform mounds were the residential domains of elite leaders who ruled socially complex groups, or platform mounds were non-residential ceremonial centers used by groups of low social complexity. These theories were based almost exclusively on archaeological data because platform mounds were not constructed by any historic period Southwestern group.

To better understand the nature of these features and the groups that used them, a cross-cultural analysis is undertaken of historic groups with platform mounds from the Pacific Ocean region, South America, and the southeastern United States. Seven groups are examined in detail using ethnographic and ethnohistoric accounts, and common attributes of these mound-using groups are abstracted and synthesized. Insights gained through this analysis are then applied to a prehistoric settlement system in the Eastern Tonto Basin of central Arizona. This system was most intensively occupied during the Roosevelt phase (A.D. 1250–1350), when it contained four platform mounds within a 6-km stretch along the Salt River.

A new model for Roosevelt phase settlement is presented that suggests that the platform mounds were constructed by two competing descent groups. Although the mounds were not residential, the groups that used them were socially complex with well-defined, institutionalized leadership positions. Through ceremonies revolving around ancestor worship and glorification of the descent group, the platform mounds played a role in the management of irrigation and other subsistence systems and were used to integrate immigrant groups of different cultural backgrounds and to mark descent group territory.

Resumen

La función de las plataformas en la región Hohokam del suroeste norteamericano ha sido tópico de intenso debate arqueológico por más de cien años. En previas investigaciones de estas plataformas arqueólogos propusieron dos teorías básicas: las plataformas fueron áreas residenciales de los líderes de la élite, quienes controlaron grupos sociales complejos o, las plataformas constituyeron centros ceremoniales no residenciales utilizados por grupos sociales poco complejos. Estas teorías se basaron casi exclusivamente en datos arqueológicos debido a que ningún grupo del suroeste construyó este tipo de montículo en el período histórico.

Para comprender mejor la naturaleza de estos rasgos arquitectónicos y los grupos que los usaron, se conduce un análisis croscultural de grupos históricos con plataformas en las islas del Océano Pacífico y en Sudamérica y el sureste de los Estados Unidos. Se examinan en detalle siete grupos usando crónicas etnográficas y etnohistóricas, y se sintetizan los atributos comunes a estos grupos que usaron plataformas. La información así obtenida se aplica al sistema de asentamiento prehistórico en la zona este de la cuenca Tonto en Arizona central. Este sistema fue ocupado más intensivamente durante la fase Roosevelt (1250–1350 d.C.), cuando contuvo quatro plataformas en un tramo de 6 km. a lo largo del Río Salt.

Se presenta un nuevo modelo de asentamiento durante la fase Roosevelt, el cual sugiere que las plataformas fueron construidas por dos linajes competitivos. Aunque las plataformas no fueron residenciales, los grupos que las usaron fueron socialmente complejos y con posiciones de liderazgo definidas e institucionalizadas. A través de rituales enfocados en el culto a los ancestros y la glorificación del linaje, las plataformas jugaron un papel significativo en el manejo de la irrigación y otros sistemas de subsistencia, y fueron usadas para integrar grupos de inmigrantes con diferentes antecedentes culturales y para marcar el territorio de cada linaje.

ANTHROPOLOGICAL PAPERS OF THE UNIVERSITY OF ARIZONA

1. Excavations at Nantack Village, Point of Pines, Arizona.   David A. Breternitz. 1959. (O.P.)

2. Yaqui Myths and Legends.   Ruth W. Giddings. 1959. *Now in book form.*

3. Marobavi: A Study of an Assimilated Group in Northern Sonora.   Roger C. Owen. 1959. (O.P.)

4. A Survey of Indian Assimilation in Eastern Sonora.   Thomas B. Hinton. 1959. (O.P.)

5. The Phonology of Arizona Yaqui.   Lynn S. Crumrine. 1961. (O.P., D)

6. The Maricopas: An Identification from Documentary Sources.   Paul H. Ezell. 1963. (O.P.)

7. The San Carlos Indian Cattle Industry.   Harry T. Getty. 1964. (O.P.)

8. The House Cross of the Mayo Indians of Sonora, Mexico.   N. Ross Crumrine. 1964. (O.P.)

9. Salvage Archaeology in Painted Rocks Reservoir, Western Arizona.   William W. Wasley and Alfred E. Johnson. 1965.

10. An Appraisal of Tree-Ring Dated Pottery in the Southwest.   David A. Breternitz. 1966. (O.P.)

11. The Albuquerque Navajos.   William H. Hodge. 1969. (O.P.)

12. Papago Indians at Work.   Jack O. Waddell. 1969.

13. Culture Change and Shifting Populations in Central Northern Mexico.   William B. Griffen. 1969.

14. Ceremonial Exchange as a Mechanism in Tribal Integration Among the Mayos of Northwest Mexico.   Lynn S. Crumrine. 1969. (O.P.)

15. Western Apache Witchcraft.   Keith H. Basso. 1969. (O.P., D)

16. Lithic Analysis and Cultural Inference: A Paleo-Indian Case.   Edwin N. Wilmsen. 1970. (O.P.)

17. Archaeology as Anthropology: A Case Study.   William A. Longacre. 1970.

18. Broken K Pueblo: Prehistoric Social Organization in the American Southwest.   James N. Hill. 1970. (O.P., D)

19. White Mountain Redware: A Pottery Tradition of East-Central Arizona and Western New Mexico.   Roy L. Carlson. 1970. (O.P., D)

20. Mexican Macaws: Comparative Osteology.   Lyndon L. Hargrave. 1970.

21. Apachean Culture History and Ethnology.   Keith H. Basso and Morris E. Opler, eds. 1971. (O.P., D)

22. Social Functions of Language in a Mexican-American Community.   George C. Barker. 1972.

23. The Indians of Point of Pines, Arizona: A Comparative Study of Their Physical Characteristics.   Kenneth A. Bennett. 1973. (O.P.)

24. Population, Contact, and Climate in the New Mexico Pueblos.   Ezra B. W. Zubrow. 1974. (O.P.)

25. Irrigation's Impact on Society.   Theodore E. Downing and McGuire Gibson, eds. 1974. (O.P.)

26. Excavations at Punta de Agua in the Santa Cruz River Basin, Southeastern Arizona.   J. Cameron Greenleaf. 1975.

27. Seri Prehistory: The Archaeology of the Central Coast of Sonora, Mexico.   Thomas Bowen. 1976. (O.P.)

28. Carib-Speaking Indians: Culture, Society, and Language.   Ellen B. Basso, ed. 1977. (O.P.)

29. Cocopa Ethnography   William H. Kelly. 1977. (O.P.)

30. The Hodges Ruin: A Hohokam Community in the Tucson Basin.   Isabel Kelly, James E. Officer, and Emil W. Haury, collaborators; Gayle H. Hartmann, ed. 1978. (O.P.)

31. Fort Bowie Material Culture.   Robert M. Herskovitz. 1978. (O.P.)

32. Artifacts from Chaco Canyon, New Mexico: The Chetro Ketl Collection.   R. Gwinn Vivian, Dulce N. Dodgen, and Gayle H. Hartmann. 1978. (O.P.)

33. Indian Assimilation in the Franciscan Area of Nueva Vizcaya.   William B. Griffen. 1979.

34. The Durango South Project: Archaeological Salvage of Two Late Basketmaker III Sites in the Durango District.   John D. Gooding. 1980.

35. Basketmaker Caves in the Prayer Rock District, Northeastern Arizona.   Elizabeth Ann Morris. 1980.

36. Archaeological Explorations in Caves of the Point of Pines Region, Arizona.   James C. Gifford. 1980.

37. Ceramic Sequences in Colima: Capacha, an Early Phase.   Isabel Kelly. 1980.

38. Themes of Indigenous Acculturation in Northwest Mexico.   Thomas B. Hinton and Phil C. Weigand, eds. 1981.

39. Sixteenth Century Maiolica Pottery in the Valley of Mexico.   Florence C. Lister and Robert H. Lister. 1982.

40. Multidisciplinary Research at Grasshopper Pueblo, Arizona.   William A. Longacre, Sally J. Holbrook, and Michael W. Graves, eds. 1982.

41. The Asturian of Cantabria: Early Holocene Hunter-Gatherers in Northern Spain.   Geoffrey A. Clark. 1983.

42. The Cochise Cultural Sequence in Southeastern Arizona.   E. B. Sayles. 1983.

43. Cultural and Environmental History of Cienega Valley, Southeastern Arizona.   Frank W. Eddy and Maurice E. Cooley. 1983.

Anthropological Papers listed as O.P., D are available as Docutech reproductions (high quality xerox) printed on demand. They are tape or spiral bound and nonreturnable.

THE UNIVERSITY OF ARIZONA PRESS

1230 North Park Avenue, Tucson, Arizona 85719